Global Perspectives on Wealth and Distribution

This is a broad-ranging and interdisciplinary series dedicated to studying the fundamental economic issue of inequality, including wealth inequality, wage and earnings differentials, and inequality in alternative measures of well-being. The series focuses on studies of developed nations as well as volumes focusing on recent research on inequality in the developing world. Gender- and racial-based inequality and the intra-household division of resources are addressed as well as inequality associated with technological change and globalization and the persistent problem of poverty. The economics of human rights addresses the problems of the most vulnerable members of society and considers policies to alleviate human rights violations.

More information about this series at
http://www.palgrave.com/gp/series/15384

Gordon Anderson

Multilateral Wellbeing Comparison in a Many Dimensioned World

Ordering and Ranking Collections of Groups

palgrave
macmillan

Gordon Anderson
Department of Economics
University of Toronto
Toronto, ON, Canada

ISSN 2662-382X ISSN 2662-3838 (electronic)
Global Perspectives on Wealth and Distribution
ISBN 978-3-030-21132-5 ISBN 978-3-030-21130-1 (eBook)
https://doi.org/10.1007/978-3-030-21130-1

This Palgrave Macmillan imprint is published by the registered company Springer Nature Switzerland AG.
The registered company address is: Gewerbestrasse 11, 6330 Cham, Switzerland

This book is about measuring differences between many things. Sometimes such differences are welcomed and to be celebrated, sometimes they are unwelcome and to be scorned. It is dedicated to my grandchildren, Sarah, Naomi, Bella, Marah, Josie, Taliah, Riel, Michael and Zachary, in the hope that they will come to know when to celebrate and when to scorn.

Acknowledgments

This book was written toward the end of my academic career and, as a consequence, I have a legion of people to thank, all too numerous to mention individually. From the community college teacher whose unbounded enthusiasm for economics inspired this high school dropout to somewhat belatedly study the subject at university, to the legendary faculty instructing the Econometrics and Mathematical Economics MSc and PhD programs at the London School of Economics in the 1970s, to my colleagues at the Universities of Southampton, McMaster and Toronto where I have taught, to all I owe a considerable debt of gratitude for providing such an intellectually enriching environment. To my many co-authors and collaborators, in particular Richard Blundell, Ian Crawford, Kinda Hachem, David Hendry, Teng Wah Leo, Oliver Linton, Grazia Pittau, Thierry Post, Yoon Jae Whang and Roberto Zelli, thanks so much for your generosity, encouragement and collegiality. I'm sure you've all made me look somewhat better than I really am and I have been truly blessed to have worked with you all.

Contents

List of Figures

List of Tables

Introduction

Throughout the social sciences, collections or groups of subjects are categorized, compared and contrasted with respect to some characteristic or characteristics of interest they possess. The process is multilateral, that is to say it is a simultaneous comparison exercise between many, that is, more than two groups. Generally, each group can be characterized by a statistical distribution describing the relative frequency with which the various subject characteristics occur and the groups will differ in nature as their respective distributions differ. Usually measures summarizing particular aspects of group distributions are employed in the comparison process but, by their very nature, they cannot fully capture the extent of distributional differences within a collection of groups. Questions thus arise as to whether such measures are adequate for the purpose and whether there are alternative approaches to the comparison process.

At the heart of the multilateral comparison problem is the notion that a family of perfectly reasonable, theoretically justifiable and hence equally appropriate, ordering instruments will very often yield conflicting results which engenders uncertainty as to the correct ranking of the subgroups. This is entirely a consequence of the particular orientation of the subgroup distributions of the characteristic under comparison. It is not simply a matter of the statistical uncertainty that arises from sampling variability; the problem would exist even if the subgroup distributions were known with absolute certainty. It is an uncertainty that transcends statistical niceties that is inherent in the structure of the problem and can be construed as "structural uncertainty" arising from the ambiguity that is a feature of a particular configuration of distributions. It would be useful to have a measure of the extent to which such "structural uncertainty" is a problem.

Multilateral between-group comparisons are ubiquitous; the activity appears in international, regional and local comparisons of all kinds, be it health, wealth, education, income, wellbeing and so on, where indices reflecting a nation's achievements or failings are ranked, ordered and contrasted. Within a society, individuals or households are classified, compared and contrasted by their social, income, educational or other such group status. In finance, returns of a variety of distinct portfolios (here the groups are the portfolio management agencies) are compared and contrasted on a risk and return basis. In the social and physical sciences, treatment effects, event study and policy evaluation literatures compare outcomes from different treatment, event or policy types. In convergence/polarization and equal opportunity/social justice literatures, the extent of outcomes of different groups circumscribed by particular sets of circumstances is measured.

Underlying each of these activities is some criterion function related to the variable or variables of interest which provides a rationale for the type of comparison process and governs the way in which the variables are to be employed in comparing the groups. The extent to which the groupings can be distinguished depends very much on the nature of the variables and how they are distributed over the respective groups. Variables can be categorical, ordinal or cardinal, discretely or continuously measured, singular or many in number, and the manner in which they are distributed across groupings will vary accordingly as will the juxtapositions of the respective distributions. One of the tasks confronting the investigator is distinguishing these various group distributions which will in turn depend upon the extent to which they vary.

Frequently, between-group comparisons are facilitated by summarizing group outcomes with statistics which provide a complete ordering. Often it is the case that alternative summarizing statistics are available, raising questions as to: "Which measures are appropriate and to what extent are they adequate?", "What if they are contradictory or inherently ambiguous?" and "Can the ambiguity situation be resolved?" It turns out that this is also dependent on the extent of distributional variability in the collection. Sometimes constituencies or groupings are easily identifiable with well-defined membership criteria or boundaries, and at other times, they are less well defined and fuzzy in nature, their identification becoming an integral part of the comparison problem. In this case, issues arise as to how the fuzzy nature of groupings can be resolved in terms of determining the number and size of groups and the extent to which they can be compared.

This book is about the issues surrounding the multilateral comparison process. While its focus is on wellbeing measurement, since most of the ideas have been drawn from that literature, hopefully it will become apparent that their application transcends that field. Directed at practitioners interested in applying these ideas in any field where multilateral comparisons have to be made, it presents a not too technical discussion of the principles and techniques involved, discusses some of the challenges of application and offers some resolution or at least some pointers to where some resolution may be found.

Frequently researchers embark upon a comparison process without clearly articulating the nature of their objective, criterion or value function: Are preferences over outcomes within and across groups increasing and concave or increasing and convex? Should downside versus upside risks or differences be viewed differently? In what sense can equality of opportunity be judged to have improved? Given the need to establish an objective function index underlying the comparison activity, in a peremptory outline of the evolution of interest in wellbeing measurement, Chap. 1 discusses the articulation, nature and development of such a criterion function and its implications for directing analysis and choosing comparators.

Probability distributions are used to describe the way that attributes are allocated across the agents within a group, and many of the ideas employed in the comparison process are founded in basic probability distribution and statistical inference theory. For an understanding of some of the statistically oriented details employed in the ensuing chapters, the fundamental statistical ideas employed are outlined in Chap. 2. Some reliance is placed upon rudimentary knowledge of the calculus but the intent is to cover all that is necessary for the non-specialist to follow the discussion.

When it comes to ranking or ordering groups, two approaches are available. Choosing an indicator suitable for the task at hand will facilitate a complete ordering of the collection in question in the sense that groups will be definitively ordered. Frequently more than one indicator is available and often alternatives yield contradictory orderings so that unless the choice is well founded and unequivocal, this approach will be fraught with problems of ambiguity with different but no less appropriate indicators yielding contradictory orderings. To avoid these issues, researchers have turned to partial ordering techniques which, when an ordering has been achieved, yield unambiguous results. The downside of this approach is that it is only partial, frequently resulting in a "no decision". Chapters 3 and 4 respectively discuss complete and partial ordering approaches, their relative merits and disadvantages.

All of the foregoing discussion relates to the comparison of well defined, identifiable groups; however, frequently groupings are not so well defined, but latent in nature and their structure is a matter for empirical investigation and determination in itself. Semi-parametric approaches for dealing with situations where groupings are not clearly delineated are presented in Chap. 5. Ideas about measuring distributional differences and exploring the closely related ambiguity issue are discussed in Chap. 6 and five examples based upon the ideas and techniques developed in the book are presented and reviewed in Chap. 7.

CHAPTER 1

Measuring the Wellbeing of Groups

1.1 Introduction

Multilateral comparisons of collections or groups of things are ubiquitous. League tables of national (or regional) education levels, health outcomes, income levels, average self-reported happiness levels, poverty and inequality measures and sports team performance abound. In other spheres, asset returns distributions of portfolio managers are compared; school based student educational attainments are contrasted; and treatment effects, the result of controlled experiments, are compared, ordered and contrasted. Degrees of societal generational income persistence are correlated with the levels of relative inequality in those societies. In other paradigms, the persistence of class membership over generations or the dependence of outcomes on different sets of circumstances is of interest. All of these pursuits relate to ranking, ordering or assessing the extent of differences between, groups or collections of things according to some implicit or explicit underlying criterion function. This book is about this generic activity as seen through the lens of wellbeing measurement, largely because researchers in that particular sphere have given a great deal of thought to the matter; however, it should be stressed that these ideas have application in many spheres beyond that of wellbeing.

G. Anderson, *Multilateral Wellbeing Comparison in a Many Dimensioned World*, Global Perspectives on Wealth and Distribution,
https://doi.org/10.1007/978-3-030-21130-1_1

Invariably group comparisons are based upon measures, usually summary statistics, of varying degrees of sophistry[1] that summarize and represent an aspect (or aspects) of interest that prevail in each of the groups under comparison. As such, they provide a complete ordering of the groups in that any one group is measurably worse, better or the same as any other group in the comparison set. The choice of statistic is based on an implicit or explicit criterion function underlying the process. It should be noted that the generality of the criterion function can often be a source of confusion because the particular configuration of groups being compared inherently engender ambiguity or conflict between alternative comparison instruments appropriate for a particular criterion function. Indeed, this particular problem has led to an alternative comparison methodology offering an unambiguous but only partial ordering of groups in the sense sometimes one group is revealed as not definitively better, worse or the same as another group. Interestingly it transpires that the partial ordering methodology can inform the complete ordering methodology as to the potential for ambiguity in the ranking process. These issues will be explored in the book.

When comparing groups, a basis for comparison has to be established at the outset. Are the group aspects being compared reflective of some quality of "goodness" or "badness" of the group? If so, does it matter how that "goodness" or "badness" is shared within a group? Are there mitigating features which mean that individual impoverishment or overabundance of the quality needs to be compensated for? When studying the effectiveness of a collection of treatments is the spread of outcomes of a particular treatment a matter for concern? Does the relative size of the groups matter? These questions have to be addressed by the investigator in articulating the criterion function and contemplating potential comparison approaches if a complete ordering of the groups is to be attempted, formulating the sort of index or indicator that is to be used in the process. A field of economics that has paid some attention to the appropriate criterion function is welfare economics and social choice theory; however, its deliberations are relevant and applicable in fields far beyond comparison of group wellbeing.

[1] Simple examples are averages, medians, coefficients of variation, Gini coefficients; somewhat more sophisticated measures would be inequality compensated average income levels or risk adjusted average returns.

In truth, in wellbeing measurement, these summary statistics are attempts at reflecting aspects of something that is inherently unmeasurable; the criterion function is in effect a measure of the aggregate wellbeing of a group or its "common good". However, formulating an idea of what should be embedded in such a function can inform the choice of summary statistic (or whether some other approach should be taken). Indeed, outside the realm of wellbeing measurement, it makes much sense for an investigator to articulate the criterion function underlying the comparison exercise since it will lend clarity to the choice of comparison instrument and methodology. So, before embarking upon a study of the measurement and comparison exercise, the nature of a "welfare", "common good" or criterion function which underlays the many different notions of the wellbeing measurement exercise (together with some of the objections that economists have made to such a comparison activity) will be explored later in this introductory chapter.

1.2 An Outline of What Follows

Since much of the following relies upon statistical constructs (i.e. probability distributions) which describe of the manner in which the aspect of interest is allocated across groups, Chap. 2 provides some necessary background for the various applied statistical components that later chapters rely upon. It outlines the very basic concepts regarding the nature, properties and use of probability distributions which treat the variables of interest as random and describe their allocation across the groups under comparison. Generally, for practical comparison purposes, distributions are not known a priori and have to be estimated, and so the chapter moves on to distinguish between parametric versus non-parametric investigative approaches to estimating distributions. When there is no information about a parametric distributional structure, or at least an unwillingness on the part of the investigator to make assumptions about parametric structure, probability distributions can be estimated using kernel techniques, the basic essentials of which are also outlined. The book is focused on multilateral comparisons; however, from a wellbeing comparison perspective, the main approach is to test for stochastic dominance relations which, together with overlap and Transvariation methods, are bilateral comparison techniques. The basic essentials of these bilateral comparison techniques are described in this chapter with a view of extending them to multilateral comparisons in later chapters. This family of techniques can sometimes fall foul of the test inconsistency problem which, together with some of the solutions to it, are described in the final section.

The most common practice is to formulate an index, frequently on an axiomatic basis, which provides a complete ordering for the ranking process and this, together with some of the pitfalls of this activity, is what is discussed in Chap. 3. After an introduction which deals with some of the difficulties associated with formulating and employing indices, Sects. 3.3 and 3.4 discuss some basic level of wellbeing and unit free inequality indices which leads to a discussion of inequality adjusted wellbeing level measures in Sect. 3.5. Notions of segmentation and polarization are distinguished in Sect. 3.6 with multivariate extensions of these being considered in Sect. 3.7. Poverty measurement and equality of opportunity and mobility indices are discussed in Sects. 3.8 and 3.9. Having alluded to the ambiguity problem in the introduction it is illustrated in the final section of the chapter.

An alternative comparison strategy is outlined in Chap. 4. Stochastic dominance criteria are used to study the orientation of group distributions to see if, given the nature of the chosen criterion function class, the juxtaposition of the group distributions will admit an unambiguous ordering. Sometimes they will, sometimes they won't, in effect the ordering is only partial; however, in the event that an unambiguous ordering is not admitted, a similar exercise can be pursued in the light of a more restrictive criterion function class. This chapter outlines some basic dominance criteria and the way in which successive orders of dominance restrict the nature of the criterion function. Based upon these concepts, Chap. 4 then considers techniques for revealing the extent of ambiguity surrounding the comparison exercise, develops some ideas for establishing unambiguous groupings and formulates a general family of ordering indices that reflect restrictions implied on the criterion function implied by the level of stochastic ordering. The relationships between stochastic dominance and inequality and poverty orderings are covered in later sections as is the special case of polarization. The problem of ambiguity and how to measure the extent to which it prevails are discussed and some tools for dealing with these issues are provided in the later sections.

The preceding chapters have relied upon the groups under comparison being identified in the sense that every data element has been unequivocally drawn from an identified group. Often groups are less well defined, in effect, they are latent; however, if the investigator is willing to make some assumptions about the commonality of behavior within each latent subgroup, it is possible to get some information about these latent subgroups that can be used in analysis. Generally, complete categorical classification is not possible, but the shape of the latent class distributions, the size of the classes and the probability of class membership can be determined. Chapter 5 addresses the issue of determining the number, size and distributional shape of latent subgroups using semiparametric mixture distribution techniques. Section 5.2 lays out the basic semiparametric mixture distribution model and in that context the probability of class membership for an individual with a given characteristic is developed in Sect. 5.3. Estimation of the model is discussed in Sect. 5.4 and methods for determining the number of classes are discussed in Sect. 5.5. Section 5.6 develops some ideas for studying factors relating to class membership in terms of the correlates of class membership probabilities. Section 5.7 briefly extends the ideas for comparing subgroups in the previous chapters to latent subgroups.

When assessing differences and similarities or ordering a collection of groups, be they identified or latent, the orientation of their respective distributions can engender ambiguity and comparability problems in the context of a particular criterion function. Chapter 6 offers an analysis of this problem in comparing the household income distributions of 18 Eurozone nations. Section 6.2 outlines some criteria for the absence of ambiguity with respect to a particular criterion function and the manner in which the problem has been dealt with in the bilateral comparison case is discussed in Sect. 6.3. It turns out that the potential for ambiguity in a collection of distributions can be measured and two “ambiguity indices” are proposed in Sect. 6.4. While these ideas have been applied to problems with indices of wellbeing levels they can equally be applied to measures of inequality, Sect. 6.5 discusses this issue. The concept of partitioning a collection of groups into sets within which there may be some ambiguity but between which there is no ambiguity is explored in Sect. 6.6 and all of these ideas are exemplified in the Eurozone application in Sect. 6.7.

To illustrate the generality of the comparison techniques developed in the book, Chap. 7 presents five very diverse examples of multilateral comparisons from a variety of situations. The first, drawn from Anderson et al. (2019), is a comparison of Canadian income distributions drawn across aboriginal-non aboriginal, gender and urban-rural lines, the application highlights the polarization—inequality distinction in revealing a society that is becoming more unequal overall yet more similar across its various divides. The second application, drawn from Anderson et al. (2019), examines how progress with the equal opportunity social justice imperative can be examined in the context of the German education system which had invested heavily in improving the outcomes of high school students in the early part of the twenty-first century. It provides an illustration of a multidimensional application of multilateral comparison techniques. An application evaluating portfolio manager performance drawn from Anderson et al. (2019) is the subject matter of the third example. An analysis of crop yields in Sub Sahara East African irrigation schemes which appear to disadvantage female (as opposed to male) farm managers is reported in the fourth example where another equal opportunity based analysis is performed. The fifth example is an illustration of how the techniques can be used in a multivariate dynamic setting looking at the progress of the Human Development Index for 164 nations over a period of 24 years.

1.3 Measuring Wellbeing: The Social Welfare Function

Generally, in the case of societal wellbeing measurement, the criterion function, denoted $\underset{\sim}{U}$, would be a measure of the aggregate wellbeing of a society and as such it would be some function of the wellbeing of its I individuals indexed $i = 1,\ldots,I$, so that $\underset{\sim}{U} = \underset{\sim}{U}[\,U_1(\ ),\ U_2(\ )\ \ldots\ U_I(\ )]$, where $U_i(\ )$ is the wellbeing of the ith individual. Generally $U_i(\ )$ is unobservable, but it is considered to be a function of a set of observable variables y_i. By endowing the function $U_i(y_i)$ with a particular structure based upon reasonable assumptions about rational behavior of the ith individual, inferences about U_i can be based upon what is observed, namely y_i. The classical example of this is the Theory of Consumer Demand (Deaton and Muellbauer 1980) wherein the most restrictive model all agents are assumed to have the same preferences, that is to say $U_i(y_i) = U(y_i)$ for all I, and y_i is the vector of goods consumed by individual i.[2] Given appropriate properties of $U()$, agents are expected to maximize it subject to the constraint that $c_i = p'y_i \leq x_i$ where p is the vector of prices faced by all consumers and, c_i and x_i are respectively the consumption expenditure and after tax income of the ith consumer. Generally, by thinking in terms of the indirect utility function $V(p,x_i) =$

[2] Some variation in wellbeing functions across individuals i can be achieved by assuming $U()$ varies by type of individual and including individual characteristics in the vector y.

$U(y_i)$,[3] this facilitates formulation of a system of consumer demand equations $x_i = h(p, y_i)$ which have certain testable properties.

Ideally when comparing the wellbeing of a collection of societies indexed $k = 1,\ldots,K$, one would like to compare $\underset{\sim}{U}_k$, $k = 1,\ldots,K$. Clearly such a comparison is extremely complex and in need of a good deal of simplification. Since x_i is an upper bound for c_i, and both are observable, wellbeing of the ith individual is frequently simplified to be a function of either c_i or x_i as in $U_i = U(c_i)$ or $V_i = V(x_i)$. In such a case, making some assumptions about the structure of $V(x_i)$ (or $U(c_i)$) will allow comparison of wellbeing in societies $k = 1,\ldots,K$ by comparing the vectors x^k (or c^k) where x^k (c^k) is the list of incomes (consumptions) x_i (c_i) for individuals $i = 1,\ldots,I_k$ in society k.

Going back to Adam Smith and beyond, there has been a long tradition in economics of concern for "The Common Good" which recognized heterogeneity in peoples' tastes and choices but simply construed the criterion function concept as the sum of individual happinesses. Comparatively recently, this tradition culminated in Samuelson (1947, 1977) and Bergson (1938) articulating "The Common Good" in terms of a "Social Welfare Function" (SWF). They imagine a society of N people named $i = 1,\ldots,N$ where the i'th persons utility or happiness is measured as $U_i(x)$, where the society is completely described by the vector x, an enormous list of things describing what each person has, does and is. In this world, everyone knows what every other person has, is and does. So, x defines a particular state of society for each and all individuals and $U_i(x)$ measures the ith persons' overall happiness with respect to that state, which may vary over individuals (hence the subscript "i"). Now imagine a benign impartial administrator (this could be the Government, God, the Price System, An Artificial Intelligence Instrument or any combination of the five) who, subject to some constraints, will choose x so as to maximize the Social Welfare Function (SWF) which is an aggregation of everyone's happiness, so SWF $= F(U_1(x), U_2(x),\ldots,U_N(x))$ where F is some monotonic non-decreasing aggregating function of the U_i's, $i = 1,\ldots,N$ which means increases in a $U_i(x)$ will generally increase (but at least never decrease) the SWF value.

Having articulated the problem, the real difficulties become clear. To start with, $F(\ )$ is a function of a collection of individuals $U_i(x)$'s, the

[3] In essence, to get $V()$ the values of the elements of y_i in the $U()$ function are replaced by the corresponding combination of prices p and aggregate consumption level c_i that determine them.

Happinesses, Felicities, Satisfactions, Utilities, Well-beings, Ophelimities that individuals experience (it's amazing that there are so many words for something ($U(x)$) that cannot be cardinally measured or observed!). Note that this issue transcends arguments about what exactly the x's should be). Robbins (1935, 1938) and Samuelson (1947) argued that, while it is reasonable to expect agents to be able to rank satisfactions, it is not reasonable (and therefor "unscientific") to expect them to be able to quantify their degree of satisfaction. Thus statements like "Agent i is happier than agent j under x" did not make sense and invalidated interpersonal utility comparisons which is precisely what $F(\ )$ does.

Robbins (1935, 1938) in particular argued that rigorous adherence to the strictly ordinal notion of utility precluded any interpersonal comparisons of utility so we cannot add up utilities like the Utilitarians did. Thus, the only societal welfare improvements or deteriorations that economists could proclaim were Paretian ones whereby if, in comparing the present state to the past, no one is worse of and at least one person is better (or no one is better off and at least one person is worse off) then Social Welfare can be deemed to have improved (diminished). In fact, the problem is even more serious than this! The problem for Robbins was that a numeric value cannot be assigned to $U(x)$ in any sense so that, somewhat importantly for measurement purposes, it could not be measured! Let's suppose for the moment that we could, what about SWF = $F(U_1(x), U_2(x),\ldots, U_n(x))$?

Arrow (1950) posited a set of "reasonable" conditions that a SWF should satisfy in the event that the $U(x)$'s could be measured—namely Collective Rationality, Universal Domain, Pareto Inclusiveness, Independence of Irrelevant Alternatives and Anonymity—and showed that such a SWF was not universal. Let's briefly consider the conditions:

Collective Rationality argues that the SWF can distinguish between states so that: The collective choice is represented by an ordering over all states that is complete and transitive thus for any x_1, x_2 and x_3, either $F(x_1) \leq F(x_2)$ or $F(x_1) \geq F(x_2)$ and, if $F(x_1) \leq F(x_2)$ and $F(x_2) \leq F(x_3)$ then $F(x_1) \leq F(x_3)$.

Universal Domain argues that all possible x's can be compared: The domain of the welfare function should contain all logically possible orderings of individuals (i.e. all possible x's could be ordered).

Pareto Inclusiveness argues that if a change is universally approved of then the SWF should reflect this: If all individuals prefer a to b then the welfare function should prefer *a* to *b*. Here if for x_1 and x_2 if $U_i(x_1) \leq U_i(x_2)$ for all $i = 1,\ldots,N$ then $F(x_1) \leq F(x_2)$.

Independence of Irrelevant Alternatives argues that a direct comparison should not be influenced by comparison to a third unrelated state. In essence, the ranking of two alternatives depends solely on information on how individuals rank those alternatives (i.e. not on an indirect comparison of the individual's happiness).

Anonymity argues that names of individuals should not matter: No identifiable individual should be able to determine the social choice in all circumstances.

While these conditions appear eminently reasonable, Arrow's results imply that the only SWF satisfying all these conditions must make all Pareto incomparable states socially indifferent, that is Pareto comparisons which make no one worse off and at least one person better off are the only basis for social choice. Thus, even if only one agent has the mildest preference for x_a whereas all other agents have a strong preference for state x_b, x_a and x_b must be declared socially indifferent. It also rules out democracies and dictatorships as social planning mechanisms.

There followed a huge debate over the nature and very existence of the SWF in the mid-1900s and many views as to what form it should take, how it should be represented, how it could be measured and whether or not such a thing could possibly exist were articulated. The point is this, when contriving some sort of indicator with respect to a characteristic of a population, one should be mindful of the fact that one is really constructing a basis for comparison which is in essence a type of Social Welfare Function so that some of the foregoing issues are pertinent. When formulating the analysis, of necessity many of the forgoing problems are implicitly assumed away, in justifying such an approach it is important to understand what is being assumed.

Harsanyi (1953, 1955) and later Rawls (1971, 2001) suggested that a just society would be one where individuals made allocative decisions from an original position of ignorance in which they would not be aware of where they would be in the list of allocations after the choice had been made. It is presumed that societal decision makers would act in a similar fashion. Known as a "Veil of Ignorance", all the decision maker knows at the point of decision is the shape and location of the new distribution over the group; their location in the distribution would only be revealed after the choice had been made. This requires an understanding of the nature of statistical distributions and the nature of their own preferences or utility functions. Typically, if individuals had a simple preference for more, they would choose the distribution with the highest average outcome, since given knowledge of the distribution but not of their likely place in it, their expected income would be the average income. On the other hand, if they preferred more but were risk averse, they would choose the distribution with the highest average outcome provided its variation was not too great in a risk modified expected outcome format. All of this is in the realm of expected utility theory but it doesn't really avoid the idea that individual utilities are being summed in some sense which was the concern of Robbins.

Here, ignoring arguments about its existence, three examples or traditions (with some extensions) regarding the underlying nature of the SWF or what will henceforth be referred to as the criterion function, will be outlined in order to understand what they imply for analysis. The Benthamite, Daltonian and Rawlsian positions that have dominated the empirical welfare analysis stage have been cited as the basis for very distinct approaches to measuring the relative wellbeing of groups.

1.4 Measuring Wellbeing: The Benthamite Tradition

People have been thinking about the "common good" for a long time. Jeremy Bentham [1748–1832],[4] a Philosopher and Lawyer with a keen interest in prison reform, led the way as a Utilitarian and can be considered as one of the first "Welfarists" and perhaps can be considered a founding father of the discipline. The early "Welfarists" did not contemplate measurement or the existence of a utility function as a problem and advocated "The Greatest Good for the Greatest Number" (Bentham's phrase). They

[4] Born to a wealthy family Bentham was a child prodigy; he studied Latin at the age of 3, attended Westminster School and, at age 12, attended Queens College Oxford, where he completed his bachelor's and master's degrees and trained as a lawyer. He was associated with University College London and the foundation of London University, his belief in the universal, low cost availability of education inspiring the founders of London University. Bentham was interested in prison reform and designed many prisons throughout the British Empire, indeed one of his designs can be seen in the early British Colonial Settlement of Fremantle Australia! If you visit London and go to the University College quadrangle, as you enter the gate in the far right hand corner you can meet him—his preserved body is in a glass case.

would simply add up utilities across the population, so that the Social Welfare Function was simply $F((U_1(x) + U_2(x) + \ldots + U_N(x)))$ where $F(\ )$ is monotonic increasing in its argument. Actually the ideas associated with the notion of Utilitarianism were born in the Scottish Enlightenment[5] in the mid-1700s (Hume [1711–1776] e.g. sketched the ideas that Bentham pursued in his many philosophical writings). However, the first formal articulation was by Jeremy Bentham in "An Introduction to the Principles and Morals of Legislation (1789)"; it was developed and extended further by Mill, Edgworth, Sidgwick and Pigou through the later 1800s and early 1900s. This very simple notion hides a huge number of difficulties, many of which we'll be discussing later on, simply put it, requires that we can identify and calculate "Happiness" or "Utility" and add it up across individuals, which turns out to be no mean trick! This tradition laid the foundation for using the simplest of criterion functions with constructs like average, median or other quantile income when comparing societies.

1.5 The Pigou-Dalton Principle: "Inequality Is a Bad Thing"

For the Utilitarians, the notion of inequality, that different people had different utilities, was not of concern (so e.g. the fact that I had 2.1 "Utes" and you had none was considered a better state than where we each had 1 "Ute"), this was addressed by Pigou in his books *Wealth and Welfare* (1912) and *The Economics of Welfare* (1920), and later by Dalton (1920).[6] For them, the Social Welfare Function was greatly simplified with x simply being a list of individual incomes and the sum of the elements of *x*, aggregate income, being an important feature. The basic notion was that inequality was a bad thing so that for a constant aggregate income level, a more equal distribution of utility is to be preferred (see Foster and Sen 1996 for a comprehensive discussion). This was captured in the Pigou-Dalton Principle of Transfers (any mean preserving transfer from a poor man to a rich man increases inequality and diminishes aggregate wellbeing).

[5] Yet another thing the Scots can be blamed for beyond Whisky, Golf and Haggis!

[6] Arthur Pigou came to economics through the study of philosophy and ethics under the Moral Science Tripos at Cambridge. He studied economics under Alfred Marshall, whom he later succeeded as Professor of Political Economy. Hugh Dalton, the son of a Church of England clergyman who ultimately became chaplain to Queen Victoria, studied and lectured at the London School of Economics and served in the Royal Artillery in the First World War. He served as Chancellor of the Exchequer during the Second World War.

Essentially this sentiment requires a Social Welfare Function which adds up the $U_i(x)$s but diminishes that sum by an amount that reflects the adverse effect of the extent of differences between the $U_i(x)$s. Actually for a society of agents with identical monotonically increasing concave preferences with $U' > 0$ and $U'' < 0$, and a "fixed cake" of total income, Utilitarianism has a Daltonian flavor since an equal distribution of aggregate income will maximize aggregate utility. It should be noted here that inequality refers specifically to differences between individuals in a society. Poverty is a related, but completely different topic which will be discussed later as an aspect of societal wellbeing (or lack of it).

1.6 Polarization

There is a suspicion that the conventional "man in the street" common parlance view of inequality has a "them and us" flavor. It is a "polarized" view of differences wherein the more clearly the "them" and the "us" are identified, (or the more closely the "them's" associate with each other and the more closely the "us's" associate with each other) the more clearly will inequality be perceived. There is an irony here in that such trends of increasing within-group association will often engender reduced inequality as it is conventionally measured. The point is, it may well be the case that the perception of inequality that the person in the street has is quite different from the one that is used by researchers, politicians and policy makers. The average citizen may well be more concerned with the thing called "polarization" than the thing called inequality and in some sense, it is that average citizens view that the Social Welfare Function should be trying to reflect.

Polarization, or the tendency of economic agents to collect into different groups and sense increasing differences between those groups and increasing commonality within groups, is both cause and consequence of much economic behavior. The first rigorous discussion of polarization appeared in Esteban and Ray (1994) (see also Duclos et al. 2004); the idea concerns informal and formal group formation and the notion that polarization is born of an increasing sense of identity or "likeness" between the members of a group and an increasing sense of distance between members of different groups. The terminology is gaining increasing currency in economics; it has been employed in describing the diminution of the middle class in wage, income and wealth distributions, in studying growth and convergence issues, in examining the plight of the poor, in the study of intergenerational income relationships and in discriminating between competing matching models of marriage partners.

When related to two perhaps latent or identified groups in a society, these studies broadly interpret polarization as the disappearance of mass at the center of the pooled empirical distribution of some characteristic that individuals possess, a bi-polarization process. When related to many groups, it concerns the multilateral segmentation and increasing distance between and intensity of, multiple points of modality of the distribution as it evolves through time. As an idea, it is related to the idea of segmentation of groups and can be applied to many, that is, more than two groups that are simultaneously moving apart in some sense. It is an inherently dynamic process involving the comparison of the anatomy of states at different points in time, essentially comparing how the shape of the distribution of a characteristic (or a collection of characteristics) has evolved during the process. Thus the objective is to detect trends in shapes of distributions over time that reflect the polarization or de-polarization (sometimes referred to as convergence) of that group of agents. Though the polarization phenomenon is closely associated with trends in inequality it is distinguishable from, and quite different to, changes in inequality in that increased polarization can induce either an increase, reduction or no change in inequality as it is conventionally measured.

Polarization, in the way it is measured, is generally viewed symmetrically between groups with members of rich and poor groups each recognizing similarly the growing distance between the groups and increasing within-group commonalities. However, it may be the case that one group, let's call them the poor may be increasingly aware of an increasing distance between them and the other group (the rich, say) as well as an increasing sense of commonality among themselves while the rich may be much less aware of such changes. That is to say, there could be an asymmetry in perception with one group feeling excluded from the other whereas the other is not so aware of such differences. This is very much the realm of social exclusivity.

1.7 Social Exclusion

Since the introduction of the notion of social exclusion[7] in the 1970s, there has been a great deal of work both directly and indirectly related to conceptualizing, identifying and measuring degrees of social and eco-

[7]The terminology is thought to have been first introduced in the French Parliament in the 1970s (Lenoir 1974), Lenoir, then Secretary of State in the Chirac government, referred to

nomic exclusion in societies. Sociologists concern with the closely related issue of social deprivation (indeed economists have usually identified exclusion in terms of deprivation) has a longer history with Runciman (1966) (see also Walker and Smith 2001) articulating the concept as follows:

> We can roughly say that [a person] is relatively deprived of X when (i) he does not have X, (ii) he sees some other person or persons, which may include himself at some previous or expected time, as having X, (iii) he wants X, and (iv) he sees it as feasible that he should have X. (Runciman 1966, p. 10)

The concept is distinct from, but very closely related to, notions of relative poverty, inequality and polarization and research into exclusion has been pursued in a similar fashion to those topics at theoretical, statistical and practical levels. The meaning of the term "social exclusion" has evolved to include all individuals and groups that are wholly or partly prevented from participation in their society and in various aspects of cultural and community life and, broadly interpreted it represents a progressive process of marginalization leading to economic deprivation and various other forms of social and cultural disadvantage. As such it is a dynamic concept, in that an individual can become socially excluded if his condition of deprivation is sustained or worsens over time and in this sense the literature on social and economic mobility between groups should become relevant (though the connection does not appear to have been made much in the literature to date). It is a relative concept in that an individual can be socially excluded only in comparison to a particular social group at a given place and time and in this sense the polarization and relative poverty literatures are relevant in quantifying relative social distanced. Finally, it is a multidimensional concept that includes economic, social and political

the excluded as consisting not only of the poor but of a wide variety of people, including social misfits. Social exclusion is of increasing interest because it has gained a primary role in official documents and in the political debate in Europe. In the Treaty of Amsterdam, signed in 1997, the European Union included the reduction of social exclusion among its objectives. The design of policies aimed at combating social exclusion is at the heart of the "Lisbon strategy" agreed upon during the European Council of March 2000 (Deroose et al. 2008).

aspects of life so that the multidimensional poverty inequality and polarization literatures become relevant.

A cursory survey suggests that there are three prevailing philosophical views underlying the theory of social exclusion and the problems of measurement which are the points of focus of this book appear to be convoluted with the normative issues that are of concern in those literatures. The first, what may be termed a "State—Agency" position, sees social exclusion as a dynamic process of social disqualification or disaffiliation which leads to the breakdown of the relationship between some individuals and the society in which they live. In this paradigm, the State is responsible of preserving social links connecting individuals and society and is responsible for promoting social integration; but individuals have to respect social norms and are expected to participate in the labor market in order to benefit from such social protection. Social exclusion is caused not only by the behavior of each individual but also by the State being incapable of guaranteeing social cohesion.

The second, what may be described as a "Laissez-Faire" alternative, tradition sees no role for the State in socially integrating society. In this tradition, society is perceived as a set of atomized individuals, each in competition within the market place, having rights and duties. In this paradigm, social links are simply interpreted as voluntary exchange contracts between individuals. In this society no one is responsible of the social position of the others and there are two types excluded: those who are discriminated against due to market failures, unprotected rights or the lack of necessary capabilities due to handicaps or other disadvantages; and those that freely choose not to actively participate in the society, that is to say those who choose to opt out.

The third tradition, which may be referred to as the monopoly paradigm sees the society as composed of different groups, the "insiders" who have control over resources, and the outsiders who do not. In this context, social exclusion is determined by the behavior of groups that restrict access to resources in order to maximize their welfare, giving rise to a hierarchy in the society. If the State is not able to counteract this phenomenon social cohesion vanishes while solidarity within each group increases, this is very much a polarization situation with a political science orientation though the tools of polarization measurement which will be outlined later seldom seem to have been employed in these literatures.

1.8 Equality of Opportunity and Social Mobility

With roots in recent egalitarian political philosophy,[8] the Equal Opportunity imperative sees differential outcomes as ethically acceptable when they are the consequence of individual choice and action but not ethically acceptable when they are the consequence of circumstances beyond the individual's control. So, for example, inequality of incomes may not be a bad thing if they are a matter of individual choice (such as two agents with equal skills and opportunities making different labor-leisure choices). Since a large portion of an individual's circumstances have to do with their gender and the parents they were blessed with, equal opportunity policies have to address the extent to which a child's status when adult is related to their gender and the status of their parents at a similar stage in their life cycle. As Kanbur and Stiglitz (1982, 1986) observe, the issue is in essence one of generational mobility (or the lack of it) and the way that it engenders a dynastic aspect to poverty and wealth over generations.

From the perspective of societal wellbeing, if mobility were an adjunct to material wellbeing in equalizing the opportunity for consuming the same pie, there would probably be trade-offs or qualifications for the policy maker to consider. To be extreme and somewhat trite, there are many ways to level a playing field: one approach is to cut off everyone's legs, but it would hopefully be eschewed by the policy maker on the grounds of its impact on material wellbeing. Piketty (2000) noted as much in his interpretation of the conservative, right wing view that, if generational mobility is low because of the high heritability of ability and the distortionary costs of welfare redistributions are high, it is reasonable to argue that low mobility is acceptable. Friedman (2005) nicely presents the other side of this coin in conjecturing (with a substantial degree of supporting evidence) that economic growth facilitates the equalizing of opportunities (among other improvements in social justice). Indeed, the pursuit of an equal opportunity goal has not been unequivocal, Cavanagh (2002) expresses some philosophical reservations, Jenks and Tach (2006) question whether an equal opportunity imperative should require the elimination of "…all sources of economic resemblance between parents and children. Specifically …(it)… does not require that society eliminate the effects of either inherited differences in ability or inherited values regarding the importance of economic success relative to other goals." In a similar vein, Dardanoni et al.

[8] See Arneson (1989), Cohen (1989) and Dworkin (1981a, b, 2000 and 2011).

(2006) question how demanding the pursuit of equal opportunity should be in terms of the feasibility of such a pursuit.

Erikson and Goldthorpe (1992) highlight the tension between Liberal and Marxist theories of societal mobility in observing that both sides make ethical judgments to the effect that high mobility is desirable, the dispute, as to whether it is or not, is essentially an empirical one.[9] However, it is not clear that this is the case. In essence, the Marxian aspiration is based on an objective of destroying inherited class; it does not necessarily come with any concern for overall economic wellbeing. It is a desire to break the connection between all parent and child outcomes and involves breaking the "good" connects (productive parents producing productive kids) as well as "bad" connects (unproductive parents producing unproductive kids). Breaking good connects and breaking bad connects are of equal value and "extreme" communal policies such as separating children from their parents reflect these aims and the fact that the wellbeing costs of breaking the child-parent connects are not deemed too high to increase mobility under such regimens.[10]

It is much more difficult to associate the attachment of equal value to "breaking good connects" and "breaking bad connects" with Liberal aspirations. As a matter of casual empiricism Liberal policy proposals, generally of an affirmative action flavor, reveal a predominant concern with breaking "bad" connects, focusing on improving the life chances of the "inherited poor" rather than diminishing the life chances of the "inherited rich". In focusing only on elevating the prospects of the poorly endowed the liberal policymaker is in effect responding to a second imperative, a sort of Pareto condition wherein the lot of the poorly endowed is improved without diminishing the lot of the richly endowed. Indeed, just breaking the bad connects elevates overall wellbeing which may be construed as the liberal policymaker following a Utilitarian mandate. In essence, increased mobility of those poor in circumstance is revealed to have greater societal

[9] Liberals claim that societies are characterized by "high and rising rates of social mobility and equality of opportunity as procedures of selection become more rational" whereas the Marxists would claim that they are not, essentially because "societies are characterized by class reproduction".

[10] "Extreme" expressions of the desire to break "bad connects" have not been confined to Marxian regimes. The eugenics movement of the twentieth century may be seen as an attempt at breaking such connections, and eugenic sterilizations continued to be carried out in the United States, Scandinavia, Switzerland and Canada (Alberta) up to 1970s and China's Law on Maternal and Infant Health Care was enacted in 1995 (Mao 1997).

value than increased mobility of those rich in circumstance (which in the face of constraints will almost by definition be increased downward mobility which lowers aggregate material wellbeing). Furthermore, in terms of societal wellbeing, consuming resources in disinheriting the "well endowed" (or destroying inherited human capital) can be seen as doubly perverse and the concomitant distortionary wellbeing costs considered too high.

1.9 The Rawlsian Principle and the Focus on Poverty

John Rawls, an American philosopher, in his book the Theory of Justice 1971 interpreted Social Welfare as simply the welfare of the poorest person or the poorest group. An overly simple interpretation of his operating rule for the benign administrator was that he advocated The Maxi-Min Rule which maximizes the income of the poorest person. Again for a society of identical agents with $U' > 0$ and $U'' < 0$, Utilitarianism also has a Rawlsian flavor since an equal distribution of aggregate income will maximize aggregate utility. Sometimes in his book, the object of attention is the poorest group, so that the "Welfarist" who is a Rawlsian will focus on the plight of the poor and the measurement of poverty to the complete exclusion of the state of the rich. He has provided us with a philosophical foundation for the focus axiom of poverty measurement to be discussed later. The broader takeaway is that poverty measurement somehow defined should be part of the conversation in multilateral comparison procedures.

1.10 What to Do Now?

Robbins has argued that wellbeing is not measureable, interpersonal comparisons cannot be made and individual happiness cannot be added up, Arrow's theorem makes Pareto Judgments the only basis for social choice, all of which is a recipe for doing nothing. If we want to be Democrats or Dictators, Utilitarians, Daltonians or Rawlsians for that matter, we have to reject at least one of Arrow's principles. Harsanyi did come up with an alternative "Veil of Ignorance" postulate in which individuals are asked to choose between two possible distributions or allocations without knowing where in the distributions they would be assigned and their preferred distribution reflects a welfare improvement on the lesser preferred distribution. Thus, hiding behind Sen (1963, 1982, 1984) (it was his idea!), we'll reject the no interpersonal comparisons constraint and follow Harsanyi and think about a society's wellbeing in terms of its average happiness or the expected value of $U(x)$ over the collection of groups which make up a society. This requires a basic understanding of statistical distribution theory which will be the topic for the next chapter.

References

Arneson, R. (1989). Equality and Equality of Opportunity for Welfare. *Philosophical Studies, 56*, 77–93.

Anderson, G. J., & Thomas, J. (2019). Measuring Multi-Group Polarization, Segmentation and Ambiguity: Increasingly Unequal Yet Similar Constituent Canadian Income Distributions. *Social Indicators Research*.

Anderson, G., Pittau, M. G., Zelli, R., & Fruehauf, T. (2019). *Educational Reform and Equal Opportunity in Capability Acquisition in 21st Century Germany: New Tools for Quantifying Distributional Differences in the Absence of Cardinal Comparability*. Toronto: University of Toronto, Department of Economics. Mimeo.

Arrow, K. J. (1950). A Difficulty in the Concept of Social Welfare. *Journal of Political Economy., 58*(4), 328–346. https://doi.org/10.1086/256963.

Bentham, J. (1789). An Introduction to the Principles and Morals of Legislation. London: Athlone.

Bergson, A. (1938). A Reformulation of Certain Aspects of Welfare Economics. *Quarterly Journal of Economics, 52*(2), 310–334.

Cavanagh, M. (2002). *Against Equality of Opportunity*. Oxford: Oxford University Press.

Cohen, G. A. (1989). On the Currency of Egalitarian Justice. *Ethics, 99*(4), 906–944.

Dalton, H. (1920). The Measurement of the Inequality of Incomes. *Economic Journal, 30*, 348–461.

Dardanoni, V., Fields, G. S., Roemer, J. E., & Puerta, M. L. S. (2006). How Demanding Should Equality of Opportunity Be, and How Much Have We Achieved? In S. L. Morgan, D. B. Grusky, & G. S. Fields (Eds.), *Mobility and Inequality: Frontiers of Research from Sociology and Economics* (pp. 59–82). Chicago: Stanford University Press.

Deaton, A., & Muellbauer, J. (1980). *Economics and Consumer Behaviour*. Cambridge: Cambridge University Press.

Deroose, S., Hodson, D., & Kuhlmann, J. (2008). The Broad Economic Policy Guidelines: Before and After the Re-launch of the Lisbon Strategy. *Journal of Common Market Studies, 46*, 827–848.

Duclos, J.-Y., Esteban, J., & Ray, D. (2004). Polarization: Concepts, Measurement, Estimation. *Econometrica, 72*(6), 1737–1772.

Dworkin, R. (1981a). What Is Equality? Part 1: Equality of Welfare. *Philosophy and Public Affairs, 10*(3), 185–246.

Dworkin, R. (1981b). What Is Equality? Part 2: Equality of Resources. *Philosophy and Public Affairs, 10*(4), 283–345.

Dworkin, R. (2000). *Sovereign Virtue: The Theory and Practice of Equality.* Cambridge, MA: Harvard University Press.

Dworkin, R. (2011). *Justice for Hedgehogs.* Cambridge, MA: Harvard University Press.

Erikson, R., & Goldthorpe, J. (1992). *The Constant Flux: A Study of Class Mobility in Industrial Societies.* Oxford: Clarendon Press.

Esteban, J.-M., & Ray, D. (1994). On the Measurement of Polarization. *Econometrica, 62*(4), 819–851.

Foster, J. E., & Sen, A. (1996). *On Economic Inequality*, expanded edition with annexe, ISBN 0-19-828193-5. Oxford: Clarendon Press.

Friedman, M. (2005). *The Optimum Quantity of Money.* books.google.com

Harsanyi, J. C. (1953). Cardinal Utility in Welfare Economics and in the Theory of Risk Bearing. *Journal of Political Economy, 61*, 434–435.

Harsanyi, J. C. (1955). Cardinal Welfare, Individualistic Ethics, and Interpersonal Comparisons of Utility. *Journal of Political Economy, 63*, 309–321.

Jenks, C., & Tach, L. (2006). Would Equal Opportunity Mean More Mobility, Chapter 2. In S. L. Morgan, D. B. Grusky, & G. S. Fields (Eds.), *Mobility and Inequality: Frontiers of Economics.* Stanford: Stanford University Press.

Kanbur, R., & Stiglitz, J. E. (1982). *Mobility and Inequality: A Utilitarian Analysis.* Economic Theory Discussion Paper No. 57, Department of Applied Economics, University of Cambridge.

Kanbur, R., & Stiglitz, J. E. (1986). *Intergenerational Mobility and Dynastic Inequality.* Woodrow Wilson School Discussion Paper in Economics, Number 111, Princeton University.

Lenoir, R. (1974/1989). *Les Exclus: Un Francais sur Dix.* Paris: Editions du Seuil.

Mao, X. (1997). Chinese Eugenic Legislation. *The Lancet, 349*, 139.

Pigou, A. C. (1912). *Wealth and Welfare.* London: Macmillan.

Pigou, A. C. (1920). *The Economics of Welfare.* The Liberty Fund.

Piketty, T. (2000). Theories of Persistent Inequality and Intergenerational Mobility, Chapter 8. In A. Atkinson & F. Bourguignon (Eds.), *Handbook of Income Distribution, Vol. 1* (pp. 429–476). Amsterdam: Elsevier.

Rawls, J. (1971). *A Theory of Justice.* Cambridge, MA: Belknap Press. ISBN 0-674-00078-1.

Rawls, J. (2001). *Justice as Fairness: A Restatement.* Cambridge, MA: Belknap Press.

Robbins, L. (1935). *An Essay on the Nature and Significance of Economic Science* (chap. 6, 2nd ed.). London: Macmillan.

Robbins, L. (1938). Interpersonal Comparisons of Utility: A Comment. *Economic Journal, 43*(4), 635–641.

Runciman, W. G. (1966). *Relative Deprivation and Social Justice: A Study of Attitudes to Social Inequality in Twentieth-Century England.* Berkeley: University of California Press.

Samuelson, P. A. (1947). *Foundations of Economic Analysis* (pp. xxi–xxiv, chap. VIII, Enlarged ed. 1983). Cambridge, MA: Harvard University Press. ISBN 0-674-31301-1.

Samuelson, P. (1977). Reaffirming the Existence of 'Reasonable' Bergson–Samuelson Social Welfare Functions. *Economica, N.S., 44*(173), 81–88. Harvard University Press

Sen, A. K. (1963). Distribution, Transitivity and Little's Welfare Criteria. *Economic Journal, 73*(292), 771–778.

Sen, A. (1982). *Choice, Welfare and Measurement.* Cambridge, MA: MIT Press.

Sen, A. (1984). Collective Rationality (chap. 3.). In *Collective Choice and Social Welfare.* Cambridge, MA: Harvard University Press. ISBN 0-444-85127-5.

Walker, I., & Smith, H. J. (2001). *Relative Deprivation: Specification, Development, and Integration.* Cambridge: Cambridge University Press. ISBN 0-521-80132-X.

CHAPTER 2

Statistical Matters

2.1 Introduction

For the reader unfamiliar with statistical ideas, this chapter provides necessary background for the many different applied statistical contexts of later chapters. It is by no means a rigorous discussion, for that the reader should refer to one of the many statistical theory texts available (Linton 2017, McLachlan and Peel 2000, Poirier 1995, Rao 1973, Silverman 1986 and Whang 2019 are particularly useful resources for the material in this book), but it does present enough information in order to understand the process of comparing groups using probability distributions later in the book.

Section 2.2 outlines the very basic essentials of the nature of the mathematical function (the probability distribution) used to describe how both continuously and/or discretely measured group outcomes are allocated across those groups in possibly many dimensions. It deals with the relationship between the probability density function and the cumulative distribution function, the concept of a conditional distribution and the idea of independence. In addition, it outlines some of the measures of location and dispersion which feature later in the book.

Since an ultimate objective is the comparison of collections of groups in some fashion, this frequently involves comparison of their respective distribution functions which requires estimation of said distribution functions. Section 2.3 distinguishes between parametric versus non-parametric investigative approaches to data with a view to estimating group distribu-

G. Anderson, *Multilateral Wellbeing Comparison in a Many Dimensioned World*, Global Perspectives on Wealth and Distribution,
https://doi.org/10.1007/978-3-030-21130-1_2

tions. (There is an intermediate Semi-Parametric Mixture Distribution Approach which is not discussed here. Since it involves the determination of the number, size and nature of groups it warrants a later chapter all of its own.) The section goes on to give some examples of discrete and continuous distributions for illustrative purposes paying particular attention to the normal distribution and the central limit theorem, a primary motivator for the normal distributions employed in Semi-Parametric mixture modeling, and outlines some basic ideas relating to estimation of parameters when the parametric structure of the distribution is known.

When there is no information about the parametric distributional structure (or at least when there is an unwillingness on the part of the investigator to make assumptions about parametric structure!), probability distributions can be estimated using kernel techniques, the basic essentials of which are outlined in Section 2.4. Comparing collections of groups is generally a multilateral exercise though there is a paucity of multilateral comparison techniques in the literature, mostly they are bilateral in nature and one objective of the book is the extension of these techniques to a multilateral paradigm. From a wellbeing comparison perspective, the main bilateral approach is to test for a stochastic dominance (SD) relation, the basic essentials of which are described in Section 2.5. The alternative bilateral comparators are overlap and Transvariation measures which are described in Section 2.6. This family of techniques can sometimes fall foul of the test inconsistency problem, which, together with some solutions to it, is described in the final section.

2.2 Probability Distributions

Typically, groups are compared and contrasted with regard to some aspect or aspects of the individuals in the group (usually individuals will be people or households), commonly referred to as their characteristic or characteristics which become the variables of interest in the analysis. The variables can be categorical (gender, race, occupation, employed/not employed and educational status are all categorical examples) or numerical (income, hours of work and age are numeric examples). To facilitate analysis, categories are usually converted into numbers rendering the variables of interest are numeric so for example, the probability of a randomly selected person being female is translated into the probability that the random variable X is 1 where $X = 1$ when the person is female $X = 0$ when the person is not female. Analysis is facilitated by describing the allocation of the variables of interest over a groups population using an algebraic expression, a mathematical function referred to as a statistical probability distribution. Groups are compared by comparing the features and properties of their respective probability distributions.

Generally, an individual's characteristic or variable of interest (for arguments' sake suppose its household income or the number of people in the household) is treated as a **random variable**, typical values of which are represented by a lower case letter, say x, with its corresponding uppercase letter X representing shorthand for the phrase "the random variable X". The way X is spread across the collection of individuals that constitute a group is described by a **probability density function,** an algebraic expression, denoted here as $f_X(x)$ and referred to as a "pdf" (it may be interpreted as "a function of X evaluated at the value x") which maps the value x onto the real line recording the values $f_X(x)$. In what follows for notational convenience, and without loss of generality, X will be assumed to exist on the positive orthant R^+, that is, $X \in [0,\infty]$. In effect, groups are compared by comparing their respective pdfs or functions thereof.

Basically, random variables come in many flavors, but fundamentally they are of two types, discrete and continuous. If the above mentioned mapping is from a finite (or countably infinite) set of points (usually the integer set), X is said to be a discrete random variable, otherwise, if the mapping is from an uncountably infinite set of points, it is said to be continuous. The nature of the pdf differs according as the variable is discrete or continuous. When X is discrete, with typical outcome x_i, $i=1,\ldots,J$ (assume for convenience that the x_is are ordered with i from the smallest to largest and there are J distinct outcomes), the probability density function $f(x_i)$ corresponds to "the probability that X is equal to the value x_i" (which may be written $P(X=x_i)$) so that $f(x_i) = P(X = x_i)$. Basically, the pdf for a discrete random variable obeys two rules:

$$f(x_i) \geq 0 \text{ for } i = 1,\ldots,J \tag{2.1}$$

$$\sum_{i=1}^{J} f(x_i) = 1 \tag{2.1a}$$

Taken together ((2.1) and (2.1a) imply that $f(x_i) \leq 1$ for all $i = 1,\ldots,J$. In the continuous case, it is not possible to interpret the pdf in the same way; indeed, since X can take on any one of the uncountably infinite set of values, we cannot give it a subscript "i". When X is continuous with typical value x, $f(x)$ is such a function that, when integrated over the range (a, b), it will yield the probability that x would fall in that range. In this case, the pdf will obey three basic rules.

$$f(x) \geq 0 \tag{2.2}$$

$$\int_0^\infty f(x)\,dx = 1 \tag{2.2a}$$

$$\int_a^b f(x)\,dx = P(a \leq X \leq b). \tag{2.2b}$$

Notice that in this case the value of $f(x)$ for a given value of x could be greater than 1. Associated with these probability density functions are cumulative distribution functions $F(x)$ (referred to as cdfs) which in each case yield the probability that the random variable X is less than some value x. In the discrete case, when the xs are indexed in order of size so that $h > k \leftrightarrow x_h \geq x_k$:

$$F(x_j) = \sum_{i=1}^{j} f(x_i) = P(X \leq x_j)\, j = 1,\ldots,I \tag{2.3}$$

In the continuous case:

$$F(x) = \int_0^x f(z)\,dz = P(X \leq x) \tag{2.3a}$$

Note that in the case of discrete random variables $F(x)$ is defined over the whole range of the random variable and is thus piecewise continuous. In the case of continuous distributions, $dF(x)/dx = f(x)$, that is, the derivative of the cdf of x gives us the pdf of x. For later purposes higher order cumulants will be useful where, in the case of continuous X, $F^j(x)$ is defined as:

$$F^j(x) = \int_0^x F^{j-1}(z)\,dz \text{ for } j = 1,\ldots \quad \text{with } F^0(z) = f(z)$$

Multivariate Considerations

Sometimes interest focuses on more than one variable, (e.g. the United Nations Human Development Index has three basic components: Income, Health and Education) and the notions of pdfs and cdfs need to be extended to account for a multidimensional situation. Consider the jointly distributed collection of continuous random variables X, Y,..., Z each defined on the positive orthant then the probability density function written as $f(x,y,\ldots,z)$ obeys rules similar to (2.2), (2.2a) and (2.2b) which is written as:

$$f(x,y,\ldots,z) \geq 0;$$

$$\int_0^\infty \int_0^\infty \cdots \int_0^\infty f(x,y,\ldots,z)\,dxdy\ldots dz = 1;$$

Letting the symbol "$\cap$" mean "and" note that:

$$\int_{a_X}^{b_X} \int_{a_Y}^{b_Y} \cdots \int_{a_Z}^{b_Z} f(x,y,\ldots,z)\,dxdydz = P\left(a_X \leq X \leq b_X \cap a_Y \leq Y \leq b_Y \cap \ldots \cap a_Z \leq X \leq b_Z\right).$$

So that the analog of (2.3a) may be written as:

$$F(x,y,\ldots,z) = \int_0^x \int_0^y \cdots \int_0^z f(p,q,\ldots,r)\,dpdqdr = P\left(X \leq x \cap Y \leq y \cap \ldots \cap Z \leq z\right) \tag{2.3b}$$

In this context, it may be necessary to consider one variable on its own; to reduce notation suppose X and Y are jointly distributed as $f(x,y)$, then the marginal distribution of X, $f_X(x)$, may be derived by integrating out Y, that is:

$$f_X(x) = \int_0^\infty f(x,y)\,dy$$

Also, the notion of the conditional distribution of one variable given another will be useful; in this instance, contemplate the joint distribution of X and Y given by $f(x,y)$, then the conditional distribution of X given Y, written as $f(x|y)$, is of the form:

$$f(x|y) = \frac{f(x,y)}{f_Y(y)}$$

where $f_Y(y)$ is the marginal distribution of Y. This should be interpreted as the statement "When the value of Y is y, the distribution of X is given by the formula $f(x|y)$." It follows that:

$$f(x|y)f_Y(y) = f(y|x)f_X(x) = f(x,y)$$

Which broadly interpreted means that the probability of x given y times the probability of y is always equal to the probability of y given x times the probability of x, so that given three of the four pieces of information, the fourth is readily computed. This relationship is at the heart of what is known as Bayes Theorem.

Multivariate discrete random variables have similar probability distributions functions with similar definitions for marginal and conditional probability density distributions and cumulative distributions. Indeed, joint distributions of a mixture of discrete and continuous random variables can also be contemplated. Let (w,z) be respectively the continuous w and the discrete z vectors of random variables and let the vector $= \begin{pmatrix} w \\ z \end{pmatrix}$. Suppose the joint density of the ws for a given configuration of the zs is $f(w|z)$ and the joint density of the zs is given by $p(z)$, then $f(x)$ the joint density of $x\left(=\begin{pmatrix} w \\ z \end{pmatrix}\right)$ is $f(x) = f(w,z) = f(w|z)p(z)$. Furthermore, subgroups in a population may have different distributions, suppose there are K subpopulations indexed $k = 1,\ldots,K$ with probability distributions $f_k(x)$ where the proportion of the population in the kth subgroup is w_k then the populations' probability density function $f(x)$ is given by:

$$f(x) = \sum_{k=1}^{K} w_k f_k(x)$$

Note that $f(x)$ retains all of the properties of a probability distribution function, in particular:

$$E(x) = \mu = \sum_{k=1}^{K} w_k \mu_k$$

Statistical Independence

When examining the nature of a particular distribution or comparing groups with respect to a variable or variables of interest, an important aspect for consideration is the extent to which things are related. Both exercises will be based upon samples of data drawn from the group or groups being studied and the extent to which samples are independently drawn has implications for the way in which comparisons are made. Some types of group comparison, for example equality of opportunity, also draw on the concept of independence. If knowing the value of *X* tells us exactly what *Y* is, then *X* and *Y* are completely dependent, if knowing the value of *X* reveals nothing about *Y*, then *X* and *Y* are deemed to be independent. Statistical independence has to do with the relationship between a joint distribution and its marginal distributions so that if given knowledge of *y*, nothing is learned about the distribution of *x* then:

$$f(x|y) = \frac{f(x,y)}{f_Y(y)} = f_X(x)$$

It follows that when *X* and *Y* are independent:

$$f(x,y) = f_X(x) f_Y(y)$$

In general, when a collection of distributions are mutually independent their joint distributions will be the product of their marginal distributions so that:

$$f(x,y,\ldots,z) = f_X(x) f_Y(y) \ldots f_Z(z)$$

Similarly:

$$F(x,y,\ldots,z) = F_X(x) F_Y(y) \ldots F_Z(z)$$

So that (2.3b) becomes:

$$\begin{aligned} F(x,y,\ldots,z) &= \int_0^x f_X(p)\,dp \int_0^y f_Y(q)\,dq \ldots \int_0^y f_Z(r)\,dr \\ &= P(X \le x) P(Y \le y) \ldots P(Z \le z) \end{aligned}$$

Independence and Random Samples

When the members of a group are independently randomly sampled each member of the group has the same chance of being drawn and no member is drawn on the basis of another member having been or not been drawn. Suppose for algebraic simplicity *x* is discrete with pdf $f_X(x)$ and suppose an independent random sample of size *N* is drawn with individual elements x_n, indexed $n = 1,\ldots,N$ will be such that the probability of drawing such a sample (referred to as the likelihood *L*) would be the product of their individual probabilities:

$$L(x_1, x_2, \ldots, x_N) = f_X(x_1) f_X(x_2) \ldots f_X(x_n)$$

This has implications for the properties of estimators of unknown parameters and summary statistics used in the comparison process and prompts a word of warning here. The statistical properties of estimators of unknown parameters and summary statistics are derived on the assumption that the data collection process has been based on random sampling. Very often the agencies that perform these tasks do not use random sampling techniques; rather, usually for reasons of economy, they will use representative sampling techniques known as Stratified or Cluster sampling techniques. In the former, the population is split into mutually exclusive and exhaustive strata and each strata randomly sampled, and in the latter the population is split into small clusters and randomly picked clusters are sampled (or a census is taken). The point is these approaches do not provide the investigator with genuine random samples and the usual properties of estimators using such samples do not naturally carry over.

Independence and Groups

What independence implies for between-group analysis can be understood by letting *Υ* be an integer random variable that determines group membership so that, given *K* groups indexed $y = 1,\ldots K$, the probability of being in group *k* is $P(y = k) = f_Y(y)$. Now suppose *X* represents household income and *Υ* represents the social class of a household, $f(x,y)$ corresponds to the joint distribution of household income and class and $f(x|y)$ is the probability density function (income distribution) of household incomes in class *y* and $f(y|x)$ is the probability density function (distribution) of households with income *x*. When *X* and *Υ* are independent $f(x|y) = f_X(x)$ and $f(y|x) = f_Y(y)$ which means that all household classes have the same income distribution and the distribution of households is the same at every income level. Alternatively put, the class of a household reveals nothing about its income and the income of a household reveals nothing about its class. These ideas are used extensively in Equality of Opportunity and Social and Economic Mobility and Generational Persistence studies.

Measures of Location and Dispersion

Very often, dependent on the matter at hand, collections of variables will be compared in terms of statistics which summarize a particular aspect of their respective distributions such as their general locations or spreads. For example, a collection of societies are frequently compared using their respective average, median or modal incomes or wages; sometimes attention focuses on comparison of their spreads using measures of their respective variation. Generally, these measures will be discussed in the following chapters but the mean and variance, summary statistics basic to the exercise, happen to be related to specific features of the pdfs of those variables, some of which depend upon a notion of the expectations operator.

Means and Variances and the Expectations Operator

The expected value of any function of X say $g(x)$, is denoted by $E(g(x))$. $E(\ )$ should be thought of as a mathematical operator or instruction, just as $\frac{dg(x)}{dx}$, the derivative operator, is an instruction which says "take the derivative of $g(x)$" according to a well specified set of rules, and so $E(g(x))$ is an instruction to perform the operation "take the expected value of the g function of X" which is:

$$E(g(x)) = \int_0^\infty f(x)g(x)dx$$

In the discrete case when X has cardinal measure, it is defined as:

$$E(g(x)) = \sum_{\text{over all } i} f(x_i)g(x_i)$$

So $E(g(X))$ tells us to perform one of the above calculations dependent on whether X is continuous or discrete. Like the derivative and integral operators, the expectations operator is a linear operator so that the expected value of a linear function of random variables is the same linear function of the expected values of those random variables. Aside from the general applicability of the above formulae for developing concepts of statistical interest like moment generating functions and characteristic functions, there are forms of $g(\ )$ that are of particular interest. For example $g(x) = x$ yields the first moment or expected value of X, namely $E(X)$, and $g(x)=(x-E(x))^2$ yields the variance of X, namely $V(X)$.

$E(X)$, the expected value, is frequently referred to as the mean and represented by the Greek character μ, a constant providing a measure of where the center of the distribution is located. The metric here is the same as that of the random variable so that, if $f(x)$ is an income distribution measured in US\$, then its location will be in terms of a US\$ value. Of use later on is the relationship between the $E(X)$ and $F(X)$. Suppose the income distribution has a finite upper bound of $b < \infty$ and a lower bound of 0 so that $E(X)=\int_0^b xf(x)dx$ then integrating by parts[1] yields:

$$\int_0^b xf(x)dx=\left[xF(x)\right]_0^b-\int_0^b 1.F(x)dx=b-\int_0^b F(x)dx=\int_0^b (1-F(x))dx$$

So another formula for $E(X)$ is:

$$E(X)=\int_0^b (1-F(x))dx$$

The usefulness of the linearity property of the expectations operator can be seen by letting $g(X) = a + bX$ where a and b are fixed constants. Taking expectations of this $g(X)$, yields the expected value of a linear function of X which, following the respective rules of summation and integration, can be shown to be the same linear function of the expected value of X as follows:

[1] Integration by parts is a mathematical trick for developing a formula that is based on the convolution of two functions $u(x)$ and $v(x)$ defined on $[0,b]$ such that $\int_0^b u(x)v'(x)dx=\left[u(x)v(x)\right]_0^b-\int_0^b u'(x)v(x)dx$ letting $u(x) = x$ and $v(x) = F(x)$ and substituting yields the result.

$$E(a+bX)=\int_0^\infty (a+bx)f(x)dx=a\int_0^\infty f(x)dx+b\int_0^\infty xf(x)dx=a+bE(X)$$

What the above demonstrates is two basic rules for expectations operators regardless of whether random variables are discrete or continuous:

1. E(a) = a "The expected value of a constant is a constant".
2. E(bX) = bE(X) "The expected value of a constant times a random variable is equal to the constant times the expected value of the random variable".

More generally let X, Y and Z be three random variables each with their own density functions and let $W = aX + bY + cZ$, then $E(W) = aE(X) + bE(Y) + cE(Z)$.

For completeness note that the median, denoted μ_{med}, is the value of X such that:

$$\int_0^{\mu_{\text{med}}} f(x)dx = 0.5$$

And the mode, which is denoted μ_{mode} and defined for unimodal or single peaked distributions, is that value of X which maximizes $f(x)$. For univariate distributions either $\mu \le \mu_{\text{med}} \le \mu_{\text{mode}}$ or $\mu \ge \mu_{\text{med}} \ge \mu_{\text{mode}}$ dependent on whether $f(x)$ is left skewed or right skewed, when $f(x)$ is symmetric $\mu = \mu_{\text{med}} = \mu_{\text{mode}}$.

Functions of the form $g(x)=(x-E(x))^i$ $i = 1,\ldots$ yield the "ith" moments about the mean. The metric here is the ith power of that of the original distribution so that if $f(x)$ relates to incomes measured in US$ then the ith moment about the mean is measured in $(\text{US\$})^i$. Sometimes the ith root of $g(X)$ is employed since it yields a measure of the appropriate characteristic in terms of the original units of the distribution. Furthermore, to make distributions measured under different metrics comparable, the function $g(X)$ deflated by the appropriate power of $E(X)$ (provided it is not 0) is considered, providing a metric free comparator. The second moment ($i = 2$) is of particular interest[2] since as the variance

[2] The third moment provides a measure of skewness or how asymmetric a distribution is and the fourth, a measure of kurtosis or how peaked a distribution is, but these will not be considered here.

(frequently represented as σ^2 or $V(X)$, its square root σ is referred to as the standard deviation) it provides a measure of how spread out a distribution is.

From a practical perspective when confronting a data set (which we refer to as "a sample" drawn from "the distribution") measures reflecting the location and dispersion of the distribution are required. For convenience it will be assumed that the sample is indexed in ascending order so that in a sample of N incomes x_n, for $n = 1,\ldots, N$, x_1 is the smallest and x_N is the largest and for any $x_i, x_j\ i > j => x_i \geq x_j$.

Location Measures

The two most popular location measures are the mean $\bar{X} = \frac{1}{N}\sum_{n=1}^{N} x_n$ and median $\bar{\bar{X}} = x_{n^*}$ where $x_{n^*} = x_{\frac{N+1}{2}}$ for N odd $= x_{\frac{N}{2}} + x_{\frac{N}{2}+1}$ for N even, the other location measure, the mode, which requires estimates of $f(x)$ denoted $\hat{f}(x)$ is the value of x which maximizes $\hat{f}(x)$.

Inequality Measures

Classic measures of distributional inequality such as the range $(x_N - x_1)$, the interquartile range (the range of the middle 50% of the population), the variance $\hat{\sigma}^2 = \sum_{n=1}^{N} \frac{(x_i - \bar{X})^2}{N-1}$ (where $\bar{X} = \sum_{n=1}^{N} \frac{x_n}{N}$) and standard deviation $\sqrt{\hat{\sigma}^2}$ are absolute measures of inequality, reflecting the scale of X, what is usually required for inequality adjusted wellbeing measurement are relative, or unit free, measures which facilitate comparison across diverse domains.[3]

Some Unit Free Inequality Measures

The relative range $\left(R = \frac{x_n - x_1}{\mu}\right)$, the span of incomes divided by a location measure, or inter-decile ($R_{10\%}$) and interquartile ($R_{25\%}$) relative ranges are used as substitutes where:

[3] If, for example, a comparison of income inequality in the United States (measured in US$) with that of Bangladesh (measured in Takas) is required, a unit free measure will do the trick since currency values cancel out.

$$R_{10\%} = \frac{F^*(0.9) - F^*(0.1)}{\mu} \text{ and } R_{25\%} = \frac{F^*(0.75) - F^*(0.25)}{\mu}$$

Also of interest is the Coefficient of Variation (CV) given by $CV = \sqrt{\frac{E\left((X - E(X))^2\right)}{(E(X))^2}}$ which may be interpreted as a metric free measure of relative dispersion. Alternative unit free measures that arise in the literature are the Relative Mean or Median Deviation $\left(D = \sum_{i=1}^{n} \frac{|\mu - x_i|}{n\mu}\right)$, which is the average deviation from a location measure divided by that same location measure is not unlike the Coefficient of Variation. Also deserving of a mention are the Standard Deviation of Logarithms $L = \sqrt{\frac{\sum_{i=1}^{n}(\ln\mu - \ln x_i)}{n}}$, Theils Entropy $T = \sum_{i=1}^{n} \frac{x_i}{n\mu} \ln\left(\frac{x_i}{\mu}\right)$ (which is related to the Generalized Entropy Class of measures[4] $GE = \frac{1}{n}\sum_{i=1}^{n}\left[\frac{1}{\alpha^2 - \alpha}\left[\left(\frac{x_i}{\mu}\right)^{\alpha} - 1\right]\right]$), Atkinsons' family of measures $1 - \frac{\left[\sum_{i=1}^{n} \frac{1}{n} x_i^r\right]^{1/r}}{\mu}$ for $(0 < r < 1)$ and the Shutz coefficient $S = \frac{1}{n\mu}\sum_{i=1}^{n}(\mu - x_i)I(\mu - x_i)$ where $I(.)$ is an indicator function which is 0 when its argument is negative and 1 otherwise. Perhaps the most popular unit free measure of inequality is the Gini coefficient G, which for a collection of n incomes is given as $G = \frac{\sum_{i=1}^{n}\sum_{j=1}^{n}|x_i - x_j|}{n^2\mu}$ or the average absolute

[4] The parameter α (>1) is a "tail sensitivity" parameter chosen by the investigator, T can be obtained by taking the limit of GE as α = >1.

difference in a set of numbers divided by their average. It has many alternative forms, for example when the *x*s are ordered it may be written as:

$$G = \frac{1}{n\overline{X}} \sum_{i=1}^{n} \left(x_i - \overline{X}\right) F\left(x_i\right)$$

and it can also be written in distribution function form as[5]:

$$G = \frac{\int_0^\infty \int_0^\infty f(x) f(y) |x - y| dy dx}{\mu}.$$

Returning to the variance, regardless of whether the variable is discrete or continuous, notice that:

$$\begin{aligned} V(X) &= E\left(\left(X - E(X)\right)^2\right) \\ &= E\left(X^2 - 2E(X)X + \left(E(X)\right)^2\right) \\ &= E\left(X^2\right) - 2E\left(E(X)X\right) + \left(E(X)\right)^2 \\ &= E\left(X^2\right) - \left(E(X)\right)^2 \end{aligned}$$

so that the variance is equal to the expected value of X^2 less the square of the expected value of X. Furthermore, again regardless of whether the random variable is discrete or continuous notice that for $Y = a + bX$:

$$\begin{aligned} V(Y) &= E\left(\left(Y - E(Y)\right)^2\right) \\ &= E\left(\left(a + bX - \left(a + bE(X)\right)\right)^2\right) \\ &= E\left(\left(bX - bE(X)\right)^2\right) \\ &= b^2 E\left(\left(X - E(X)\right)^2\right) \\ &= b^2 V(X) \end{aligned}$$

[5] Note that this form can be generalized to a multivariate Gini by thinking of the integration signs as multiple integrals relating to the vector x thinking of $|x - y|$ as the Euclidean norm and replacing μ with the Euclidean norm of the vector $E(x)$.

so that the variance of a constant is zero and the variance of a constant times a random variable is the square of the constant times the random variable. The variance of a linear function of several random variables is a little more complicated, depending as it does on the relationships between the random variables it will be dealt with when multivariate analysis is considered later on.

There are numerous discrete and continuous probability density functions to suit all kinds of purposes, one of the arts in practicing statistics is that of choosing the one most appropriate for a particular problem.

2.3 Parametric and Non-Parametric Distributions

Often a theory, be it social, economic, political or statistical will be informative as to the specific parametric nature of the distribution of a particular random variable such as its parametric form, the only thing missing is the values of the parameters that define the distribution. Other times no information will be available and resort will have to be made to non-parametric distributions. Linton 2017 and Poirier 1995 provide detailed discussion of these issues from somewhat different perspectives, here for illustrative purposes an example each of discrete and continuous distributions will be outlined to get an idea of what they are like and how they work.

An Example of a Discrete Probability Density Function: The Poisson Distribution

The Poisson distribution is employed in situations where the object of interest is the number of times a given event occurs in a given amount of space or period of time. Thus for example it could be used to study the number of crashes that take place at a particular spot over a period of a week or it could be used to investigate the number of faults in a fixed length of steel or it could be used to study the number of children in households which have completed their fertility decisions. The presumption in this model is that successive weeks, or successive lengths of steel or different households are independent of one another and that the same probability model is applicable in each successive observation. Suppose X is the number of occurrences of the event, then the pdf is given by:

$$f(x,\gamma) = \frac{\gamma^{x} e^{-\gamma}}{x!}$$

where γ is a parameter (whose value is unknown) such that $E(X) = V(X) = \gamma$.

Figures 2.1 and 2.2 illustrate the changing shape of Poisson pdfs and cdfs for values of γ = 2, 3 and 4 denoted respectively as POI(2), POI(3) and POI(4).

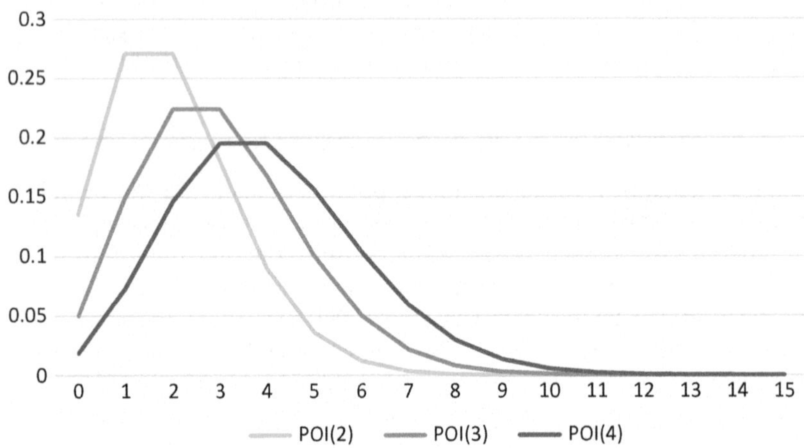

Fig. 2.1 Poisson pdfs. (Source: Author's calculations)

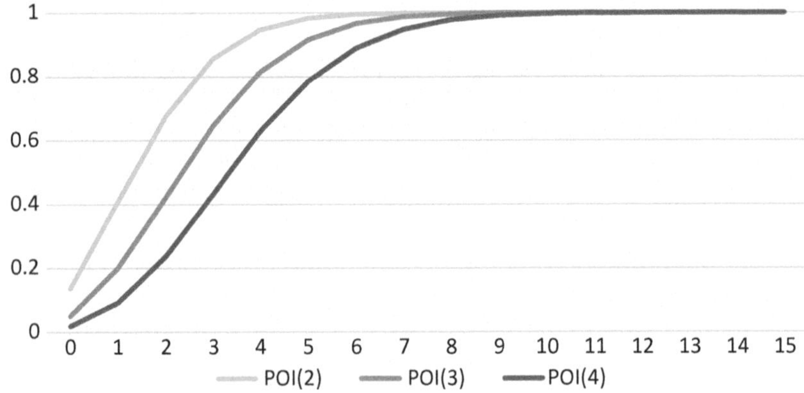

Fig. 2.2 Poisson cdfs. (Source: Author's calculations)

An Example of Continuous Probability Density Function: The Normal Distribution

The normal distribution is probably the most frequently employed distribution in statistics with good reason; there are sound theoretical reasons why it can be employed in a wide range of circumstances where averages are used. Its pdf is of the form:

$$f\left(x, \mu, \sigma^2\right) = \frac{1}{\sqrt{2\pi\sigma^2}} e^{-\frac{(x-\mu)^2}{2\sigma^2}}$$

The parameters μ and σ^2 respectively correspond to the mean $E(X)$ and variance $V(X)$ of X. The fact that X is normally distributed with a mean μ and a variance σ^2 is often denoted by $X \sim N(\mu, \sigma^2)$. The normal distribution does not have a closed form representation for the cumulative density $F(X)$ (i.e. we cannot write down an algebraic expression for it) but this will not present any difficulties since it is tabulated and most statistical software packages are capable of performing the appropriate calculations. The distribution is symmetric about the mean, bell shaped with extremely thin tails to the extent that more than 99% of the distribution lays within $\mu \pm 3\sigma$. In fact, as a basic rule 65% lays within $\mu \pm 1\sigma$ and 95% lays within $\mu \pm 2\sigma$. As an illustration, and for comparison purposes, the pdfs, cdfs and integrated cdfs of 3 normal distributions N(3.8, 0.5), N(4.0, 0.5) and N(4.0, 0.7) are exemplified in Figs. 2.3, 2.4 and 2.5. Note the differences that small changes in parameter values make to location and spread.

Normal random variables possess the very useful property that their linear functions are also normal. Hence if X is normal then $Z = a + bX$ is also normal and, using our rules for expectations, $E(Z) = a + bE(X)$ and $V(Z) = b^2 V(X)$. Letting $a = -\mu/\sigma$ and $b = 1/\sigma$, $Z \sim N(0,1)$ which is referred to as a Standard Normal Random Variable (indeed the standard normal variable is frequently referred to with the letter *z*, hence the term "*z* score"). This is most useful since $N(0,1)$ is the distribution that is tabulated in textbooks and programmed in software packages. Suppose we need to calculate $P(X < x_0)$ where x_0 is some known value and $X \sim N(\mu, \sigma^2)$ and since $Z = (X - \mu)/\sigma$:

$$P\left(X < x_0\right) = P\left(\frac{(X-\mu)}{\sigma} < \frac{(x_0-\mu)}{\sigma}\right) = P\left(Z < \frac{(x_0-\mu)}{\sigma}\right)$$

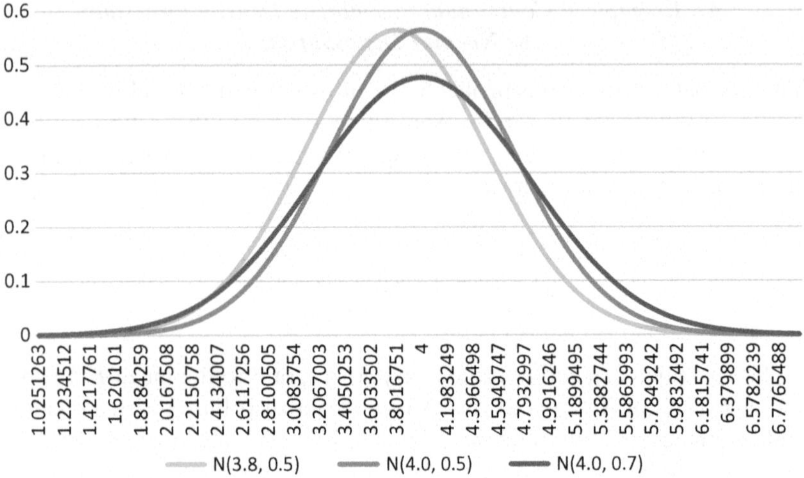

Fig. 2.3 Normal pdfs. (Source: Author's calculations)

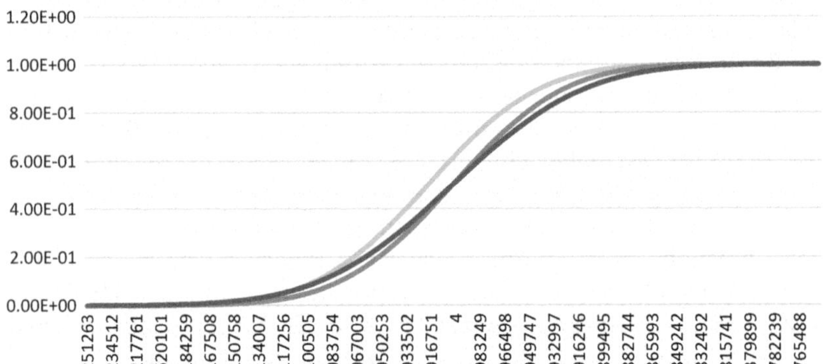

Fig. 2.4 Normal cdfs. (Source: Author's calculations)

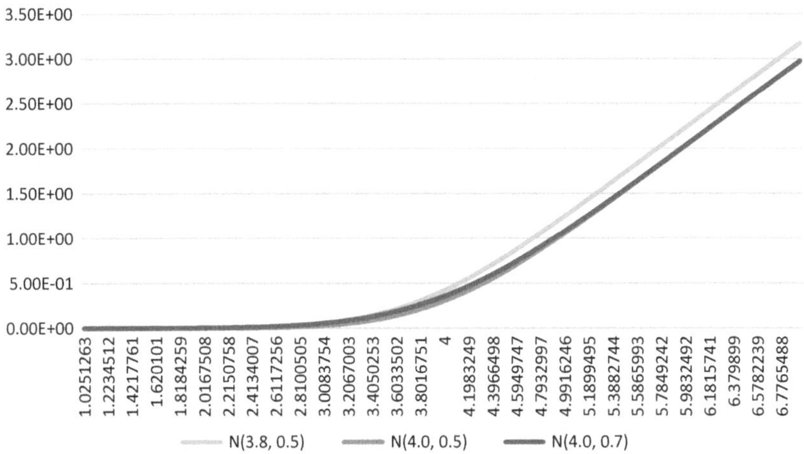

Fig. 2.5 Integrated normal cdfs. (Source: Author's calculations)

so all that is needed is to calculate the value $(x_0 - \mu)/\sigma$ and employ the standard normal tables or software package to evaluate the probability.

Multidimensional Considerations

Multidimensional versions of parametric distributions are readily available, although their algebraic representation can be complicated.

A Note of Caution

Much of the business of ordering or ranking groups has to do with comparing their respective distributions. As the dimensions of analysis increase, distinguishing between groups becomes more difficult. To see this consider the K dimensioned standard normal distribution whose pdf $f(x_1, x_2, \ldots, x_K)$, is given as:

$$f(x_1, x_2, \ldots, x_K) = \frac{1}{\sqrt{2}^K} e^{-0.5\sum_{k=1}^{K} x_k^2}$$

The height of the distribution at its peak (when $x_k = 0$ for all $k = 1, \ldots, K$) will be $\frac{1}{\sqrt{2}^K}$, so as K gets large the surface flattens in that the peak tends toward zero. As a general principle, this is true of all symmetric unimodal distributions, as their dimensionality increases their surfaces flatten. When distinguishing between two groups each described by K dimensioned probability distributions, it is the distance between their respective surfaces that facilitates distinction, it follows that as K increases this distance will automatically be compressed and differences between the distributions much harder to detect as a consequence.

The Normal Distribution and Central Limit Theorems

The normal distribution has a special place in the statistical lexicon because of a family of mathematical/statistical theorems known as central limit theorems (see Rao 1973 for details) which predict that, under very general circumstances, averages of things turn out to be normally distributed, indeed they are the basis of Gibrat's law (1931) which will be invoked in later chapters. The very basic idea is that, given a sequence of random variables X_n for $n = 1, \ldots, n$, drawn from any distribution where $E(X_n) = \mu$ and $V(X_n) = \sigma^2$ (imagine, e.g. the n elements of a random sample of X), the average of the xs, $\bar{X}_n = \frac{\sum_{i=1}^{n} X_i}{n}$ is such that $\sqrt{n}\frac{(\bar{X}_n - \mu)}{\sigma}$ is $N(0,1)$ for n sufficiently large, regardless of the original distributions of the underlying Xs. This implies that $\bar{X}_n$ is distributed $N\left(\mu, \frac{\sigma^2}{n}\right)$ as the sample size gets large ($\bar{X}_n$ is said to be "asymptotically normal") which is important for inference and confidence interval purposes. The theorems are quite general and can be developed for quite general non-independent sequences of xs, the important point being that knowledge of the distribution underlying the Xs is not required.

This is a quite different situation from the sample median $\bar{M}_n$ which is asymptotically normally distributed $N\left(M, \frac{1}{4nf(M)^2}\right)$. Here $\bar{M}_n$ is the sample median estimate of the true median M and $f(x)$ is the distribution underlying the *X*s. So here, knowledge of the underlying distribution of the random variables is required.

Estimation of Unknown Parameters

The statistical methodology literature for estimation is extensive and will not be summarized here—most commonly Maximum Likelihood methods, which choose those parameter values which maximize the chance of observing the sample that was observed; and Method of Moments methods, which choose those parameter values which equate the theoretical moments with the sample moments. When parameters of a distribution represent means or variances they are typically estimated using the sample mean $\left(\bar{X} = \frac{\sum_{i=1}^{n} x_i}{n}\right)$ and sample variance $\left(\sigma^2 = \frac{\sum_{i=1}^{n}\left(x_i - \bar{X}\right)^2}{n-1}\right)$ of a random sample $x_i; i = 1, \ldots, n$ drawn from the population described by the distribution. These estimators have good properties as any good statistical textbook would indicate.

2.4 Kernel Estimation

Non-Parametric Distributions

Sometimes information about the parametric structure of a distribution is not available and resort has to be made to non-parametric distributions, distributional structures which don't rely upon information about parametric structures. In this case, the probability functions need to be estimated which is in the realm of non-parametric statistics (excellent resources for this material Pagan and Ullah 1999 and Silverman 1986). Multilateral comparison of groups frequently involves comparing their respective distributions when little is known about their nature or shape in which case the distributions have to be estimated non-parametrically.

The issue to be addressed here is the estimation of some unknown density function $f(x)$ which underlies a sample of observations on x and since this situation arises frequently in multilateral comparisons it will be outlined in some detail here. Given such a sample x_i, $i = 1,\ldots,n$, the generation of a naive estimate of $f(x)$ is straightforward. If the random variable X has the density $f(x)$ then:

$$f(x) = \lim_{h \to 0} \frac{1}{2h} P(x - h < X < x + h)$$

for given h we can estimate $P(x - h < X < x + h)$ by the proportion of observations falling into the interval $x - h$, $x + h$. Letting $I(\ )$ be an indicator function where $I(z) = 1$ if z is true and 0 otherwise, our estimator of $f(x)$ (call it $f^e(x)$) may be written as:

$$f^e(x) = \frac{1}{n} \sum_{i=1}^{n} \frac{1}{2h} I\left(\left|\frac{x - x_i}{h}\right| < 1\right)$$

There is a connection with histograms, suppose no x_i lands exactly on the boundary of a bin, then this estimator corresponds to splitting the range of the random variable into bins of width 2 h allowing x to be the "center" of each bin and treating $f^e(x)$ as the ordinate of the histogram. The problem with this type of estimator is that it is not "smooth" but consists of a sequence of jumps at $x \pm h$ with a zero derivative everywhere else. Kernel estimators get around this problem by replacing .5I( ) in the above formula by a **kernel function** $K(\ )$ with certain desirable properties that to some degree resolve the "smoothness" problem. So that our estimator looks like:

$$f^e(x) = \frac{1}{nh} \sum_{i=1}^{n} K\left(\frac{x - x_i}{h}\right)$$

where h is usually referred to as the band width, window width or smoothing parameter.

The Kernel Function

Generally, a kernel function would be selected so that it satisfies:

$$\int_{-\infty}^{\infty} K(y)dy = 1$$

making the vast array of continuous density functions suitable candidates. Provided $K(\ )$ is everywhere non-negative (making it a density function)

$f^e(\ )$ will itself be a density function and will inherit all of the continuity and differentiability properties of K.

Three Examples:

In each of the following h is the bandwidth and $t_i = (x - X_i)/h$. The **Epanechnikov** Kernel $K_E(t_i)$ is of the form:

$$K_E(t_i) = \frac{.75(1-.2t_i^2)}{\sqrt{5}} t_i^2 < 5$$
$$= 0 \text{ otherwise}$$

The **Gaussian** Kernel $K_G(t_i)$ is of the form:

$$K_G(t_i) = \frac{1}{(2\pi)^{.5}} e^{\frac{t_i^2}{2}}$$

The **Biweight** Kernel $K_B(t_i)$ is of the form:

$$K_B(t_i) = \frac{15}{16}(1-t^2)^2 \mid t \mid < 1; 0 \text{ otherwise.}$$

Note also that the original naive estimator is like a rectangular kernel with $K(t) = .5$ It $I < 1$, 0 otherwise.

Choosing the "H" and the Kernel

$$\text{MISE}(f^e) = E\int(f^e(x) - f(x))^2 dx$$

Thinking about the mean integrated squared error of the estimator defined by the above-mentioned equation note that, since the integrand is non-negative the order of integration and expectation can be reversed, note also that $E(f^e - f)^2 = E(f^e - E(f^e) + E(f^e) - f)^2 = (E(f^e) - f)^2 + E(f^e - E(f^e))^2 = \text{bias}^2 + \text{var}(f^e)$ yielding:

$$\text{MISE}(f^e) = \int(E(f^e(x)) - f(x))^2 dx + \int \text{var}(f^e(x))dx$$

which is the integrated squared bias plus the integrated variance. This would conceptually be a useful thing to minimize in choosing h and the Kernel. Rewriting $K^* = K/h$ it can be noted that:

$$E\left(f^e\right)=\frac{1}{n}\sum_{i=1}^{n}E\left(k^*\left(t_i\right)\right)=\int k^*\left(t\right)f\left(x\right)dx$$

which, for given *f*, does not depend upon *n* but only on *K* and *h*. This indicates that taking larger samples alone will not reduce the bias, attention has to be focused on the choice of *h* and *K*!

Confining attention to Kernels symmetric about zero with continuous derivatives at all orders with a variance v_k, it can be shown that that the optimal *h* is equal to:

$$v_k^{-\frac{2}{5}}\left(\int K\left(t\right)^2 dt\right)^{\frac{1}{5}}\left(\int f''\left(x\right)^2 dx\right)^{\frac{-1}{5}} n^{\frac{-1}{5}}$$

Unfortunately "optimal *h*" here depends upon knowledge of the unknown *f*( ) we are attempting to estimate; however, it does tell us that the optimal window gets smaller as the sample size grows (last term) and as the degree of fluctuation of the unknown function increases (penultimate term). Substituting the value of the optimal *h* back into the formula for the mean integrated squared error and minimizing with respect to *K* results in the Epanechnikov Kernel. The relative efficiencies of other kernels can be shown to be 0.9512 for the Gaussian kernel, 0.9939 for the Biweight kernel and 0.9295 for the rectangular suggesting that there is little to choose between kernels on efficiency grounds.

Choosing "H"

Referring to the normal family of distributions with a variance σ^2 yields a value of "optimal *h*" of $1.06\,\sigma n^{-0.2}$. One could then estimate σ from the data and, on the presumption that the distribution being estimated was like the normal, use this as the value for *h*. When the underlying distribution is not normal this tends to result in over-smoothing (especially when bi-modality is present). A safe alternative, based on a sample standard deviation of σ and a sample inter-quartile range of ξ, the bandwidth "*h*" is specified as:

$$h=\frac{.9\min\left(\sigma,\frac{\xi}{1.34}\right)}{n^{\frac{1}{5}}}$$

Least Squares Cross Validation

Noting that the integrated squared error may be written as:

$$\int\left(f^{e}-f\right)^{2}=\int f^{e2}-2\int f^{e}f+)\int f^{2}$$

and that the last term does not depend upon f^e and hence h's interest focuses on minimizing an approximation to the first two terms with respect to h. After some tedious argument, it may be shown that a good approximation to these two terms is:

$$\frac{1}{n^{2}h}\sum_{i}\sum_{j}K^{c}\left(\frac{X_{i}-X_{j}}{h}\right)+\frac{2}{nh}K(0)$$

where K^c is defined as:

$$K^{c}(t)=K^{2}(t)-2K(t)$$

and $K^2(t)$ is the convolution of the Kernel with itself. Numerical methods for minimizing this with respect to h can easily consume inordinate amounts of time; however, Fourier transform methods can be used to substantially reduce computations (see Silverman pages 61–66). Nonetheless, the computational burden remains considerable.

Likelihood Cross Validation

Let $f_{-i}(\ )$ be the Kernel estimate calculated by missing out observation x_i then $\ln f_{-1}(x_i)$ is the log- likelihood of f as the density underlying the independent additional observation x_i. We can think of maximizing this with respect to h; indeed, why not maximize:

$$CV(h)=\frac{1}{n}\sum_{i=1}^{n}\ln f_{-i}(x_{i})$$

This is related to the Kullback-Leibler Information distance $I(f, f^e)$ where:

$$I\left(f,f^{e}\right)=\int f(x)\ln\frac{f(x)}{f^{e}(x)}dx$$

Thinking of $E(CV(h))$ as the expectation of f^e for some arbitrary j we have:

$$E\left(\ln f_{-j}^{\ e}\right)=\int f\ln f_{-j}^{\ e}dx=\int f\left(\ln f_{-j}^{\ e}-\ln f\right)dx$$
$$+\int f\ln f dx\approx -I\left(f,f^{e}\right)+\int f\ln f dx$$

Thus, we are minimizing the Kullback-Leibler information distance plus a constant. Alternatively, one can eyeball the problem. Plot out a selection of curves based upon different *h*s and choose the one that best suits ones prior beliefs.

A Variable Bandwidth H: The Adaptive Kernel

One of the problems with the above estimators is that the degree of smoothing is constant over all *x*, the same value in regions densely populated with *x* as it is in regions sparsely populated with *x*. This can lead to over-smoothing in the dense areas (removing bumps that should be there) and/or under-smoothing in sparse areas (failing to remove bumps that should not be there). To solve this problem a variable bandwidth estimator has been developed. Essentially, in this case our estimator f^{ae} is of the form:

$$f^{ae}(x)=\frac{1}{n}\sum_{i=1}^{n}\frac{1}{h_i}K\left(\frac{x-x_i}{h_i}\right)$$

where h_i is usually referred to as the local band width, window width or smoothing parameter. Various methods are available for estimation in this case; one of the simplest, most practical and most effective is the following. Compute f^e in one of the preceding methods which yields a fixed bandwidth h. Calculate f^{gm} the geometric mean of f^e for the sample given by:

$$f^{gm}=\prod_{i=1}^{n}f^{e}(X_i)^{\frac{1}{n}}$$

Set h_i as:

$$h_i = h\left(\frac{f^e(X_i)}{f^{gm}}\right)^{-a}$$

where a is a sensitivity parameter chosen by the investigator. Most applications seem to choose $a = 0.5$.

Consistency of the Kernel Estimator

Under apparently very mild conditions on the kernel convergence in probability of $f^e(x)$ to $f(x)$ (convergence at a point) can be established. Essentially the requirement on h is that it does not converge to 0 as rapidly as n^{-1} ensuring the expected number of points in $x \pm h_n$ tends to infinity with n. Further, and more importantly, under similar conditions $\sup_x|f^e(x) - f(x)|$ can also be shown to converge to 0. A note of caution, the rate of convergence is often very slow so that in this instance consistency is by no means a warranty for good estimates!

Kernel estimates of the cumulative density function are facilitated by noting that $F^e(x) = \int f^e(x)dx = \int \frac{1}{nh}\sum_{i=1}^{n} K\left(\frac{x - x_i}{h}\right) = \frac{1}{nh}\sum_{i=1}^{n}\int K\left(\frac{x - x_i}{h}\right)$ so that a judicious choice of kernel with a closed form integral solution such as the Biweight or Epanechnikov kernels makes for easy computation.

2.5 Stochastic Dominance Relations

Using summary statistics to rank a collection of societies can present difficulties. Whilst always yielding a definitive ranking for comparison purposes (referred to as a complete ordering) alternative summary statistics (such as the mean the median and the mode), can give contradictory rankings, in essence there is an ambiguity problem here. A partial solution to this problem is to compare the complete distributions over all values of X using stochastic dominance comparisons (For a detailed discussion of these techniques see Whang 2019). The solution is partial in the sense that the comparison is only pairwise and the comparison is not always conclusive.

Consider two pdfs of X, $f(x)$ and $g(x)$ representing income distributions of France and Germany. Define $F^h(x) = \int_0^x F^{h-1}(z)dz$ with $F^0(x) = f(x)$

and similarly define $G^h(x)=\int_0^x G^{h-1}(z)dz$ with $G^0(x)=g(x)$. Then France is said to dominate Germany at the *h*th order when:

$$F^h(x)\le G^h(x)\,\text{for all}\,x\,\text{with strict inequality somewhere}$$

These conditions were developed in finance theory as being necessary for establishing that the average value of some function *U*(*x*) was greater under distribution *f*(*x*) than it was under *g*(*x*) where $(-1)^{i+1}\dfrac{\partial^h U(x)}{\partial x^h}>0\ h=1,\ldots$ which are standard assumptions for actors with risk averse preferences. Similar conditions can be developed for risk lovers (see Levy 1998).

These ideas can be extended to many dimensions. Atkinson and Bourguignon (1982) extended SD techniques to more than one dimension but things get much more complicated both theoretically (largely due to the conditions for concavity and convexity in multidimensional functions being much more complicated) and for empirical practicality reasons (curse of dimensionality); see Anderson (2007).

2.6 Comparing Distributions

Two concepts that are useful for comparing groups are (1) the extent to which their respective distributions Overlap (OV) and (2) their Transvariation (TR).[6] These are two closely related concepts: for Distributional Transvariation, see Gini (1916, 1959); for Distributional Overlap, see Anderson et al. (2012). Consider two groups whose continuous distributions are represented by *f*(*x*) and *g*(*x*), each defined on the closed interval [a,b]. Overlap (OV) is a measure commonality between the groups where:

$$OV=\int_a^b \min\left(f(x),g(x)\right)dx$$

Whereas the Transvariation (TR) is a measure of the lack of commonality:

$$TR=0.5\int_a^b\left\{\max\left(f(x),g(x)\right)-\min\left(f(x),g(x)\right)\right\}dx=0.5\int_a^b\left|f(x)-g(x)\right|dx$$

[6]These concepts can be more generally applied to transformed distributions which facilitate focus on particular aspects of distributional differences/similarities (see for example Tukey 1977, Handcock and Morris 1999 and Anderson et. al. 2017).

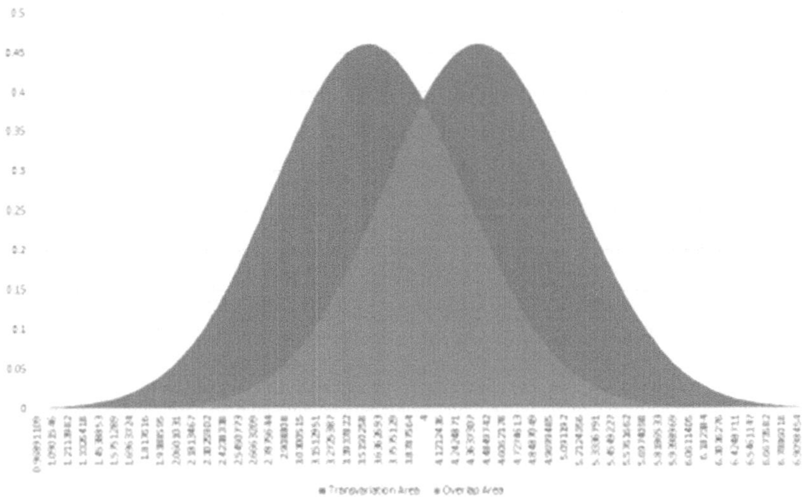

Fig. 2.6 Transvariations and Overlaps for two distributions with different means. (Source: Author's calculations)

Note that $0 \leq OV, TR \leq 1$. When the groups are perfectly segmented (i.e. when $f(x) > 0$, $g(x) = 0$ and when $g(x) > 0$ $f(x) = 0$) $OV = 0$ and $TR = 1$, when the distributions are identical (i.e. $f(x)= g(x)$ for all x) $OV = 1$ and $TR = 0$. It is also the case that TR = 1-OV. The Overlap (orange) and the Transvariation in blue are illustrated in Figs. 2.6 and 2.7.

Tests for Similarity of Two Distributions

There are many alternative tests for examining differences between distributions with very different properties (Anderson 2006). Two classic tests for the difference between two distributions are the Pearson type tests and Kolmogorov-Smirnov type test. The former family of tests is based on choosing a set of points to partition the range of the random variable into mutually exclusive and exhaustive sectors and comparing differences in the probability of the random variable falling into those sectors. Many tests of this form, (Pearson Goodness of Fit tests, Tests for Differences in Distributional Form and Stochastic Dominance Tests) suffer the possibility of inconsistency or at least of not being as powerful as they could be because of an injudicious choice of partition points. The latter family of tests compares the cumulative distribution functions of two densities focusing on the maximum vertical distance

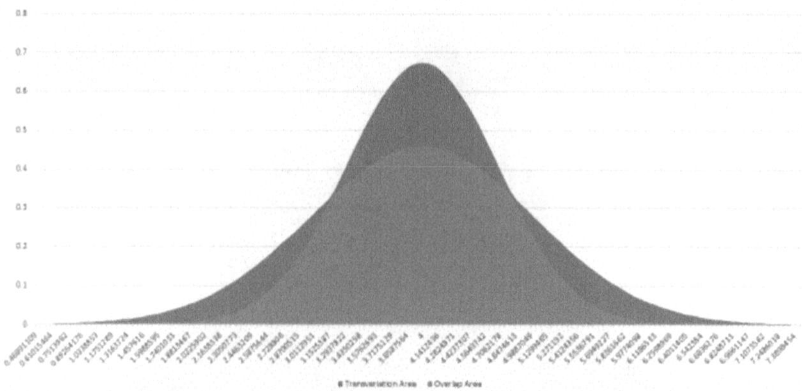

Fig. 2.7 Transvariations and Overlaps for two distributions with common means. (Source: Author's calculations)

between their respective cdfs; they tend to have lower power (the chance of correctly rejecting the null of no difference). The Kolmogorov-Smirnov test is simply employed. Let $\hat{F}_a(x), \hat{F}_b(x)$ be the respective estimates of the cdfs of distributions $f_a(x)$ and $f_b(x)$, the comparator. $D\left(\hat{F}_a(x), \hat{F}_b(x)\right) = \sup_x \left|\hat{F}_a(x) - \hat{F}_b(x)\right|$ is compared to a critical value $c(n_a n_b \alpha) = \sqrt{-0.5\ln(\alpha)}\left(\frac{n_a + n_b}{n_a n_b}\right)$, where n_a and n_b are the respective sample sizes and α is the chosen size of the test. The null hypothesis of commonality is rejected if $D > c$. Stochastic dominance tests can be contrived using $D\left(\hat{F}_a(x), \hat{F}_b(x)\right) = \sup_x \left(\hat{F}_a(x) - \hat{F}_b(x)\right)$ and $D\left(\hat{F}_a(x), \hat{F}_b(x)\right) = \inf_x \left(\hat{F}_a(x) - \hat{F}_b(x)\right)$. Rejection of one together with non-rejection of the other indicates a first order dominance relation.

Here the potential for inconsistency is examined and recommendations for maximizing power are made. Tests based on the overlap statistic or equivalently Gini's Transvariation are found to avoid the test inconsistency problem and maximize power.

2.7 The Test Inconsistency Problem

A consistent test is one for whom the probability of correctly rejecting a fixed untrue hypothesis increases to one as the sample size grows without bound (Dodge 2003); on the other hand the power of an inconsistent test will fail to respond to such an increase in sample size in certain circumstances. Many of the tests proposed for examining equality (or otherwise) between two functions over a range by examining their proximity at a sequence of points or regions within that range are potentially inconsistent in this sense.[7] It can be shown that generally choice of the regions and the juxtaposition of the null and "true" alternatives is critical in this regard as it will affect the power and inconsistency properties of such tests.

For a simple demonstration of the effect of interval choice on the power of a test we consider a Pearson test of H_0: $x \sim U(0,1)$ against H_1: x not $U(0,1)$. For power considerations, suppose the true alternative is at $U(0.25,0.75)$ so the two distributions intersect at $x = 0.25$ and $x = 0.75$. Partitions for a three interval ($\chi^2(2)$) test are chosen at $0.5 \pm \delta$ for $0 \leq \delta \leq 0.5$. After some algebra, the corresponding goodness of fit test statistic "chi" may be written as a function of δ as:

$$\begin{aligned} \text{Chi} &= \frac{n\delta}{0.5-\delta} \text{ for } \; 0 \leq \delta \leq 0.25 \\ &= \frac{n\left(2\delta - 4\delta^2 + 0.25\right)}{2\delta} \text{ for } \; 0.25 < \delta \leq 0.5 \end{aligned}$$

The function is discontinuous at $\delta = 0.25$ and reaches a maximum there which is where the partition points coincide with the intersection points of the two distributions. For $\delta = 0$ there is just one partition point at $x = 0.5$ reducing the test to a two interval $\chi^2(1)$ test which will have a value 0 for all n and is thus an inconsistent test. In illustration of these points, Fig. 2.8 plots Chi/n for values of δ between zero and 0.5.

Note the distributional overlap test (Anderson et al. 2012) or equivalently Gini's Transvariation (Gini 1916) will have a value 0.5 for all n and

[7] Tests based on the structure of the Pearson Goodness of Fit test (Pearson 1900) including its modifications and extensions (Anderson 1996, 1988), Contingency Table and Homogeneity of Parallel samples tests that are applied to continuous distributions are all potentially inconsistent tests (Rao 1973), as are Lorenz and Generalized Lorenz Dominance tests (Beach and Davidson 1983), and Stochastic Dominance Tests in the Poverty, Inequality and Finance Literature (Anderson 1996, Davidson and Duclos 2000).

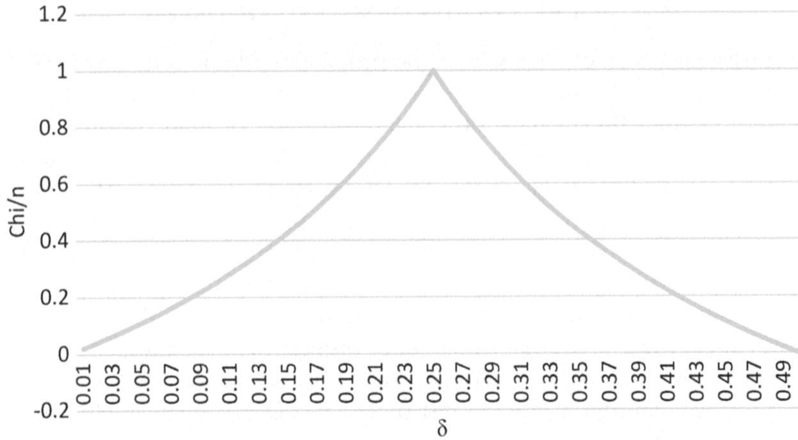

Fig. 2.8 $x^2(3)/n$ Test Statistic H_0:$X \sim U(0,1)$ v $H1$ $X \sim U(0.25,0.75)$. (Source: Author's calculations)

thus provides a consistent test in this case for n sufficiently large, that is, these tests do not suffer the test inconsistency problem. However, test inconsistency need not be much of a problem.

Generally, for two smooth and continuous probability density functions $f(x)$ and $g(x)$, defined for $x \in [a, b]$, based on a random sample (or samples) of a size that grow uniformly with the population size T, the family of tests in question can be generically represented by:

$$\text{GFT} = H(T)\sum_{k=1}^{K+1}\left(\sum_{j=1}^{K} I(j,k)\int_{y_{j-1}}^{y_j}\left(f(x)-g(x)\right)dx\right)^2 G_k + O\left(\frac{1}{T}\right) \quad (2.4)$$

where, y_j, $j = (1,\ldots,K)$ represents K mutually exhaustive ordered partition points (such that $y_1 < y_2 < ::: < y_K$), and together with $y_0 = a$ and $y_{K+1} = b$ fully partitions the support $[a; b]$ into $K + 1$ intervals. G_k is a function of the appropriate elements of the inverse of the covariance matrix of integrals of differences that appear in the test and are zero otherwise, and $I(j,k)$ is an indicator function equaling 1 when $j = k$ and 0 otherwise. The elements G_k are $O(1)$ asymptotically and may be thought of as a weighting factor for the kth comparison and $H(T)$, the sample size factor, is monotonically increasing and at least $O(T)$.

As examples, in goodness of fit tests, $f(x)$ corresponds to an empirical density function, $g(x)$ to the theoretical density under the null. In the parallel samples tests, $f(x)$ and $g(x)$ are two empirical densities being compared, in both cases $I(j) = 1$ for $j = k$, 0 otherwise ($H(T) = T$ in the former and $T_f T_g/(T_f + T_g)$ in the latter where T_f and T_g are the sample sizes from the respective distributions). In First Order Stochastic Dominance (and Lorenz) tests, $f(x)$ and $g(x)$ correspond to empirical density functions (or monotonic transformations of them) with $I(j) = 1$ for all j. In higher order dominance tests, $f(x)$ and $g(x)$ correspond to higher order integrals Anderson (1996) or incomplete moment estimates (Davidson and Duclos 2000) again with $I(j) = 1$.

Given the sample size factor is $H(T)$ and the covariance factors are $O(1)$, inconsistency of the Goodness of Fit Tests (GFT) in 2.4, when $f(x) \neq g(x)$ except for a finite K set of intersection points y_k $k = 1,\ldots,K$ requires that:

$$\int_{y_{k-1}}^{y_k} \left(f(x) - g(x)\right)dx = 0 \text{ for all } y_k \; k =,1,\ldots,K+1 \tag{2.5}$$

The partition points y_k chosen by the investigator are the source of potential inconsistency. In the case of goodness of fit tests, advice abounds as to what and how many y_ks should be chosen (see, e.g. Andrews (1988) but it largely focuses on power issues and ignores the potential inconsistency problem. The following lemma shows that, if the points at which $f(x)$ and $g(x)$ intersect are finite (M) in number, then there are a finite (K) number of partition points that generate the inconsistency property and furthermore $K <$ M.

Test Inconsistency for Smooth Continuous Alternatives

Intuition can be gleaned from the goodness of fit example in the Introduction. The two substantially different functions $f(x)$ ($U(0,1)$ and $g(x)$ ($U(0.25,0.75)$ intersect at two points on the interior of the range of the null. x^* is chosen such that the integral of the difference between the function up to x^* (0.5) and the integral of the difference between them from x^* up to 1 both are equal to 0. If x^* is chosen as the partition point, tests of differences of the two functions based on areas between them over the two segments will be inconsistent, which is to say the probability of detecting that the functions are different will be 0 at all sample sizes. On the other hand, if the range is partitioned at the intersection points and the test is based on integrals of differences over the three segments the probability of rejecting the null of no difference will be maximized at each value of n.

Lemma 2.1 For smooth, continuous functions $f(x)$ and $g(x)$ defined on $[a, b]$, let there be M ordered interior intersection points z_m, such that $f(x) = g(x)$ when $x = z_m$, $m = (1, 2,..., M)$ and $f(x) \neq g(x)$ otherwise, except possibly at $x = a$ and $x = b$. Then the partitions, y_k $k = (1, 2,..., K)$, satisfying eq. (2.5) number at most K where $K < M$.

Proof. Suppose without loss of generality, $f(x) > g(x)$ for $x \varepsilon [a; z_1)$, then from the smoothness and continuity assumptions for $f(x)$ and $g(x)$, $|f(x) - g(x)| > 0$ for $x \varepsilon (z_m; z_{m+1})$, $m = 1, 2,..., M-1$. Since:

$$\int_{a}^{y<z_1} \left(f(x) - g(x)\right) dx > 0 \tag{2.6}$$

There can be no partition point in $[a; z_1)$, otherwise a term of $O(1)$ remains in the extreme left tail of the region $[a; b]$. Similarly, since:

$$(-1)^M \int_{y>z_M}^{b} \left(f(x) - g(x)\right) dx > 0 \tag{2.7}$$

There can be no partition point in $(z_M; b]$, otherwise a term of $O(1)$ remains at the extreme right tail of the region $[a; b]$. Finally, since:

$$(-1)^M \int_{y_L}^{y_U} \left(f(x) - g(x)\right) dx > 0 \text{ for all } y_L < y_U, \text{with } y_L, y_U \in [z_M, z_{M+1}] \tag{2.8}$$

There can be at most one partition point in (z_m, z_{m+1}) for $m = (1, 2,..., M-1)$, otherwise a term of $O(1)$ remains within the region. Hence, there are at most M-1 partition points satisfying (2.5).

Though the result is "simple", its practical implications are significant. For test inconsistency the set of points satisfying eq. (2.5), or a subset of them, have to be chosen exclusively. The number of points, located on an infinite space, has been shown to be finite and bounded from above by the number of intersections of $f(x)$ and $g(x)$ so that, in the assumed circumstances, the probability of choosing them is for all intents and purposes arbitrarily close to zero. In any event, as long as there are at least M partition points, there will be no inconsistency problem. Alternatively, following Lemma 2.1 of Davidson and Duclos, which can be interpreted as proving that the number of intersection points reduces as the order of integration increases, one could consider comparing the functions at some higher order of integration.

The result also highlights when inconsistency can arise. If for example $f(x) = g(x)$ over some substantive range of x (as would occur if a policy transferred income from people immediately above some poverty line to people immediately below it whilst leaving the rest of the income distribution unaltered) then an injudicious selection of y_ks, specifically not having a y_k at the poverty line, will engender inconsistency when comparisons are made over the whole distribution. Clearly the y_ks need to be located more intensely within the range over which curves potentially differ. Evidently smoothness and continuity properties are crucial since when distribution functions exhibit substantial mass at a point the potential for inconsistency increases. In short, when distributions are smooth and continuous it takes very special circumstances for inconsistency in these tests to arise, either a freakish coincidence or else something that can readily be spotted in advance of testing.

Maximizing the Power of a Test

Having seen the implications of test inconsistency concerns for partition choice we now turn to power considerations and show that power can be maximized when partition points coincide with intersection points.

Lemma 2.2 For smooth, continuous functions $f(x)$ and $g(x)$ defined on $[a, b]$, let there be M ordered interior intersection points z_m, such that $f(x) = g(x)$ when $x = z_m$, $m = (1, 2,\ldots, M)$ and $f(x) \neq g(x)$ otherwise, except possibly at $x = a$ and $x = b$. Then the power of the test is maximized for a given sample size when the partition points y_k, $k = (1, 2,\ldots, M)$ are such that $y_k = z_k$ for $k = (1, 2,\ldots, M)$.

Proof. Suppose without loss of generality, $f(x) > g(\mathrm{x})$ for $x \; \varepsilon \; (z_i, z_{i+1})$, and $f(x) < g(x)$ for $x \; \varepsilon \; (z_{i+1}, z_{i+2})$ and consider the partition scheme y_i, y_{i+1}, y_{i+2} where $y_{i+1} = z_{i+1} - \delta$, $y_{i+2} = z_{i+2}$ where $\delta > 0$ is small relative to the intervals (z_i, z_{i+1}) and (z_{i+1}, z_{i+2}) such that:

$$\int_{z_{i+1}-\delta}^{z_{i+1}} (f(x)-g(x))dx > 0, \int_{z_{i+1}}^{z_{i+2}} (f(x)-g(x))dx$$

$$\text{and} \left| \int_{z_{i+1}-\delta}^{z_{i+1}} (f(x)-g(x))dx \right| < \left| \int_{z_{i+1}}^{z_{i+2}} (f(x)-g(x))dx \right|$$

Noting that:

$$\int_{z_i}^{y_1}(f(x)-g(x))dx + \int_{y_1}^{z_{i+2}} (f(x)-g(x))dx =$$

$$\int_{z_i}^{y_2}(f(x)-g(x))dx + \int_{y_2}^{z_{i+1}} (f(x)-g(x))dx + \int_{z_{i+1}}^{z_{i+2}} (f(x)-g(x))dx$$

Consider components in (2.4) of the form:

$$C_i = \frac{\left(\int_{z_i}^{y_1}(f(x)-g(x))dx\right)^2}{\int_{z_i}^{y_1} g(x)dx} + \frac{\left(\int_{y_1}^{z_{i+2}}(f(x)-g(x))dx\right)^2}{\int_{y_1}^{z_{i+2}} g(x)dx} =$$

$$\frac{\left(\int_{z_i}^{z_{i+1}-\delta}(f(x)-g(x))dx\right)^2}{\int_{z_i}^{y_1} g(x)dx} + \frac{\left(\int_{z_{i+1}-\delta}^{z_{i+1}}(f(x)-g(x))dx + \int_{z_{i+1}}^{z_{i+2}}(f(x)-g(x))dx\right)^2}{\int_{y_1}^{z_{i+2}} g(x)dx}$$

Observe that:

$$\frac{d\int_{z_1}^{y_2}(f(x)-g(x))dx}{dy_2} = (f(x)-g(x)) >, \le 0 \quad \text{for } y_2 <, \ge z_2 \text{ and}$$

$$\frac{d\int_{y_2}^{z_{i+1}}(f(x)-g(x))dx}{dy_2} = -(f(x)-g(x)) <, \ge 0 \quad \text{for } y_2 <, \ge z_2$$

So that

$$\frac{dC_i}{dy_{i+1}} >,=,< 0 \quad \text{as } y_{i+1} <,=,> z_{i+1}$$

Implying C_i is at a maximum when $y_{i+1} = z_{i+1}$ similar symmetric arguments demonstrate C_i is at a maximum for all $i = 0$ to K-1, that is, all such components of (2.4)

Relationship of Gini's Transvariation and Anderson et al. (2012) Overlap measure:

$$\text{GINIT} = 0.5\int_a^b \left|f(x) - g(x)\right| dx = 1 - OV$$

When $f(x)$ and $g(x)$ are kernel estimates, OV can be shown to be asymptotically normally distributed as:

$$OV - OV + a \sim N(0,v)$$

Here, a (a bias correction term) and v (the variance) are dependent on the "contact set", the set of points where $f(x) = g(x)$, when this set is empty or of measure 0 the bias term is 0 and v is given by:

$$v = h(n)\left\{p_f\left(1 - p_f\right) + p_g\left(1 - p_g\right) + \left(p_{fg} - p_f p_g\right)\right\}$$

where $h(n)$ is a sample size factor and p_f is the estimated probability that $f(x) - g(x) < -c$, p_g is the estimated probability that $f(x) - g(x) > c$ and p_{fg} is the estimated probability that $-c < f(x) - g(x) < c$ for some tuning parameter c. (Note this last term is omitted if the random variables under f and g are not jointly distributed.)

References

Anderson, G. (1996). Nonparametric Tests for Stochastic Dominance in Income Distributions. *Econometrica, 64*, 1183–1193.

Anderson, G. (2006). The Power and Size of Nonparametric Tests for Common Distributional Characteristics. *Econometric Reviews, 20*(1), 1–30. https://doi.org/10.1081/ETC-100104077.

Anderson, G. J. (2007). Indices and Tests for Multidimensional Inequality: Multivariate Generalizations of the Gini Coefficient and Kolmogorov-Smirnov Two Sample Test. *Journal of Economic Inequality, 6*(1), 73–87.

Anderson, G., Linton, O., & Whang, Y. J. (2012). Nonparametric Estimation and Inference about the Overlap of Two Distributions. *Journal of Econometrics, 171*(1), 1–23.

Anderson, G., Linton, O., & Thomas, J. (2017). Similarity, Dissimilarity and Exceptionality: Generalizing Gini's Transvariation to Measure "Differentness" in Many Distributions. *Metron, 759*(2), 161–180.

Andrews, D. W. K. (1988). Chi-Squared Diagnostic Tests for Econometric Models: Theory. *Econometrica, 56*, 1419–1453.

Atkinson, A. B., & Bourguignon, F. (1982). The Comparison of Multidimensioned Distributions of Economic Status. *Review of Economic Studies, XLIX*, 183–201.

Beach, C. M., & Davidson, R. (1983). Distribution-Free Statistical Inference with Lorenz Curves and Income Shares. *Review of Economic Studies, 50*(4), 723–735.

Davidson, R., & Duclos, J.-Y. (2000). Statistical Inference for Stochastic Dominance and for the Measurement of Poverty and Inequality. *Econometrica, 68*, 1435–1464.

Dodge, Y. (2003). *The Oxford Dictionary of Statistical Terms.* Oxford: Oxford University Press.

Gini, C. (1916). Il concetto di transvariazione e le sue prime applicazioni. *Giornale degli Economisti e Rivista di Statistica., 5*, 1–35.

Gini, C. (1959). *Transvariazione.* Rome: Libreria Goliardica.

Handcock, M., & Morris, M. (1999). *Relative Distribution Methods in the Social Sciences. Statistics for Social Science and Public Policy.* Berlin: Springer.

Levy, H. (1998). *Stochastic Dominance Investment Decision Making Under Uncertainty.* Boston: Kluwer Academic Publishers.

Linton, O. (2017). *Probability, Statistics and Econometrics.* London: Academic Press.

McLachlan, G., & Peel, D. (2000). *Finite Mixture Models.* New York: Wiley.

Pagan, A., & Ullah, A. (1999). *Nonparametric Econometrics.* Cambridge: Cambridge University Press.

Pearson, K. (1900). On the Criterion that a Given System of Deviations from the Probable in the Case of a Correlated System of Variables Is Such that it Can Be Reasonably Supposed to Have Arisen from Random Sampling. *Philosophical Magazine Series, 5*(50), 157–175.

Poirier, D. J. (1995). *Intermediate Statistics and Econometrics: A Comparative Approach.* Cambridge, MA: MIT Press.

Rao, C. R. (1973). *Linear Statistical Inference and its Applications* (2nd ed.). New York: Wiley.

Silverman, B. W. (1986). *Density Estimation for Statistics and Data Analysis.* London: Chapman and Hall.

Tukey, J. W. (1977). *Exploratory Data Analysis.* Reading: Addison-Wesley.

Whang, Y.-J. (2019). *Econometric Analysis of Stochastic Dominance: Concepts, Methods, Tools, and Applications.* Cambridge: Cambridge University Press.

CHAPTER 3

Complete Orderings: Index Types and the Ambiguity Problem

3.1 Chapter Outline

When ordering or comparing a collection of groups, the most common practice is to formulate an index, frequently on an axiomatic basis, which provides a complete ordering for the ranking process and this, together with some of the pitfalls of this activity, is what is discussed in this chapter. After an Introduction which deals with some of the difficulties associated with formulating and employing indices, Sect. 3.3 discusses some basic level of wellbeing indices such as the mean, median and mode. These measures do not reflect the extent of inequality in a group and, if the criterion function requires acknowledgment of the Pigou-Dalton principle of transfers, the extent of inequality within a group needs to be addressed. Usually inequality measures are developed on an axiomatic basis, Sect. 3.4 outlines some unit free inequality indices and the axioms upon which they are founded. This leads to a discussion of inequality adjusted wellbeing level measures in Sect. 3.5. Notions of segmentation and polarization are distinguished in Sect. 3.6 with multivariate extensions of these being considered in Sect. 3.7. Poverty measurement and equality of opportunity and mobility indices are discussed in Sects. 3.8 and 3.9. Having alluded to the ambiguity problem in the Introduction, it is illustrated in the final section of this chapter.

G. Anderson, *Multilateral Wellbeing Comparison in a Many Dimensioned World*, Global Perspectives on Wealth and Distribution,
https://doi.org/10.1007/978-3-030-21130-1_3

3.2 Introduction

Throughout the empirical sciences, situations arise where collections of things, alternative states, regions, classes or groups have to be grouped and ordered with respect to some attribute or attributes of the members of the collection. In the social, health and physical sciences "league tables" of health, wealth, income, education, treatment impacts and so forth abound, usually based on statistics summarizing aspects of the distribution of the attributes over the individuals each group. Though the differences between any two group distributions can take on a variety of forms, they are usually represented by the change in a single statistic which often conceals important distinctions between groups.

For example, in modeling of alternative treatment effects (nation incomes) {asset portfolio returns}, whereas different treatments may influence the distribution of outcomes in a variety of ways, their effects are usually summarized in terms of differences in conditional means of the treated and the untreated groups. Durlauf and Quah (2002) and Carneiro, Hansen, and Heckman (2002, 2003) have effectively argued that such summary statistics are uninformative as to general mass relocation, losing important information about outcome state differences and creating a "veil of ignorance" which can only be countervailed by comparing complete outcome distributions. Figure 3.1 illustrates the problem in three paradigms, suppose the Blue distribution records the test outcome (income) {investment portfolio returns} distribution of the treated group (nation A) {portfolio

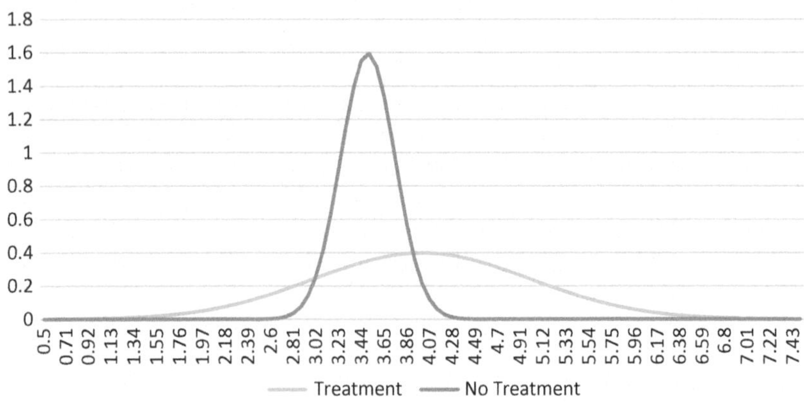

Fig. 3.1 A two-group comparison. (Source: Author's calculations)

A} and the Red distribution, the initial or untreated group (nation B) {portfolio B}. While the average treatment effect (average income difference) {average return} is positive (4–3.5), roughly 10% of the treated group (nation A) {portfolio returns} end up worse off than they would have been be if they were not treated (in nation B) {from portfolio B}. Clearly, there is benefit in moving from Red to Blue, but it is not universal; some subjects actually end up worse off and this is not truly reflected in the simple difference of an elementary location statistic, a measure that somehow accounts for the deleterious effect of the move is preferable. In the treatment effect case, the pertinent questions are, how serious is the worsening outcome for the lower 10% of the population? Does the benefit gained by the rest of the population warrant this cost that is felt by the lowest 10% and how could the mean difference be adjusted so as to reflect this downside risk discrepancy? A pure difference in means calculation yields no information on the matter. In the nation income scenario, if inequality matters then some inequality adjusted average income measure is to be preferred. In the asset portfolio context, the average return has increased but at the expense of increased risk and some risk adjusted average return measure would be a better indicator. The Carneiro, Hansen, and Heckman (2002, 2003) point is that in treatment effect studies something more than simple differences in treatment means is needed.

Many alternative indices appropriate for the task of adjusting location measures for the degree of spread in a distribution are available. Frequently they yield conflicting orderings. For instance, to get a sense of the overall level of household income wellbeing in a nation, measures of central tendency such as the mean, median or, modal income level are used. However, when comparing adult equivalent purchasing power parity (PPP) adjusted household income levels of Eurozone nations in 2015 (Anderson and Thomas 2018), mean household income records Latvia (9.28) as better off than Greece (9.16) and Portugal (11.89) as better off than Slovakia (11.41); on the other hand median income records Latvia (7.27) as worse off than Greece (8.10) and Portugal (9.98) as worse off than Slovakia (10.61). Similarly, with respect to relative inequality, Belgium appears more equal than Slovenia using the Coefficient of Variation, whereas Slovenia appears more equal than Belgium using Atkinson's measure with an inequality aversion parameter of 0.25. The problem here is the structural ambiguity that resides in the juxtaposition of distributions which, even with full knowledge of their shape and location, engenders contradictory summary statistics appropriate for a given comparison class prompting uncertainty and debate about which instrument to use.

3.3 Indices for the Level of Wellbeing

Probably the most commonly used measure of societal economic wellbeing is its average income per capita (frequently characterized by net national income per capita). This is very much a Benthamite measure, born of the idea that individual wellbeings can be summed; it is a reflection of the center of the income distribution. Suppose for a moment that a society is comprised of N individuals labeled $i = 1,\ldots, N$ and their unmeasurable happiness $U_i(x_i)$ depends solely on their income x_i. Furthermore assume all agents are identical so that $U_i(.) = U(.)$ for all i and $U(x)$ is a simple linear increasing function of x say $U(x) = \alpha + \beta x$ with $\beta > 0$. Then societal wellbeing, or average utility, may be written $\frac{1}{N}\sum_{i=1}^{N} U(x_i) = \frac{1}{N}\sum_{i=1}^{N}(\alpha + \beta x_i) = \alpha + \frac{1}{N}\beta\sum_{i=1}^{N} x_i$ which is a simple linear function of average income $\bar{X}$, that is, $\bar{U}(x_i) = \alpha + \beta\bar{X}$. Thus, average income would be a good proxy for the true unmeasurable average wellbeing.

As was seen in Chap. 2, when income distributions are symmetric, mean, median and modal incomes do a similar job, though when they are asymmetric, they tell very different stories. Indeed, Stiglitz, the Nobel Prizewinning Laureate, in a New York Times Magazine article interview Gertner (2010), argued that "Americans would have had a much clearer picture of our progress over the past decade if we had focused on median income rather than G.D.P. per capita .... When you have increasing inequality, median and average behave differently". Actually, this is not quite right: if increasing inequality (let us call it variance for now) takes place while at the same time the symmetry of a distribution is preserved, then mean and median incomes will be the same; however, if increased inequality engenders increased skewness, they will indeed behave differently. In essence, the average or mean is overly influenced by extreme values whereas the median is less so affected and thus, in the context of skewed distributions, the median better reflects the income wellbeing of the central mass of individuals since their relative orientation is less affected by the nature and degree of skewness.

When the extent to which societal incomes are shared matters, following the ideas of Dalton (1920) and Pigou (1912, 1920), pure location measures need to be modified to account for the loss of societal wellbeing that is a consequence of a higher relative level of inequality in a society (see for example Lerman and Yitzhaki 1985; Yitzahki and Lerman 1991).[1] Indeed, this can be seen in the context of the simple society of identical agents with additive utilities. Suppose again $U_i(.) = U(.)$ for all i and $U(x)$ is a quadratic function of x with positive but diminishing marginal utility, say $U(x) = \alpha + \beta x - \gamma x^2$ with $\gamma > 0$ and $\beta > 2\gamma x_{\max}$ where $x_{\max}$ is the maximum possible income so that $U'(x) > 0,\ U''(x) < 0$. Suppose aggregate incomes $\sum_{i=1}^{N} x_i = C$ are fixed, then average utility $\bar{U}(x_i) = \frac{1}{N}\sum_{i=1}^{N}(\alpha + \beta x_i - \gamma x_i^2)$ may be written as $\bar{U}(x_i) = \frac{1}{N}\sum_{i=1}^{N}(\alpha + \beta x_i - \gamma \bar{X}^2) - \gamma V(x_i)$, where $V(x_i) = \frac{1}{N}\sum_{i=1}^{N}(x_i^2 - \bar{X}^2)$ will be maximized when $V(x_i) = 0$, that is, aggregate income is equally shared $(\bar{U}(x_i) = \alpha + \beta \bar{X} - \gamma \bar{X}^2)$ for all i. Here, the Benthamite model with identical agents with diminishing marginal utilities has a distinctly Daltonian-Pigovian flavor since with a fixed pie equality maximizes wellbeing but note that average income on its own is no longer an adequate proxy for wellbeing; some measure of relative inequality needs to be incorporated in the calculus. To see how this can be done, a review of the relative inequality measures outlined in Chap. 2 is in order.

3.4 Some Unit Free Inequality Measures

The classic measures of distributional inequality mentioned in Chap. 2 such as the range, the inter-quartile range, the variance and standard deviation are absolute measures of inequality, reflecting the scale of X, what is required for inequality adjusted wellbeing measurement are relative, or unit free, measures which facilitate comparison across diverse domains.[2] The relative range, the span of incomes divided by a location measure, is an obvious contender, but it lacks favor among researchers and practitioners because of dependency on extreme values in the sample about which there are often concerns regarding measurement accuracy, and so on.

[1] In a similar fashion, average, median or modal returns in a portfolio say nothing about the riskiness or variability of those returns and, if this is of concern such location measures need to be modified accordingly.

[2] If, for example, a comparison of income inequality in the United States (measured in US$) with that of Bangladesh (measured in Takas) is required, a unit free measure will do the trick since currency values cancel out.

Often inter-decile ($R_{10\%}$) and inter-quartile ($R_{25\%}$) relative ranges are used as substitutes though one wonders why the mean is used in the denominator if vulnerability to extreme values is of concern, perhaps the median value would be better in its place. Clearly, this is a matter of taste for the investigator.

Alternative unit free measures that arise in the literature are the Relative Mean or Median Deviation, which is the average deviation from a location measure divided by that same location measure, which is not unlike the Coefficient of Variation, one of the more popular unit free measures of variation. Also deserving of a mention are the Standard Deviation of Logarithms, Theils Entropy (which is related to the Generalized Entropy [GE] Class of measures, see Theil 1967, 1979), Atkinsons' family of measures, the Shutz coefficient and the Gini.

Sometimes the extent to which societies vary in their unequalness is of interest in and of itself and the foregoing unit free measures can be used in this regard. However, much like instruments for measuring levels of wellbeing, they can yield contradictory orderings as we have seen with the Belgium-Slovenia comparison. Analysts have reduced the number of indices to be entertained by requiring that such indices possess certain properties thought desirable for an inequality index, called the axiomatic approach (Cowell 1980, 1985, 1989, 1995, 1999; Cowell & Jenkins 1995; Sen 1995) there are many axioms, here five are listed to give an idea of how they are employed. Perhaps the most important is the Pigou-Dalton Transfer Principle (Dalton 1920; Pigou 1912) or **principle of transfers** which requires that an inequality measure increases (decreases) in response to a mean preserving increase (decrease) in the spread of a distribution (see Atkinson 1970, 1983; Cowell 1985; Sen 1973). Other important axioms such as **Scale and Replication Independence / Invariance and Anonymity Axioms** (which require that an index be unaffected when all incomes are multiplied by a constant or when a population is replicated or when agents swap incomes) are frequently invoked. An important axiom from the perspective of studying relationships between subgroups in a population is the **subgroup decomposability axiom** which requires an overall inequality measure to be decomposable into within sub group and between sub group inequalities. Cowell (1995) shows that any measure $I(y)$ that satisfies all of these axioms is a member of the Generalized Entropy (GE) Class of inequality measures however the Atkinson family and the Gini coefficient fail with respect to this subgroup decomposability criterion.

The non-subgroup decomposability property of Gini's relative mean difference coefficient (Gini 1912, 1921) has often been cited as a criticism (Bourguignon 1979), but it can be turned into an advantage. Under certain conditions, namely when the subgroup distributions do not overlap or are segmented (i.e. subgroup distributions have mutually exclusive, closed and bounded support), Mookherjee and Shorrocks (1982) demonstrate that it is (see also Shorrocks 1982a, b, 1983, 1984). To give some context, in the following, discussion is pursued in terms of continuous distributions where $f(x)$ is considered a mixture of K subgroup distributions $f_k(x)$, $k = 1,\ldots K$, with compact support on R^+ such that:

$$f(x) = \sum_{k=1}^{K} w_k f_k(x)$$

where $f_k(x)$ is such that $E_{f_k(x)}(x) = \mu_k$; $\infty > V_{f_k(x)}(x) = \sigma_k^2 > 0$ and $\sum_{k=1}^{K} w_k = 1$ so $E_{f(x)}(x) = \mu$. For convenience let $\mu_k > \mu_j \Leftrightarrow k > j$. The formula for Gini coefficient is given by:

$$\text{GINI} = \frac{1}{E(x)} \int_0^\infty \int_0^\infty f(y) f(x) |x - y| \, dx dy \tag{3.1}$$

where $E(x) = \mu = \sum_{k=1}^{K} w_k \mu_k$.

From (3.1) it follows that:

$$\begin{aligned} \text{GINI} &= \sum_{k=1}^{K} w_k^2 \frac{\mu_k}{\mu} G_k + \frac{1}{\mu} \sum_{k=2}^{K} \sum_{j=1}^{k} w_k w_j |\mu_k - \mu_j| + \frac{2}{\mu} \sum_{k=2}^{K} \sum_{j=1}^{k-1} w_k w_j \int_0^\infty f_k(y) \int_y^\infty f_j(x)(x - y) \, dx dy \\ &= \sum_{k=1}^{K} w_k^2 \frac{\mu_k}{\mu} G_k + \frac{1}{\mu} \sum_{k=2}^{K} \sum_{j=1}^{k} w_k w_j |\mu_k - \mu_j| + \text{NSF} \end{aligned} \tag{3.2}$$

where $\text{NSF} = \frac{2}{\mu} \sum_{k=2}^{K} \sum_{j=1}^{k-1} w_k w_j \int_0^\infty f_k(y) \int_y^\infty f_j(x)(x - y) \, dx dy$.

GINI is thus a weighted sum of subgroup GINI's plus a weighted sum of subgroup "dominating mean differences" plus a component which is a weighted sum of the extent to which there are individuals in lower group j who overlap with, that is, have greater incomes than, individuals in upper group k weighted by the extent to which they have more. In essence, GINI is a linear function of within- and between-group Gini coefficients plus a term measuring the extent to which subgroups overlap or are not segmented.

Considering NSF, first note that when subgroups k and j are perfectly segmented and do not overlap so that $f_k(x)=0$ for all $f_j(x)>0$ and $f_j(x)=0$ for all $f_k(x)>0$, the corresponding term in the component vanishes. To see this, for any $j \neq k$, consider the corresponding term in NSF and observe that if $f_k(y)>0$ and $f_j(y)=0$ for $y \in Y^*$, $f_k(y)=0$ and $f_j(y)>0$ for $y \in Y^{**}$, and $f_k(y)=0$ and $f_j(y)=0$ for $y \in Y^{***}$ and $Y^* \cup Y^{**} \cup Y^{***} \equiv R^+$ then:

$$\int_0^\infty f_k(y)\int_y^\infty f_j(x)(x-y)dxdy = \int_{y\in Y^*}^\infty f_k(y)\int_y^\infty f_j(x)(x-y)dxdy + \int_{y\in Y^{**}}^\infty f_k(y)\int_y^\infty f_j(x)(x-y)dxdy$$
$$+ \int_{y\in Y^{***}}^\infty f_k(y)\int_y^\infty f_j(x)(x-y)dxdy = 0$$

In the particular case where this is true for all $j \neq k$, observe the Mookherjee and Shorrocks (1982) result:

$$\text{GINI} = \sum_{k=1}^{K} w_k^2 \frac{\mu_k}{\mu}\text{GINI}_k + \frac{2}{\mu}\sum_{k=2}^{K}\sum_{j=1}^{k} w_k w_j \left|\mu_k - \mu_j\right|$$

Noting that in general all three components of GINI are non-negative and that $0 \leq \text{NSF} \leq \text{GINI}$, then $0 \leq \text{NSF}/\text{GINI} \leq 1$, and thus SI, a segmentation index, may be written as:

$$\text{SI} = 1 - \frac{\text{NSF}}{\text{GINI}} \tag{3.3}$$

where $0 \leq \text{SI} \leq 1$ provides an index of segmentation, a measure of the degree to which constituent groups are segmented. Thus, the possibility of examining the extent to which a collection of subgroups is segmented emerges from the non-decomposability property of the Gini.

Furthermore, the analysis can be done with respect to particular groups, so the extent to which the poor or the rich are segmented from the rest of society may be readily analyzed. Considering just the poor group $(j = 1)$ observe the component:

$$\mathrm{NSF}_{\mathrm{poor}} = \frac{2}{\mu}\sum_{k=2}^{K} w_k w_l \int_0^{\infty} f_k(y) \int_y^{\infty} f_l(x)(x-y)\,dxdy$$

This is twice a weighted sum of the (expected) average value of the excess of incomes of people in the poor group over those of people in the non-poor groups normalized by average income which is of interest in contemplating the "isolation" of the poor. Similarly, an index of the segmentation of the "rich" group $(k = K)$ can be obtained as:

$$\mathrm{NSF}_{\mathrm{rich}} = \frac{2}{\mu}\sum_{j=1}^{K-1} \int_0^{\infty} f_K(y) \int_y^{\infty} f_j(x)(x-y)\,dxdy$$

which is twice a weighted sum of the (expected) average value of the excess of incomes of people in the poor group over those of people in the richest group normalized by average income, which is of interest in contemplating the "isolation" of the rich. Clearly $\mathrm{NSF}_{\mathrm{poor}}$ or $\mathrm{NSF}_{\mathrm{rich}}$ could be inserted in place of NSF in (3.3) to obtain an index of the segmentation of the poor or rich respectively.

3.5 Inequality Adjusted Wellbeing Levels

Returning to the incorporation of an inequality component in a level of wellbeing measure, it has long been argued that for a given average level of income in a society, the more equally shared that income is the better off that society would be in a wellbeing sense. So some means of incorporating an inequality component in an aggregate wellbeing measure is required. Blackorby and Donaldson (1978) developed implicit income wellbeing level indices underlying four relative income inequality measures (Gini, Thiel's Entropy, Coefficient of Variation and Atkinson) which are outlined in Table 3.1 together with the Utopia-Dystopia index (Anderson, Post, and Whang 2018). The latter index is drawn from a family of relative income measures based upon a collection of income distributions, the family was formulated using ideas from the Stochastic Dominance literature and its development will be discussed later in Chap. 4. For present purposes think of it as measuring the notional distance from the worst

Table 3.1 Inequality measure implied income wellbeing indices

Type	*Inequality measure*	*Wellbeing measure*
GINI	$\frac{1}{\mu n^2}\sum_{i=1}^{n}\sum_{j=1}^{n}\lvert x_i - x_j\rvert$	$\frac{1}{n^2}\sum_{i=1}^{n}\left(2\left(n+1-i\right)-1\right)x_i$
Theils entropy	$\frac{1}{n}\sum_{i=1}^{n}x_i \ln\left(\frac{\mu}{x_i}\right)$	$\frac{1}{n\ln(n)}\sum_{i=1}^{n}x_i \ln\left(\frac{n\mu}{x_i}\right)$
Coefficient of variation	$\frac{\left[\frac{1}{n}\sum_{i=1}^{n}\left(x_i-\mu\right)^2\right]^{0.5}}{\mu}$	$\frac{1}{n}\sum_{i=1}^{n}x_i - \left[\frac{1}{n}\sum_{i=1}^{n}\left(x_i-\mu\right)^2\right]^{0.5}$
Atkinson	$1-\frac{\left[\sum_{i=1}^{n}\frac{1}{n}x_i^r\right]^{1/r}}{\mu}$	$\left[\sum_{i=1}^{n}\frac{1}{n}x_i^r\right]^{1/r}$ for $0 < r \le 1$ $\prod_{i=1}^{n}x_i^{1/n}$ for $r = 0$
Utopia-Dystopia (for a collection of K distributions)		$\frac{\int_a^b\left\{\max\left(F_k(x):k=1,\ldots,K\right)-F_k(x)\right\}dx}{\int_a^b\left\{\max\left(F_k(x):k=1,\ldots,K\right)-\min\left(F_k(x):k=1,\ldots,K\right)\right\}dx}$

Source: Anderson and Thomas (2019)

possible average income in a collection, some intuition can be gleaned from the following. Suppose that x corresponds to income and $f(x)$ is its probability density function, since $\mu = \int xf(x)dx = \int(1-F(x))dx$ generally $\mu_j - \mu_i = \int_0^\infty (F_i(x) - F_j(x))dx$, so that intuitively $\int_0^\infty (F_i(x) - F_j(x))dx$ corresponds to a measure of difference between distributions $f_j(x)$ and $f_i(x)$. When $f_j(x)$ first order dominates $f_i(x)$, it will be the case that $F_i(x) \ge F_j(x)$ for all x with strict inequality somewhere so that $\int_0^\infty (F_i(x) - F_j(x))dx > 0$. Writing $F^h(x) = \int_0^x F^{h-1}(z)dz$, it follows in this case that $\int_0^\infty (F_i^h(x) - F_j^h(x))dx > 0$ provides a measure of the difference between the distributions at the hth order of integration. When a dominance relation doesn't exist between distributions $f_j(x)$ and $f_i(x)$, we can contemplate $\text{FUE}(x) = \max\left(F_i(x), F_j(x)\right)$, the upper envelope of the two cumulative densities, and $\text{FLE}(x) = \min\left(F_i(x), F_j(x)\right)$, the lower envelope of the two cumulative densities. If one could imagine a combination of $f_j(x)$ and $f_i(x)$, $\text{FUE}(x)$ would correspond to the cumulative distribution of the worst set of outcomes or DYSTOPIA and $\text{FLE}(x)$ would correspond to the best set of outcomes or UTOPIA. Clearly $F_i(x), F_j(x)$ and $\text{FLE}(x)$ first order dominate $\text{FUE}(x)$ and $F_i(x), F_j(x)$ and $\text{FUE}(x)$ are dominated by $\text{FLE}(x)$. Anderson, Post, and Whang (2019) use these ideas to formulate relative wellbeing indices that are bounded between zero and one which for distribution $f_j(x)$ would look like $\int_0^\infty \left(\text{FUE}(x) - F_j(x)\right)dx / \int_0^\infty \left(\text{FUE}(x) - \text{FLE}(x)\right)dx$.

Each gives an index of wellbeing that has been adjusted in some sense for the negative impact that inequality has on overall wellbeing levels. Some, like the Atkinson measure (by choice of r), offer a means of muting the extent to which the level of wellbeing is penalized for the level of inequality and others can be modified to similar effect. The first four indices are absolute measures with potentially different ranges, when comparing a collection of K groups with distributions $f_k(x) k = 1, \ldots, K$ relative measures, like the Utopia-Dystopia index would be useful for comparability purposes. To get a relative measure any collection of K absolute wellbeing measures $U_k(x)$ $k = 1, \ldots, K$ can be converted into a collection of relative wellbeing measures by determining $U^{\text{Min}} = \min\left(U_1, U_2, \ldots, U_K\right)$ and $U^{\text{Max}} = \max\left(U_1, U_2, \ldots, U_K\right)$ and constructing $U_k^r(x) = U_k(x) - U^{\text{Min}}$ or, if indices on the unit interval are desired, constructing $U_k^{r01}(x) = \left(U_k(x) - U^{\text{Min}}\right) / \left(U^{\text{Max}} - U^{\text{Min}}\right)$. This is the basis of the Utopia-Dystopia family of indices, except that U^{Min} and U^{Max}. are determined as the minima and maxima over an amalgamation of the collection of distributions. Again, with such a variety of measures, it is no surprise that they may yield contradictory orderings. This issue will be returned to toward the end of the chapter in the meantime indices of other aspects of wellbeing will be outlined and discussed. The next family of measures relate to the extent to which a society is polarized.

3.6 Polarization Measures

The notion of polarization is closely associated with, but quite distinct from the concept of inequality, often it will be the case that societies can simultaneously become more equal yet more polarized. Unlike societal inequality, the focus of polarization has more to do with differences between the individuals in a society as they relate to their respective membership of different groups, thus the existence of subgroups and group membership is of concern here. The relatively recent literature is extensive, there have been several proposed univariate polarization indices which focus on an arbitrary number of groups and a fortiori two groups (Esteban and Ray 1994; Esteban, Gradín and Ray 2007; Zhang and Kanbur 2001; Duclos et al. 2004) and a similar number that focus on just two groups (Alesina and Spolaore 1997; Foster and Wolfson 1992; Wolfson 1994; Wang and Tsui 2000; Anderson 2004, 2004a; Anderson et al. 2012). Gigliarano and Mosler (2009) and Anderson (2010, 2012) develop a family of multivariate polarization measures based upon measures of between- and within-group multivariate variation and relative group size which exploit notions of subgroup decomposability. An excellent summary of the properties of the univariate indices is to be found in Esteban and Ray (2008) wherein the properties of indices are evaluated in terms of their coherence with some basic axioms that reflect three notions: (1) when there is only one group there is little polarization, (2) polarization increases when within-group inequality is reduced and (3) polarization increases when between-group inequality increases.

The axioms are formed around a notional univariate density that is a mixture of kernels $f(x, a)$ that are symmetric unimodal on a compact support of $[a,a + 2]$ with $E(x) = \mu = (a + 1)$ also representing the mode. The kernels are subject to slides (location shifts) $g(y) = f(y - x)$ and squeezes (shrinkages) of the form $f^{\lambda}(x) = f(\{x - [1-\lambda]\mu\}/\lambda)/\lambda\,(0 < \lambda < 1)$ and potential indices are evaluated in the context of such changes in terms of the extent to which they satisfy the following set of axioms.

Axiom 1 "A squeeze of a distribution that consists of a single basic density cannot increase polarization." In the present context, this axiom is not particularly relevant for evaluating the extent to which bi-polarization measures capture that phenomenon. Note however that if such a squeeze is applied to the mixture distribution (whose mean vector will be $(\mu_1 + \mu_2)/2$), the trapezoid measure will only be effective as long as the "bumps" remain identifiable.

Axiom 2 "Symmetric squeezes of the two kernels cannot reduce polarization." Given Bipol, the Bipolarization Trapezoidal Index, is of the form: $\text{Bipol} = 0.5\left(f\left(\mu_1\right)+f\left(\mu_2\right)\right)/\mid \mu_1 >> \mu_2 \mid$ the change in Bipol will be $\lambda\ \text{Bipol}/\left(1-\lambda\right)>0$. The extent to which the squeeze affects the overlap measure again depends upon the extent of common support, if there is common support then the overlap measure will reflect the effect of the squeeze appropriately.

Axiom 3 "Slides of the two kernels outward increases polarization." Again the impact on Bipol is fairly straightforward since Bipol is a positive linear function of $\left|\mu_1 - \mu_2\right|$ which will simply be increased by such a slide effect. With regard to the overlap measure, as long as there is common support in the two distributions this too will reflect polarization in the desired fashion.

Axiom 4 "Common population scaling preserves the ordering." Neither the overlap nor the trapezoidal measure is affected by common scaling and so ordering will be preserved in both cases.

Axiom 5 "Polarization indices have to come from a family where if x and y are independently distributed with marginal distributions $f(x)$ and $f(y)$ then the index is the expected value of some function $T\left(f\left(x\right), \mid x-y \mid\right)$ which is increasing in its second argument." While this is true for the trapezoidal measure, it is not demonstrably true for the overlap measure.

Axiom 6 "Symmetric squeezes of the sub distributions weakly increases polarization." Much like Axiom 2 in the present context and the same comments apply.

Axiom 7 "Non-monotonicity of the index with respect to outward slides of the sub distributions." Neither the trapezoidal nor the overlap measures satisfy this axiom.

Axiom 8 "Flipping the distribution around its support should leave polarization unchanged." This is satisfied by both the trapezoid and the overlap measures. (Note that polarization measures which satisfy this axiom in the present context just as well reflect the degree of advantage an agent from the rich group perceives from their position).

The general polarization index developed for discrete distributions as a consequence of these axioms (Esteban and Ray 1994) may be written as:

$$P_\alpha = \text{K}\sum_{i=1}^{n}\sum_{j=1}^{n}\left|x_i - x_j\right|\pi_i^{1+\alpha}\pi_j \tag{3.4}$$

Here K is a normalizing constant, π_i is the sample weight of the *i*th observation and where $\alpha \geq 0$ is a polarization sensitivity factor chosen by the investigator. It may readily be seen that $\alpha = 0$ and $K = 1/\mu$ yields the sample weighted Gini coefficient. The continuous distribution analog (Duclos et al. 2004) may be written as:

$$P_\alpha(F) = \int_0^\infty f(y)^\alpha \int_0^\infty |y - x| dF(x) dF(y) \tag{3.5}$$

Again, α is the polarization sensitivity factor which in this case is confined to [0.25,1]. Esteban and Ray (2008) point out that the bipolarization measures they discuss (those of Wolfson 1994; Wang and Tsui 2000; Alessina and Spolare 1997) essentially measure the difference between the empirical distribution and one which has all of the population concentrated at the median. This is most obviously seen in the Wang and Tsui index which is given by:

$$P^{WT} = K \int \left| \frac{x - M}{M} \right|^r f(x) dx \tag{3.6}$$

The Wolfson Index is given by:

$$P^W = \frac{\mu}{M} \{0.5 - L(0.5) - 0.5G\} \tag{3.7}$$

where μ is the population mean, m is the population median, $L(0.5)$ is the Lorenz ordinate at median income and G is the Gini coefficient. The Alesina and Spolare measure is essentially the median distance to the median. The extent to which these indices cohere with the axioms is discussed in (Esteban and Ray 2008) and will not be elaborated here. What should be noted is that they all work off the overall population distribution, whether the subgroups are identified or not and whether multimodality is identified in the overall population distribution or not, which, were multivariate analogs of them to exist, would represent a clear advantage over the indices and tests being proposed here.

The non-decomposability of the Gini also provides us with a polarization index based upon a segmentation factor implicit in the Gini.

To derive the non-segmentation version of GINI in the context of continuous distributions note that from (3.1):

$$
\begin{aligned}
G &= \left(E(x)\right)^{-1}\int_0^\infty\int_0^\infty f(y)f(x)|x-y|\,dxdy \\
&= \frac{1}{\sum_{k=1}^{K} w_k\mu_k}\int_0^\infty\int_0^\infty \sum_{k=1}^{K} w_k f_k(y)\sum_{k=1}^{K} w_k f_k(x)|x-y|\,dxdy \\
&= \frac{1}{\sum_{k=1}^{K} w_k\mu_k}\int_0^\infty\int_0^\infty\left[\sum_{k=1}^{K} w_k^2 f_k(y)f_k(x)|x-y| + 2\sum_{k=2}^{K} w_k f_k(y)\sum_{j=1}^{k-1} w_j f_j(x)|x-y|\right]dxdy \\
&= \frac{1}{\mu}\int_0^\infty\int_0^\infty\sum_{k=1}^{K} w_k^2\frac{\mu_k}{\mu_k} f_k(y)f_k(x)|x-y|\,dxdy + \frac{2}{\mu}\int_0^\infty\int_0^\infty\sum_{k=2}^{K} w_k f_k(y)\sum_{j=1}^{k-1} w_j f_j(x)|x-y|\,dxdy \\
&= \sum_{k=1}^{K} w_k^2\frac{\mu_k}{\mu}\mathrm{GINI}_k + \frac{2}{\mu}\int_0^\infty\int_0^\infty\sum_{k=2}^{K} w_k f_k(y)\sum_{j=1}^{k-1} w_j f_j(x)|x-y|\,dxdy
\end{aligned}
$$

Where

$$
\mathrm{GINI}_k = \frac{1}{\mu_k}\int_0^\infty\int_0^\infty f_k(y)f_k(x)|x-y|\,dxdy
$$

From the second component, consider a typical term:

$$
\begin{aligned}
\int_0^\infty\int_0^\infty w_k f_k(y) w_j f_j(x)|x-y|\,dxdy &= w_k w_j\int_0^\infty f_k(y)\int_0^\infty f_j(x)|x-y|\,dxdy \\
&= w_k w_j\int_0^\infty f_k(y)\left[-\int_0^y f_j(x)(x-y)\,dx + \int_y^\infty f_j(x)(x-y)\,dx\right]dy \\
&= w_k w_j\int_0^\infty f_k(y)\left[-\int_0^\infty f_j(x)(x-y)\,dx + 2\int_y^\infty f_j(x)(x-y)\,dx\right]dy \\
&= w_k w_j\int_0^\infty f_k(y)\left[-(\mu_j - y) + 2\int_y^\infty f_j(x)(x-y)\,dx\right]dy \\
&= w_k w_j\left[|\mu_k - \mu_j| + \int_0^\infty f_k(y)\int_y^\infty f_j(x)(x-y)\,dxdy\right]
\end{aligned}
$$

Note $\int_0^\infty f_k(y)\int_y^\infty f_j(x)(x-y)\,dxdy > 0$, so that:

$$
\begin{aligned}
\text{GINI} &= \sum_{k=1}^{K} w_k^2 \frac{\mu_k}{\mu} \text{GINI}_k + \frac{2}{\mu} \sum_{k=2}^{K} \sum_{j=1}^{k} w_k w_j \left| \mu_k - \mu_j \right| \\
&+ \frac{2}{\mu} \sum_{k=2}^{K} \sum_{j=1}^{k-1} w_k w_j \int_0^\infty f_k(y) \int_y^\infty f_j(x)(x-y)\,dx\,dy \\
&= \sum_{k=1}^{K} w_k^2 \frac{\mu_k}{\mu} G_k + \frac{1}{\mu} \sum_{k=1}^{K} \sum_{j=1}^{K} w_k w_j \left| \mu_k - \mu_j \right| + \text{NSF} \\
&= \sum_{k=1}^{K} w_k^2 \frac{\mu_k}{\mu} G_k + \text{BGINI} + \text{NSF}
\end{aligned}
\tag{3.8}
$$

Where $\text{NSF} = \frac{2}{\mu} \sum_{k=2}^{K} \sum_{j=1}^{k-1} w_k w_j \int_0^\infty f_k(y) \int_y^\infty f_j(x)(x-y)\,dx\,dy$

GINI is thus a weighted sum of subgroup GINI's plus a weighted sum of subgroup "dominating mean differences" or a BGINI, a between-group Gini plus a component which is a weighted sum of the average value of the extent to which outcomes in lower group j exceed outcomes in upper group k, which will be referred to as a Non-Segmentation Factor NSF. In essence, GINI is a linear function of within- and between-group Gini coefficients plus a term NSF which measures the extent to which subgroups overlap or are not segmented. Considering NSF, first note that when subgroups k and j are perfectly segmented (so that $f_k(x)=0$ for all $f_j(x)>0$ and $f_j(x)=0$ for all $f_k(x)>0$), the corresponding term in the component vanishes. To see this, for any $j \neq k$, consider the corresponding term in NSF and observe that if $f_k(y)>0$ and $f_j(y)=0$ for $y \in Y^*$, $f_k(y)=0$ and $f_j(y)>0$ for $y \in Y^{**}$, and $f_k(y)=0$ and $f_j(y)=0$ for $y \in Y^{***}$ and $Y^* \cup Y^{**} \cup Y^{***} \equiv R^+$ then:

$$
\begin{aligned}
\int_0^\infty f_k(y) \int_y^\infty f_j(x)(x-y)\,dx\,dy &= \int_{y \in Y^*} f_k(y) \int_y^\infty f_j(x)(x-y)\,dx\,dy + \int_{y \in Y^{**}} f_k(y) \int_y^\infty f_j(x)(x-y)\,dx\,dy \\
&+ \int_{y \in Y^{***}} f_k(y) \int_y^\infty f_j(x)(x-y)\,dx\,dy = 0
\end{aligned}
$$

In the particular case where this is true for all $j \neq k$, observe the Mookherjee and Shorrocks (1982) result holds in that the Gini coefficient is now subgroup decomposable.

For completeness, suppose all groups have identical distributions so that $f_j(y) = f_k(y)$, $\text{GINI}_k = \text{GINI}_j = \text{GINI}$ and $\mu_k = \mu$ for all j,k and all y, then (3.2) becomes:

$$\begin{aligned}\text{GINI} &= \sum_{k=1}^{K} w_k^2 \frac{\mu_k}{\mu} \text{GINI}_k + \frac{2}{\mu} \sum_{k=2}^{K} \sum_{j=1}^{k-1} w_k w_j \int_0^\infty f(y) \int_y^\infty f(x)(x-y)\,dxdy \\ &= \sum_{k=1}^{K} w_k^2 \frac{\mu_k}{\mu} \text{GINI}_k + \frac{1}{\mu} \sum_{k=1}^{K} \sum_{\substack{j=1 \\ j \neq k}}^{K} w_k w_j \int_0^\infty f(y) \int_y^\infty f(x)(x-y)\,dxdy\end{aligned}$$

Since $\text{GINI}_k = \text{GINI}_j = \text{GINI}$ and $\mu_k = \mu_j = \mu$ for all j,k, we have:

$$\text{GINI} = \sum_{k=1}^{K} w_k^2 \text{GINI} + \sum_{k=1}^{K} \sum_{\substack{j=1 \\ j \neq k}}^{K} w_k w_j \text{GINI} = \text{GINI} \tag{3.9}$$

Noting that in general all three components of GINI are non-negative and that $0 \leq \text{NSF} \leq \text{GINI}$, then $0 \leq \text{NSF}/\text{GINI} \leq 1$, and thus SI, a segmentation index, may be written as:

$$\text{SI} = 1 - \frac{\text{NSF}}{\text{GINI}} \tag{3.10}$$

where $0 \leq \text{SI} \leq 1$ provides an index of segmentation, a measure of the degree to which constituent groups are segmented or separate. Furthermore, the analysis can be done with respect to particular groups, and so the extent to which the poor or the rich are segmented from the rest of society may be readily analyzed.

To study the connection between segmentation and polarization, attention is focused on any component pair in the decomposition $f_i(x)$ and $f_j(x)$ where, conveniently assuming that $\mu_i = \int x f_i(x)dx > \int x f_j(x)dx = \mu_j$, the corresponding component in the NSF sum is given by:

$$w_i w_j \int_0^\infty f_i(y) \int_y^\infty f_j(x)(x-y)\,dxdy$$

and the corresponding component in the between-group inequality Gini is $w_i w_j (\mu_i - \mu_j)$, the weighted sum of the difference in means. Clearly, the between-group inequality component will enlarge under the θ transformation of $f_i(x)$ increasing the alienation factor. Furthermore, since First

Order Dominance implies Second Order Dominance, for $0<\theta<\theta'$ observe that, for the corresponding component of the segmentation factor:

$$\int_0^\infty f_i^{\theta'}(y)\int_y^\infty f_j(x)(x-y)dxdy \leq \int_0^\infty f_i^{\theta}(y)\int_y^\infty f_j(x)(x-y)dxdy$$

which is to say a polarizing slide increases the between-group inequality factor and reduces the non-segmentation factor. As the expected value under $f_i(y)$ of the partial moment of x above y, the NSF component is a measure of the extent to which agents in the lower income distribution f_j have higher incomes than agents in the higher distribution f_i. It follows that a sufficient (though not necessary) condition for a polarizing change is a non-decreasing change in the between-group factor standardized by the overall Gini combined with a non-decreasing change in segmentation. This would be captured by GBP, a Gini Based Polarization Index, which is a weighted sum of the between-group Gini coefficient (BGINI) and the segmentation index. The segmentation index of itself will not capture polarization when the subgroups are already segmented (clearly, although no longer overlapping, the distributions could still move further apart). Here the weighted geometric mean is chosen which, for $0<\gamma<1$, may be written as:

$$\text{GBP} = \left(\frac{\text{BGINI}}{\text{GINI}}\right)^{\gamma} \text{SI}^{1-\gamma}$$

3.7 Multivariate Polarization Indices

The multivariate polarization index provided by (Gigliarano and Mosler 2009) requires the groups to be separately identified. Their index is a function of three measures, within-group inequality W(X), between-group inequality $B(X)$ and relative group size $S(X)$, where X is the $N \times K$ overall sample matrix of N observations on K characteristics so:

$$P^{\text{GM}} = \Phi\big(W(X), B(X), S(X)\big)$$

where Φ is decreasing in its first argument and increasing in its second and third arguments. A variety of multivariate inequality measures could be employed for the first two arguments and the relative group size index has to increase with the degree of similarity of group sizes. Here two multivariate polarization measures are proposed which work off the anatomy of the subgroup distributions. As such, they are very natural measures of the notion of polarization that would cohere with the axioms mentioned earlier. For simplicity consider two distributions $f_F(x), f_G(x)$ representing France and Germany where x is now a vector of values. For example, the vector x could contain individual indicators of health education and income as is employed in the United Nations Human Development Project Index (UNPD 2016), the idea being that wellbeing is jointly determined by three factors, the health, education and income levels that an individual enjoys.

Three Measures of Multivariate Bipolarization

(a) The Overlap Measure. $\mathrm{OV} = \int_0^\infty \min\{f_F(x), f_G(x)\}\,dx$ presents one way of gaging the extent of polarization between the two groups is to measure how little they have in common. It captures the degree of commonality between two distributions so that 1-OV will measure the degree of dissimilarity. It is a very natural measure (always a number between 0 and 1), which is in effect a multivariate version of one minus a multivariate version of Gini's Transvariation measure.

(b) The Polarization Trapezoid. Letting x_{mF} be the value of the characteristic vector at the modal point of the French distribution and x_{mG} the corresponding vector for the German distribution each characterizing the representative modal agents of those distributions. In these circumstances, the area of the trapezoid formed by the heights of the distributions at their modal points and the mean normalized Euclidean distance (denoted |.|) between the two modal points provides a measure of the polarization between France and Germany as follows:

$$\mathrm{Bipol} = 0.5\left(f_F\left(x_{mF}\right) + f_G\left(x_{mG}\right)\right)\frac{\left|x_{mG} - x_{mF}\right|}{|\mu|}$$

When the groups are not separately identified, the index is calculated from the modal points of the mixture distribution.

(c) Anderson (2011) generalized the polarization measure to many dimensions some of which are discrete random variables and some of which are continuous. Let (w_i, z_i) be respectively the $k \times 1$ and $h \times 1$ jointly distributed $Q(= k + h)$ continuous and discrete vectors of the status of agent i where $i = 1,\ldots, n$ where for convenience all variables are positively related to agent i's wellbeing. The joint density of the *ws* for a given configuration of the *zs* is $f(w|z)$ and the joint density of the *zs* is given by $p(z)$ so that the joint density of w and z is $f(w_i, z_i) = f(w_i | z_i) p(z_i)$ let the stacked vector $x_i = \begin{pmatrix} w_i \\ z_i \end{pmatrix}$ then the dimension normalized Euclidean distance between agent i and agent j is given by:

$$\|x_i - x_j\| = \sqrt{\frac{\sum_{q=1}^{Q}\left(x_{iq} - x_{jq}\right)^2}{Q}}$$

Then the multidimensional polarization measure for $1 > \alpha > 0.25$ is given by:

$$P_\alpha = \sum_{z \in x} \int_{R_{k_{w_x}}^+}^{\infty} \sum_{z \in y} \int_{R_{k_{w_y}}^+}^{\infty} f(w,z)^{1+\alpha} \|x_i - x_j\| dF(w_x) dF(w_y)$$

For inference purposes, Duclos, Esteban, and Ray (2004) show that the univariate version is asymptotically normal and derive its standard error; the standard error for this multivariate version is derived in Anderson (2011). It is interesting to note that for $\alpha = 1$ this is in effect the multidimensional Gini coefficient.

As we have seen earlier Duclos, Esteban, and Ray (2004) and Esteban and Ray (1994) have evaluated polarization measures on the basis of the extent to which such measures satisfy certain axioms. For present purposes consider the population distribution to be made up of two multidimensional symmetric unimodal kernels with mean (modal) vectors μ_1 and μ_2 (with $\mu_1 >> \mu_2$ for convenience) so that x, the μs and the *a*s are $k \times 1$ vectors with λ remaining a scalar. A slide is now defined in terms of $\mu_1 - \mu_2$ becoming larger and a squeeze increases the value of the density at the mode to $f(\mu)/\lambda$.

In terms of the aforementioned axioms, in the present context this Axiom 1 is not particularly relevant for evaluating the extent to which bi-polarization measures capture that phenomenon. Note however that if such a squeeze is applied to the mixture distribution (whose mean vector will be $(\mu_1 + \mu_2)/2$), the trapezoid measure will only be effective as long as the "bumps" remain identifiable. As for Axiom 2 (and Axiom 6), given the trapezoid index is $\text{Bipol} = 0.5\left(f\left(\mu_1\right)+f\left(\mu_2\right)\right)/\left|\mu_1 >> \mu_2\right|$ the change in Bipol will be λ Bipol/(1-λ) > 0. The extent to which the squeeze affects the overlap measure again depends upon the extent of common support, if there is common support then the overlap measure will reflect the effect of the squeeze appropriately.

Axiom 3 has a fairly straightforward impact on Bipol, it is a positive linear function of $|\mu_1 - \mu_2|$ which will simply be increased by such a slide. With regard to the overlap measure, as long as there is common support in the two distributions this too will reflect polarization in the desired fashion. As for Axiom 4, neither the overlap nor the trapezoidal measure is affected by common scaling so ordering will be preserved in both cases.

Axiom 5 "Polarization indices have to come from a family where if x and y are independently distributed with marginal distributions $f(x)$ and $f(y)$ then the index is the expected value of some function $T\left(f\left(x\right), |x-y|\right)$ which is increasing in its second argument." It is satisfied by the trapezoid measure but it is not demonstrably true for the overlap measure. Neither the trapezoid nor the overlap satisfies Axiom 7 but Axiom 8 is satisfied by both the trapezoid and overlap measures.

With respect to polarization, the intensity or within-group association is represented by the averaged heights of the modal points $f_p(x_{mp})$ and $f_r(x_{mr})$ following the intuition that the greater the mass within a region close to the modal point, the greater will be the height of the pdf. That the mean normalized Euclidean distance between the two modal points represents the sense of alienation between the two groups is somewhat more obvious. It is interesting to speculate how the identity components could be interpreted. If I am poor, the poor modal height ($f_p(x_{mp})$) tells me the extent to which there are others like me or close to me, the higher it is the more identification with my group will I perceive. The rich modal height $f_r(x_{mr})$ tells me how easily I can identify "the other club" and reflects how strongly I may perceive the other group from whom I'm alienated. The higher the rich modal height the more closely associated the agents in that club are, the lower it is the more widely dispersed they are. The symmetry property attaches equal importance to them in the index reflecting its "relative" nature. If, as will be discussed below, an absolute poverty measure is desired the rich modal height should have no play and the Euclidean distance from the nearest point on a poverty frontier (rather than the modal point of the rich distribution) would correspond to a measure of alienation from the non-poor group.

Many variants of this index are possible. Note that the weights given to either the within-group association or the between-group alienation components could be varied if such emphasis is desired. Thus a general form of Bipol could be $(\text{Height}^{\alpha}\text{Base}^{1-\alpha})^2$, where $0 < \alpha < 1$ represents the relative importance of the self-identification component. Similarly, the modal point height components could be individually re-weighted to reflect the different importance of the identification component of the rich and poor groups.

3.8 Poverty Measurement

In his treatise on Justice, John Rawls (1971) argued that any social or economic inequality in a society was to be so arranged as to be "of the greatest benefit to the least-advantaged members of society". In essence, his idea was that a society was to be judged by how it treated its poor. Such expressions of concern for the poor have prompted a plethora of "the extent of Poverty measures" which will be denoted by $P(x)$, which in some sense are an increasing function of "Poverty". Taking a Rawlsian position, one could imagine a societal wellbeing index $U = -P$.

Much like inequality measures, in order to refine the class of available measures, Poverty indices have been developed over the years on an axiomatic basis. To fix ideas a brief discussion of the more important axioms is provided here, Zheng (1997) provides an excellent survey of the plethora of axioms that have been proposed and the extent to which various poverty measures are in accord with those axioms.

The **Focus axiom** simply requires that the poverty measure should be independent of the income distribution of the non-poor; essentially, it argues that only the status of the poor should matter. Note however that such an axiom would rule out a vast array of relative poverty measures. In a similar fashion to the analysis of inequality measurement, the **Anonymity or Symmetry Axiom** asserts that if poor and non-poor persons switch places the poverty measure should remain unaffected. The **Replication Invariance axiom** requires that measures should admit the comparison of different sized distributions without variation. The **Continuity Axiom** requires that small increments of income changes of the poor should not result in large changes in the poverty measure. When some sort of poverty cut-off or poverty line is invoked to identify the poor **the Increasing Poverty Line axiom** requires that when comparing two identical societies (in the sense that they have identical distributions), the one with the higher poverty line should have the higher poverty index. The **Regressive Transfer and Transfer Sensitivity Axioms** respectively require that Poverty measures should be sensitive to redistribution among the poor (thus a regressive transfer should increase the poverty index) and greater weight be given to income transfers low in the income distribution.

There is a vast array of poverty measures in the literature, (again it will be assumed that incomes are ordered in ascending order by subscript so $i > j \Rightarrow x_i \geq x_j$, an indicator function $I(a,b)$ will be employed whereby $I(a,b) = 1$ if $a \leq b$ otherwise $I(a,b) = 0$ and the poverty cut-off will be deemed to be some value z), a selection follows. Perhaps the most popular index is the headcount $H = \frac{\sum_{i=1}^{N} I(x_i, z)}{N}$ which is simply the proportion of the population or sample with incomes less than the poverty cut-off. The average income of the poor can be calculated as $\bar{X}_p = \frac{\sum_{i=1}^{N} I(x_i, z) x_i}{\sum_{i=1}^{N} I(x_i, z)}$ which can be used in various depth and intensity of poverty measures (e.g. $\left(\frac{z - \bar{X}_p}{z}\right)^k$ for some $k = 1, \ldots, K$) similar to the class of FGT measures (Foster et al. 1984). Many other variants are out there but these are the most important.

Multivariate Poverty, Deprivation and Exclusion Indices

The notions of multivariate Poverty, Deprivation and Exclusion are very similar and the development of indices via the axiomatic approach follows similar paths. The approach posits a set of conditions with which an index must comply in order for it to be a "useful" index and such conditions have been set out in Bossert, D'Ambrosio, and Peragine (2004). Here they are listed and interpreted:

1. Normalization (the index for the least excluded is zero)
2. Focus (those more excluded than i do not affect her sense of exclusion)
3. Conditional anonymity (agents changing places in the rest of society does not affect a person's degree of exclusion)
4. Homogeneity
5. Translation invariance
6. Deprivation additivity (these are essentially a group of mathematical conditions common in the poverty literature which make the indices tractable and interpretable)
7. Population proportionality and deprivation proportionality (these concern the behavior of the indices when the population size changes)

These axioms provide a useful set of criteria by which existing indices may be evaluated in a theoretical context in terms of their theoretical or mathematical construction and lead Bossert et al. to a particular formulation of an index which satisfies such conditions. But the axioms essentially relate to the mathematical structure of the index and do not relate to the types of variables or agent characteristics that should be employed. They lead Bossert et al. to propose an exclusion index formula of the form:

$$E = \frac{1}{N}\sum_{i=1}^{N}\frac{1}{T}\sum_{t=1}^{T_i} D_{it}$$

where D_{it} is the deprivation (or exclusion) that the *i*th person feels with regard to the *t*th individual (and *i* feels deprived with respect to T_i individuals).

There are many multivariate poverty indices, perhaps the gold standard is the Alkire-Foster Multivariate Deprivation Index (AFMDI), which is in essence a counting measure (Alkire and Foster 2011). To see the relationship between the index and Consumer Theory, let there be a sample of N agents with D dimensions that constitute the potential deprivation (poverty/wellbeing) measure's database. In addition, let $K \varepsilon$ 0, 1, 2,..., D-1 denote the number of dimensions in which the agent fails to meet the threshold for minimum wellbeing. Then the generalized versions of the index for the Kth level of deprivation may be written as:

$$M_K^{\alpha} = \frac{1}{N}\sum_{n=1}^{N} I\left(c_n > K\right)\sum_{d=1}^{D}\frac{w_d}{D} I\left(\frac{x_{nd}}{\underline{x}_d} < 1\right)\left(\frac{\underline{x}_d - x_{nd}}{\underline{x}_d}\right)^{\alpha} \tag{3.11}$$

where $I(.)$ is an indicator function (which is 1 when its argument is true, 0 when it is false), c_n is the count of the number of dimensions in which agent $n = 1,\ldots, N$ is deprived, w_d is a weight attached to the dth deprivation dimension, x_{nd} is the deprivation level experienced by the nth agent in the dth dimension, $\underline{x_d}$ is the deprivation threshold on the dth dimension and $\alpha = 0, 1,\ldots g$ is the parameter for the degree of aversion to poverty (deprivation/wellbeing) in the generalized Foster et al. (1984) (FGT) index.

The parameter α is most frequently set to 0 in practice, which implies that the index involves an average across agents of a weighted count of the number of dimensions in which an individual has not met the deprivation metric particular to each dimension. On closer examination of the Alkire-Foster index of eq. (3.11), one begins to observe the measure as similar to the aggregation of additively separable utility functions (see e.g. Lasso de la Vega and Urrutia (2011)), where the weights could be construed as the marginal effect of each respective dimension in the overall wellbeing index of an agent. The familiar complete union (failure to meet at least one metric, $c_n = K = 0$) and complete intersection (failure to meet all metrics $c_n > K = D$) approaches are extreme versions of the Alkire-Foster index. Complete union can be interpreted as the case where all goods are perfect complements in deprivation, so that deprivation in one good implies deprivation in all, while complete intersection can be interpreted as the case where all goods are perfect substitutes for each other, so that deprivation will only arise when there is deprivation in all. This suggests that the social planner's choice of weights, and number of deprivations for eq. (3.11) is much like approximating the deprivation/wellbeing boundary, denoted by U_, of an individual's preference function $U(x)$ over x (in the present context the vector x represents the various dimensions of functionings, and capabilities of agents). Thus, eq. (3.11) implies a very restrictive form of $U(.)$, which may not represent or be close to the true preferences or needs of agents due to the strong separability assumptions. In essence strong separability may rule out the everyday work life/home life trade-offs that people have to make at the margin (e.g. household reconciliation of the competing demands of good school districts vs. workplace location).

Strongly or additively separable structures for utility functions have played an important role in the empirical development of the theory of consumer behavior, largely as simplifying assumptions for the purposes of facilitating estimable demand equations (for an extensive discussion see Deaton and Muellbauer (1980)) in the context of very limited data sets. A widely used strongly separable utility function is the Stone-Geary utility function underlying the Linear Expenditure System (Stone 1954) which, for goods q_d, $d = 1,\ldots, D$, may be written as:

$$U\left(q_1, q_2, \ldots, q_D,\right) = \sum_{d=1}^{D} \beta_d \ln\left(q_d - \gamma_d\right) \tag{3.12}$$

For U to be appropriately concave $\beta_d \geq 0,\ \sum_{d=1}^{D} \beta_d = 1 \text{ and } q_d > \gamma_d \text{ for all } d.$

Note should be taken here of the mathematical similarity of this structure to (3.11); AFMDI is in essence, a strongly separable representation of preferences for (or aversion to) deprivations. Indeed, the AFMDI of (3.11) can be construed as the Stone-Geary utility function in the limit as consumption in every dimension tends toward their "subsistence" levels.

Stone-Geary is frequently referred to as a "want independent" model, since $\dfrac{d^2U}{\partial q_j \partial q_i} = 0 \text{ for } i \neq j$ (note the same is true for (3.11)). In a similar fashion, the subsistence levels can be considered independent in this system of preferences since the cross partials with respect to the γ_ds are also zero. Its attraction is that it requires estimation of only 2D-1 parameters, much like the deprivation weights in (3.11). The problem with the Stone-Geary utility function [3.12] in the present context is that it does not admit inferior goods, and unfortunately sustaining the concavity assumption also precludes the presence of complementary goods. This is instructive when thinking about the AFMDI, especially when considering the complementarity arguments for using the set intersection ($K = 0$) version of index (3.11). Insofar as there are no interactions between the various dimensions of the index, it does not strictly reflect any complementarity. The "complementarity" referred to when $K = 0$ is implicit, since the idea is relative to the AFMDI under other values of $K\,6 = 0$ examined by the researcher. Alternatively, when considering increasing degrees of substitutability for the respective AFMDI indices, note that the common use of positive weights for the index implies that it continues to violate concavity. Secondly, viewed from the perspective that the AFMDI is in fact a utility/welfare function, and that these weights implicitly describe the relative importance of each dimension, a subjective imposition of weights may overestimate the degree of deprivation. To see that, consider intermediate values of the cut-off K, since individual agents living in deprivation would choose to meet their more heavier weighted needs first, then an imprudent weighting scheme that weighs lower ranking needs heavier would artificially inflate the degree of deprivation because the AFMDI would be counting only those dimensions the individual have chosen not to meet yet.

Finally, insofar as the AFMDI is intended to be a tool for policymakers to focus their efforts of alleviating deprivation, and it is unlikely that every dimension's needs would be fulfilled at the same time, she would need to understand where the direst needs lie.

Given the above considerations, should an investigator consider estimating a utility function in order to derive the requisite weights for use in the AFMDI, a Stone-Geary utility function would not suffice. What is required is a more general description of the relationship between various sources of wellbeing. Furthermore, if the AFMDI is seen as representing deprivations across groups of goods, with each dimension representing several components, then additively separable preferences over the dimensions of wellbeing impose extremely strong restrictions over the substitutability between the components within each dimension, especially at the level of subsistence. Therefore, to accommodate the myriad of interrelationships that individual agents contemplate, the following modification of the AFMDI of (3.11) is proposed in the following form:

$$M_K^\alpha = \frac{1}{N}\sum_{n=1}^{N} I\left(c_n > K\right)\sum_{d=1}^{D}\frac{w_d}{D} I\left(\frac{x_{nd}}{\underline{x}_d} < 1\right)\left(\frac{\underline{x}_d - x_{nd}}{\underline{x}_d}\right)^\alpha \times\left(1+\sum_{h=d+1}^{D}\frac{w_{dh}}{D} I\left(\frac{x_{nh}}{\underline{x}_h} < 1\right)\left(\frac{\underline{x}_h - x_{nh}}{\underline{x}_h}\right)^\alpha\right)$$

where w_{dh}s are chosen to reflect the complementary ($w_{dh} > 0$) or substitutability ($w_{dh} < 0$) nature of capabilities x_d and x_h, $d \neq h$, d, $h \in \{1,\ldots,D\}$. By considering the interaction terms as a composite welfare dimension, it is clear that the axioms fulfilled by the AFMDI still hold under the modified version.

3.9 Equal Opportunity and Mobility Indices

Equality of Opportunity (EO) and Social Mobility (MO) are aspects of societal wellbeing that have received much attention recently (Arrow et al. 2000; Morgan et al. 2006 provide excellent collections of papers as a starting point). Underlying the EO paradigm is the idea that when inequality exists as a matter of choice, it should not be regarded as a bad thing; whereas, when it is the consequence of circumstances beyond an individuals' control, it is a matter of concern. With MO, interest centers on the extent to which there is fluidity in social strata Dardanoni (1993). To over simplify matters somewhat, in both paradigms the object of interest is the nature of Transition Matrix T which maps the progress from an "initial" state to a "final" state. With EO, initial and final states are circumstance and outcome classes respectively; with MO, they are agents' social classifications at point a in time and their corresponding social classification at a subsequent point b ($b > a$) in time, respectively. Suppose that s is a $c \times 1$ vector of the proportions of the population in the c circumstance classes and f is an $r \times 1$ vector of the proportions of the population in the final state or outcome classes then T is an $r \times c$ matrix with typical element t_{ij} $i = 1,\ldots, r$, $j = 1,\ldots, c$ such that $f = Ts$. In effect, t_{ij} is the conditional probability that an agent starting in circumstance class j will end up in outcome class i.

In both paradigms, the focal point is the extent to which the final state is not dependent upon the initial state and generally two approaches have been taken to assess the problem: regression, where initial conditions are regressed on final outcomes and the extent to which their coefficients are different from 0 is a measure of dependence (see e.g. Lee and Solon 2009), and an index construction based upon the anatomical structure of T (see e.g. Shorrocks 1978a).

Shorrocks (1978, 1978a) provides much background for the latter. In an axiomatic approach Shorrocks (1978) seeks indices $M(T)$ which possess the properties of normalization ($0 \leq M(T) \leq 1$), Monotonicity (when the off-diagonals in $T1$ are greater than the off-diagonals in $T2$, $M(T1) > M(T2)$), Immobility ($M(T) = 0$ when $T = I$) and Perfect Mobility ($M(T) = 1$ when T has common columns). Typically, in the mobility literature the matrices are square ($r = c$) given that social categories remain constant over time so that indices based upon square matrix formula are the norm. Indices based upon the trace or the determinant or the eigenvalues of T are popular but all have questions (see Shorrocks 1978) and depend upon the squareness of T, but in many instances, especially in the EO paradigm, the number of circumstance categories differs from the number of outcome categories. A solution to this problem is an index which measures the extent of commonality in the columns of T which will be returned to in a later chapter.

3.10 Exploring the Impact of Ambiguity

At the beginning of the chapter, it was noted that different indicators could yield conflicting orderings, in essence there is a potential for some ambiguity in the ordering process. To illustrate the possibility, data on 18 Eurozone nations over four observation years are used to compare six wellbeing indices that account for inequality to varying degrees. Five are drawn from Blackorby and Donaldson (1978) and are listed in Table 3.1 to which the second order Utopia index drawn from Anderson, Post, and Whang (2018) was added. Atkinson's index has an inequality aversion parameter "*r*" which for present purposes was set at 0.5 and 0.0. The Utopia index (Anderson, Post, and Whang 2019) $U(k)$ was also included as a second order measure, though it does not have a companion inequality measure, $U(k)$ is of the form:

$$U(k) = \frac{\int_a^b \{\max(F_1(x), F_2(x) \ldots, F_K(x)) - F_k(x)\}\,dx}{\int_a^b \{\max(F_1(x), F_2(x) \ldots, F_K(x)) - \min(F_1(x), F_2(x) \ldots, F_K(x))\}\,dx}.$$

In contrast to inequality adjusted wellbeing indices, $U(k)$ considers all feasible outcome distributions and all welfare indices that are monotonically increasing and concave in income.

In addition, seven relative inequality measures were compared, five drawn from Table 3.1 to which was added the inter-quartile range divided by the mean and the inter-quartile range divided by the median.

An indication of the magnitude of discord in ranking a collection of states using a variety of indicators can be gleaned by summing over nations the standard deviation of each nations ranking across ranking instruments in a given class. Let R_{kj} be nation k's rank for the jth ranking instrument for $k = 1, \ldots, K$ nations and $j = 1, \ldots, J$ instruments, then a Rank Variation Index, RVI, and index of the variability in ranking are given by:

$$\text{RVI} = \frac{1}{K}\sum_{k=1}^{K}\sqrt{\sum_{j=1}^{J}\frac{\left(R_{kj} - \frac{\sum_{j=1}^{J} R_{kj}}{J}\right)^2}{J-1}}$$

Clearly, when there is complete accord this average will be 0, when there is much discord the average will be large (Tables 3.2 and 3.3).

Table 3.2 Inequality adjusted income wellbeing indices

	2006						2009						2012						2015					
Nation	*A*	*B*	*C*	*D*	*E*	*F*	*A*	*B*	*C*	*D*	*E*	*F*	*A*	*B*	*C*	*D*	*E*	*F*	*A*	*B*	*C*	*D*	*E*	*F*
Austria	3	3	3	3	3	3	5	5	5	5	5	5	5	5	5	5	5	5	4	5	4	4	5	4
Belgium	5	5	5	5	5	5	8	7	8	8	8	9	7	7	8	8	7	8	7	6	7	7	7	7
Cyprus	8	8	7	8	8	7	7	8	7	7	7	7	8	8	7	7	8	7	10	11	10	10	11	10
Germany	4	4	4	4	4	4	6	6	6	6	6	6	6	6	6	6	6	6	6	7	6	6	6	6
Estonia	15	16	15	15	15	15	16	16	16	16	16	16	16	16	16	16	16	16	14	14	13	13	14	13
Greece	13	13	13	13	13	13	13	13	13	13	13	13	15	14	15	15	15	15	17	16	18	17	17	18
Spain	12	12	12	12	12	12	12	12	11	12	12	11	12	12	12	12	12	12	12	13	12	12	12	12
Finland	7	7	8	7	7	9	4	4	4	4	4	4	4	4	3	3	4	3	3	3	3	3	3	3
France	6	6	6	6	6	6	3	3	3	3	3	3	3	3	2	2	3	2	2	2	2	2	2	2
Ireland	9	9	9	9	9	8	9	9	9	9	9	8	10	11	10	10	10	10	8	9	8	8	8	8
Italy	10	10	10	10	10	10	10	11	10	10	10	10	9	9	9	9	9	9	9	8	9	9	9	9
Lithuania	16	17	16	16	17	16	17	17	17	17	17	17	17	17	17	17	17	17	16	17	16	16	16	16
Luxembourg	1	1	1	1	1	1	1	1	1	1	1	1	1	1	1	1	1	1	1	1	1	1	1	1
Latvia	18	18	18	18	18	18	18	18	18	18	18	18	18	18	18	18	18	18	18	18	17	18	18	17
Netherlands	2	2	2	2	2	2	2	2	2	2	2	2	2	2	4	4	2	4	5	4	5	5	4	5
Portugal	14	14	14	14	14	14	14	15	14	14	14	14	14	15	14	14	14	14	15	15	14	15	15	14
Slovenia	11	11	11	11	11	11	11	10	12	11	11	12	11	10	11	11	11	11	11	10	11	11	10	11
Slovakia	17	15	17	17	16	17	15	14	15	15	15	15	13	13	13	13	13	13	13	12	15	14	13	15
RVI			0.1957						0.2190						0.2733						0.4477			

Source: Anderson and Thomas (2019)

A: Atkinson Index ($r = 0.5$), B: Coefficient of Variation, C: Theils Entropy, D: Atkinson Index ($r = 0.0$), E: GINI, F: Utopia Index

Table 3.3 Inequality index rankings

	2006							2009							2012							2015						
Nation	*A*	*B*	*C*	*D*	*E*	*F*	*G*	*A*	*B*	*C*	*D*	*E*	*F*	*G*	*A*	*B*	*C*	*D*	*E*	*F*	*G*	*A*	*B*	*C*	*D*	*E*	*F*	*G*
Austria	2	3	3	2	2	4	4	6	5	5	7	6	4	4	8	8	7	9	8	5	5	6	6	6	6	6	5	5
Belgium	5	5	5	5	5	9	8	7	6	6	6	5	9	8	7	6	6	7	7	8	7	8	7	7	8	7	8	8
Cyprus	11	10	9	10	10	11	13	11	11	11	11	11	12	15	11	11	12	10	11	13	16	12	12	12	11	12	14	14
Germany	6	6	6	7	6	5	5	9	9	8	9	9	6	6	9	9	8	8	9	9	9	9	9	9	9	9	9	9
Estonia	14	15	15	14	15	12	11	14	14	15	13	14	13	13	14	15	15	14	14	16	15	15	15	15	15	15	17	17
Greece	15	14	14	15	14	15	15	13	13	13	14	13	11	11	13	13	13	13	13	10	10	13	13	14	13	13	11	11
Spain	13	13	13	13	13	13	16	15	15	14	15	15	15	17	16	14	14	16	15	17	18	14	14	13	14	14	15	16
Finland	9	8	8	8	8	6	7	8	7	7	8	8	7	7	6	5	4	6	5	7	6	5	5	4	5	5	6	6
France	7	7	7	6	7	7	6	5	4	4	5	4	5	5	4	3	3	4	4	4	4	3	2	1	2	2	4	4
Ireland	12	12	11	11	12	17	17	10	10	10	10	10	14	16	10	10	10	11	10	12	11	10	10	11	10	10	12	13
Italy	10	10	10	12	11	10	10	12	12	12	12	12	10	10	12	12	11	12	12	11	14	11	11	10	12	11	10	10
Lithuania	16	16	16	16	16	14	12	16	16	16	16	16	17	14	15	16	16	15	16	14	13	17	17	17	17	17	16	15
Luxembourg	3	2	2	4	3	8	9	3	2	2	2	2	8	9	2	2	2	2	2	6	8	4	4	3	4	4	7	7
Latvia	18	18	18	18	18	18	18	18	18	18	18	18	18	18	18	18	18	18	18	18	17	18	18	18	18	18	18	18
Netherlands	1	1	1	1	1	1	2	1	1	1	1	1	1	2	1	1	1	1	1	1	1	1	1	2	1	1	2	2
Portugal	17	17	17	17	17	16	14	17	17	17	17	17	16	12	17	17	17	17	17	15	12	16	16	16	16	16	13	12
Slovenia	4	4	4	4	4	3	3	2	3	3	3	3	2	3	3	4	5	3	3	2	2	7	8	8	7	8	3	3
Slovakia	8	9	12	9	9	2	1	4	8	9	4	7	3	1	5	7	9	5	6	3	3	2	3	5	3	3	1	1
RVI				1.296							1.244							1.161							0.964			

Source: Anderson and Thomas (2019)

A: Gini, B: Theils Entropic measure, C: The Coefficient of Variation, D: Atkinson ($r = 0.25$), E: Atkinson ($r = 0.75$), F: Inter-quartile range/average and G: Inter-quartile range/median

What can be seen from Tables 3.2 and 3.3 is an increase in the lack of accord in the wellbeing level ranking instruments and a diminution in the lack of accord in the inequality measures over the period. Chapter 5 will elaborate on the source of these discrepancies and introduce measures for the propensity for such ambiguities.

References

Alesina, A., & Spolaore, E. (1997). On the Number and Size of Nations. *The Quarterly Journal of Economics, 112*(4), 1027–1056.

Alkire, S., & Foster, J. (2011). Counting and Multidimensional Poverty Measurement. *Journal of Public Economics, 95*(7–8), 476–487.

Anderson, G. J. (2004). Making Inferences About the Polarization, Welfare and Poverty of Nations: A Study of 101 Countries 1970–1995. *Journal of Applied Econometrics, 19*, 537–550.

Anderson, G. J. (2004a). Toward an Empirical Analysis of Polarization. *Journal of Econometrics, 122*, 1–26.

Anderson, G. J. (2010). Polarization of the Poor: Multivariate Relative Poverty Measurement Sans Frontiers. *Review of Income and Wealth, 56*(1), 84–101.

Anderson, G. J. (2011). Polarization Measurement and Inference in Many Dimensions When Subgroups Can Not Be Identified. *Economics: The Open-Access, Open-Assessment E-Journal, 5*, 2011-11.

Anderson G. J. (2012). Polarization Measurement and Inference in Many Dimensions When Subgroups Cannot Be Identified. *Economics (E Journal).*

Anderson, G., & Thomas, J. (2018). Measuring Multi-Group Polarization, Segmentation and Ambiguity: Increasingly Unequal Yet Similar Constituent Canadian Income Distributions. *Social Indicators Research.* Forthcoming.

Anderson, G., & Thomas, J. (2019). *Structural Ambiguity in Wellbeing Indices.* Toronto: University of Toronto, Economics Department. Mimeo.

Anderson, G. J., Linton, O., & Leo, T. W. (2012). A Polarization-Cohesion Perspective on Cross Country Convergence. *Journal of Economic Growth, 17*, 49–69.

Anderson G. J., Post, T., & Whang, Y.-J. (2019). Somewhere Between Utopia and Dystopia: Choosing From Multiple Incomparable Prospects. *Journal of Business and Economic Statistics.* Forthcoming.

Anderson, G., Pittau, G., Zelli, R., & Thomas, J. (2018). Income Inequality, Cohesiveness and Commonality in the Euro Area: A Semi-Parametric Boundary-Free Analysis. *Econometrics, Special Issue on Econometrics of Inequality, 6*, 15.

Arrow, K., Bowles, S., & Durlauf, S. (2000). *Meritocracy and Economic Inequality.* Princeton: Princeton University Press.

Atkinson, A. B. (1970). On the Measurement of Inequality. *Journal of Economic Theory, 2*, 244–263.

Atkinson, A. B. (1983). *The Economics of Inequality* (2nd ed.). Oxford: Clarendon Press.
Blackorby, C., & Donaldson, D. (1978). Measures of Relative Equality and Their Meaning in Terms of Social Welfare. *Journal of Economic Theory, 18*, 59–80.
Bossert, W., D'Ambrosio, C., & Peragine, V. (2004). Deprivation and Social Exclusion. *Economica, 74*(296), 777–803.
Bourguignon, F. (1979). Decomposable Income Inequality Measures. *Econometrica, 47*(4), 901–920.
Carneiro, P., Hansen, K. T., & Heckman, J. J. (2002). *Removing the Veil of Ignorance in Assessing the Distributional Impacts of Social Policy* (NBER Working Paper 8840).
Carneiro, P., Hansen, K. T., & Heckman, J. J. (2003). 2001 Lawrence R. Klein Lecture Estimating Distributions of Treatment Effects with an Application to the Returns to Schooling and Measurement of the Effects of Uncertainty on College Choice. *International Economic Review, 44*, 361–422.
Cowell, F. A. (1980). On the Structure of Additive Inequality Measures. *Review of Economic Studies, 47*, 52131.
Cowell, F. A. (1985). Measures of Distributional Change: An Axiomatic Approach. *Review of Economic Studies, 52*, 135–151.
Cowell, F. A. (1989). Sampling Variance and Decomposable Inequality Measures. *Journal of Econometrics, 42*, 27–41.
Cowell, F. A. (1995). *Measuring Inequality* (2nd ed.). Hemel Hempstead: Harvester Wheatsheaf.
Cowell, F. A. (1999). Measurement of Inequality. In A. B. Atkinson & F. Bourguignon (Eds.), *Handbook of Income Distribution*. Amsterdam: North Holland.
Cowell, F. A., & Jenkins, S. P. (1995). How Much Inequality Can We Explain? A Methodology and an Application to the USA. *Economic Journal, 105*, 421–430.
Dalton, H. (1920). The Measurement of the Inequality of Incomes. *The Economic Journal, 30*, 348–361.
Dardanoni, V. (1993). Measuring Social Mobility. *Journal of Economic Theory, 61*, 372–394.
Deaton, A., & Muellbauer, J. (1980). *Economics and Consumer Behaviour*. Cambridge: Cambridge University Press.
Duclos, J., Esteban, J., & Ray, D. (2004). Polarization: Concepts, Measurement, Estimation. *Econometrica, 72*, 1737–1772.
Durlauf, S. N., & Quah, D. (2002). The New Empirics of Economic Growth, Chap. 4. In J. B. Taylor & M. Woodford (Eds.), *Handbook of Macroeconomics*. Amsterdam: North Holland.
Esteban, J., & Ray, D. (1994). On the Measurement of Polarization. *Econometrica, 62*, 819–851.
Esteban, J., & Ray, D. (2008). Polarization, Fractionalization and Conflict. *Journal of Peace Research, 45*(2), 163–182.

Esteban, J., Gradín, C., & Ray, D. (2007). An Extension of a Measure of Polarization, with an Application to the Income Distribution of Five OECD Countries. *The Journal of Economic Inequality, 5*, 1–19.

Foster, J. E., & Wolfson, M. C. (1992). *Polarization and the Decline of the Middle Class: Canada and the* US. Mimeo Vanderbilt University.

Foster, J., Greer, J., & Thorbecke, E. (1984). A Class of Decomposable Poverty Measures. *Econometrica, 52*, 761–765.

Gertner, G. (2010). The Rise and Fall of the G.D.P. *New York Times Magazine.*

Gigliarano, C., & Mosler, K. (2009). Constructing Indices of Multivariate Polarization. *The Journal of Economic Inequality, 7*, 435.

Gini, C. (1912). *Variabilità e mutabilità.* Reprinted in Pizetti, E., & Salvemini, T. (Eds.). (1955). *Memorie di metodologica statistica.* Rome: Libreria Eredi Virgilio Veschi.

Gini, C. (1921). Measurement of Inequality of Incomes. *The Economic Journal.* Blackwell Publishing, *31*(121), 124–126.

Lasso de la Vega, M. C., & Urrutia, A. (2011). Characterizing How to Aggregate the Individuals' Deprivations in a Multidimensional Framework. *The Journal of Economic Inequality, 9*, 183.

Lee, C.-I., & Solon, G. (2009). Trends in Intergenerational Income. *Mobility Review of Economics and Statistics, 91*, 766–772.

Lerman, R. I., & Yitzhaki, S. (1985). Income Inequality Effects by Income Source: A New Approach and Applications to the United States. *The Review of Economics and Statistics, 67*(1), 151–156.

Mookherjee, D., & Shorrocks, A. (1982). A Decomposition Analysis of the Trend in UK Income Inequality. *Economic Journal, 92*, 886–902.

Morgan, S. L., Grusky, D. B., & Fields, G. S. (2006). *Mobility and Inequality Frontiers of Research in Sociology and Economics.* Stanford: Stanford University Press.

Pigou, A. F. (1912). *Wealth and Welfare.* London: Macmillan.

Pigou, A. F. (1920). *The Economics of Welfare.* Indianapolis: The Liberty Fund.

Rawls, J. (1971). *Theory of Justice.* Cambridge: The Belknap Press of Harvard University Press.

Sen, A. (1973). *On Economic Inequality.* Oxford: Oxford University Press.

Sen, A. (1995). Rationality and Social Choice. *American Economic Review, Papers and Proceedings*, 85, 1–24.

Shorrocks, A. F. (1978). The Measurement of Mobility. *Econometrica, 46*, 1013–1024.

Shorrocks, A. F. (1978a). Income Inequality and Income Mobility. *Journal of Economic Theory, 19*, 376–393.

Shorrocks, A. F. (1982a). Inequality Decomposition by Factor Components. *Econometrica, 50*, 193–212.

Shorrocks, A. F. (1982b). The Impact of Income Components on the Distribution of Family Incomes. *Quarterly Journal of Economics, 98*, 311–326.

Shorrocks, A. F. (1983). Ranking Income Distributions. *Economica, 50*, 3–17.

Shorrocks, A. F. (1984). Inequality Decomposition by Population Subgroup. *Econometrica, 52*, 1369–1385.

Stone, J. R. N. (1954). Linear Expenditure Systems and Demand Analysis: An Application to the Pattern of British Demand. *Economic Journal*, 64, 511–527.

Theil, H. (1967). *Economics and Information Theory*. Amsterdam: North Holland.

Theil, H. (1979). The Measurement of Inequality by Components of Income. *Economics Letters, 2*, 197–199.

UNPD. (2016). *Human Development Report 2016*. Washington, DC: Communications Development Incorporated.

Wang, Y., & Tsui, K. (2000). Polarization Orderings and New Classes of Polarization Indices. *Journal of Public Economic Theory, 2*, 349–363.

Wolfson, M. (1994). When Inequalities Diverge. *The American Economic Review, 84*(2), 353–358.

Yitzhaki, S., & Lerman, R. I. (1991). Income Stratification and Income Inequality. *Review of Income and Wealth, 37*, 313–329.

Zhang, X., & Kanbur, R. (2001). What Difference Do Polarisation Measures Make? An Application to China. *The Journal of Development Studies, 37*, 85–98.

Zheng, B. (1997). Aggregate poverty measures. *Journal of Economic Surveys, 11*, 123–162.

CHAPTER 4

Partial Orderings

As noted at the end of Chap. 3, there are often many alternative indices suitable for a given task unfortunately they frequently yield conflicting orderings, in essence there is invariably some ambiguity in the ordering process. An alternative comparison strategy is to use stochastic dominance (SD) criteria to study the orientation of group distributions to see if, given the nature of the chosen criterion function class, the juxtaposition of the group distributions will admit an unambiguous ordering. Sometimes they will, sometimes they won't, in effect the ordering is only partial; however, in the event that an unambiguous ordering is not admitted a similar exercise can be pursued in the light of a more restrictive criterion function class. Based on the aforesaid stochastic dominance concepts, this chapter considers techniques for revealing the extent of ambiguity surrounding the comparison exercise, develops some ideas for establishing unambiguous groupings and formulates a general family of ordering indices that reflect restrictions implied on the criterion function implied by the level of stochastic ordering.

After an introduction to the partial ordering process in Sect. 4.1, Sect. 4.2 details some preliminary concepts, outlines some basic stochastic dominance criteria and provides a simple example of a first order stochastic dominance application which illustrates the sharpness (or lack thereof) of the criteria in distinguishing an unambiguous ordering. The problem is seen to be the generality of the criteria which suggests performing comparisons in environments which increasingly restrict the nature of the criterion function.

G. Anderson, *Multilateral Wellbeing Comparison in a Many Dimensioned World*, Global Perspectives on Wealth and Distribution,
https://doi.org/10.1007/978-3-030-21130-1_4

The ways in which successive orders of dominance restrict the nature of the criterion function are discussed in Sect. 4.3. The relationships between stochastic dominance and inequality and poverty orderings are covered in Sects. 4.4 and 4.5 and the special case of polarization is discussed in Sect. 4.6. The problem of ambiguity and how to measure the extent to which it prevails are discussed in Sects. 4.7 and 4.8. Some tools for dealing with these issues are provided in Sect. 4.9.

4.1 Introduction

Until now, consideration has been confined to comparing aspects of societies via instruments (usually indices) that are completely ordered and it has been seen that different indices constructed for a common purpose can produce contradictory orderings. Indeed, an index on its own can produce some confusing results. For example, the Gini coefficient, which records the average absolute distance relative to the mean between all agent incomes in a society will record definitively whether one society is more equal, less equal or the same as another society in that regard. Such a comparison is always feasible and in this sense, the ordering provided by the Gini coefficient is said to be complete. But there is a sense in which such comparisons conceal considerable ambiguity, to the extent that one may feel uncomfortable about declaring more or less equality between two states via a complete ordering system. Partial orderings avoid these ambiguities but at a cost, a definitive result is not guaranteed in the sense that some comparisons are inconclusive.

These issues are best illustrated by noting the relationship between the Lorenz curve (which can be used as a partial ordering) and the Gini coefficient. The Lorenz curve relates the proportion of the population (x) to the proportion of aggregate income (y) it possesses. In terms of a size distribution of incomes x given by f(x) where $E(x) = \mu$, the Lorenz curve may be written as:

$$L(p) = \frac{1}{\mu} \int_{0}^{y\left(=F^{-1}(p)\right)} xf(x)\,dx$$

Note that $L(p)$ is monotonic and non-decreasing with $dL(p)/dp = y/\mu$. The Gini turns out to be twice the area between this curve and the 45°

line.[1] Assume now three equal sized, equal average income societies A, B and C, where for simplicity society A has a Lorenz curve $L = 0.75p$ for $0 \leq p < 1$ and $L = p$ for $p = 1$, society B has a Lorenz curve $L = 0$ for $p \leq 0.25$ and $L = 4p/3 - 1/3$ for $0.25 < p \leq 1$ and society C has a Lorenz curve $L = 0.74p$ for $0 \leq x < 1$ and $L = p$ for $p = 1$ (i.e. C is very close to B). Fig. 4.1 illustrates these three societies.

The Gini coefficient for societies A and B is 0.25, so the "completely ordered" Gini declares the two societies equally unequal. Yet they record very different types of inequality—the first 25% of the population in B have no income whereas in A the first 25% have 18.75% of aggregate income and the highest income earner in B gets 25% of the aggregate income of the society—so one may feel uncomfortable about declaring such different societies as equal in their inequality. The fact is that all agents below the median agent in society A possess a greater share of aggregate income in society A than in society B whereas above the median agents in society A increment less than agents in society B except for the last person. Intuitively there is great inequality in the top end of the A distribution and great inequality in the bottom end of the B distribution. In short it is not at all clear that A and B are "equally unequal" there is ambiguity in the comparison. Now consider C which has a Gini coefficient

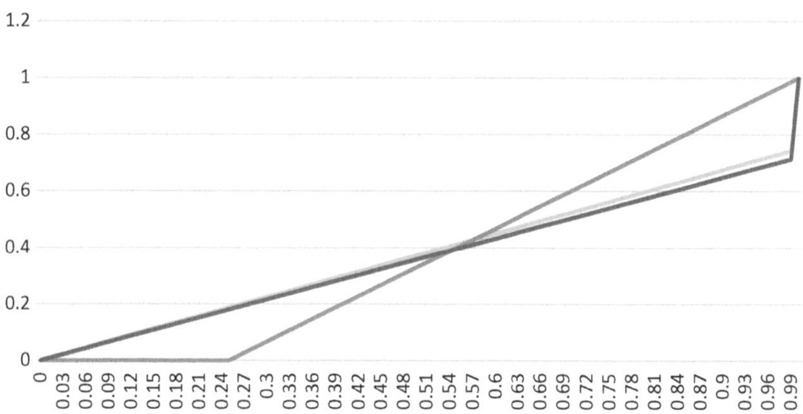

Fig. 4.1 Lorenz curves for three societies. (Source: Author's calculations)

[1] The Schutz coefficient is the maximal vertical distance between $L(p)$ and 45° line.

value of 0.27 (approximately) and so is more unequal than both A and B under the complete ordering system; however it may be argued that the lowest 25% of that population are more equally treated than the corresponding group in society B (they possess 19% of aggregate income as opposed to nothing for the B group) so the B–C comparison may again be considered ambiguous. Comparison of C with A is however unambiguous. Other than the highest income person (in C he has 27% of aggregate income), the A group has a greater share of aggregate income than C at every income strata.

What generates the ambiguities is the crossing of the Lorenz curves, notice A and B cross and B and C cross, which renders them "incomparable", the technical term in order theory. Only A and C do not cross, and they are the only unambiguous comparison. For this reason, in a system of partial orderings comparisons between A and B and B and C would not be admitted whereas A and C would (and A would be preferred to C) so that societies A, B and C are in this case only partially ordered. The Lorenz curve A is preferred to C because A is everywhere not below C and at least somewhere above C, in other words A "Lorenz Dominates" C. What this implies is that, when ordering the population in terms of their incomes, every population quantile in A enjoys at least as big a share of aggregate income as the corresponding population quantile in C with some quantiles in A enjoying a greater share than their counterparts in C.[2]

Note here that, as opposed to summarizing the difference in the two distributions by the difference in their respective summary statistics (here the Gini coefficient), the two distributions of x are being compared at every value of x which is very much the stuff of dominance relations and comparisons. The price of the lack of ambiguity is that not all comparisons are admissible, pairs of distributions can only be partially ordered. However, dominance relations provide a useful alternative set of comparison techniques which can shed a brighter light on the nature of differences between groups; what they are and what they imply are explored in this chapter.

[2] Note here the semantic similarity with the Paretian judgment that "no one should be worse of and at least someone should be better off", but beware this is not at all the same thing given the anonymity axiom.

4.2 Stochastic Dominance Criteria

In two-way comparisons, the problems with ambiguity and interpretation have led researchers to employ model-free non-parametric stochastic dominance (SD) criteria for comparing distributions (Lorenz dominance comparisons are a special case of this activity). Originally developed for studying decision making under uncertainty (Hadar and Russell 1969; Hanoch and Levy 1969; Rothschild and Stiglitz 1970; Linton et al. 2014), Atkinson (1970, 1983, 1987)[3] had the great insight to introduce dominance comparison techniques to wellbeing analysis where they provide a partial ordering for general classes of wellbeing or criterion functions discussed in Chap. 1. The ordering is partial in the sense that, when comparing two states under a particular class of criterion functions, the orientation of the two distributions can be such that the process can be inconclusive and no ranking can be made. This inconclusive nature reflects the ambiguity inherent in the process and is precisely the situation where different indices from a class could reveal contradictory orderings.[4] In these circumstances, the usual practice has been to seek compliance with the dominance criterion at some higher order since successively higher orders of dominance correspond to rankings of successively more parametrically restrictive wellbeing functions.[5] In effect, the potential for ambiguity is being constrained by successively restricting the class of indices entertained.

Some Preliminaries

Of interest is a collection of indices $U(x)$ that reflect the average quality $E(U(x))$ yielded by the random variable x where $(-1)^{i+1}(dU(x)/dx) > 0$ for $i = 1, 2,\ldots$ when comparing K distributions of x denoted $f_k(x)$ indexed $k = 1,\ldots,K$. For convenience each distribution will be defined on compact support $[0,M]$ $M < \infty$. Since the juxtaposition of distributions is relevant in developing concepts of ambiguity, stochastic dominance concepts (Levy 1998) will be useful. For notational convenience, the distributions will be ordered by their means so that:

[3] See also Atkinson and Bourguingnon (1987), Foster and Shorrocks (1988), Davies and Hoy (1994, 1995), Lambert and Ok (1999).

[4] Indeed, Atkinson (1970) expressed some scepticism regarding its use given the frequency with which he observed a "no decision".

[5] A lemma, due to Davidson and Duclos (2000), provides a rationale for this practice. It reveals that, if a distribution dominates over a restricted lower range at a given order of dominance, it will dominate over the whole range at some higher order.

$$k > j \Rightarrow E_{f_k}(x) = \int_0^M x f_k(x)\,dx \geq \int_0^M x f_j(x)\,dx = E_{f_j}(x).$$

Throughout the discussion, successive orders of integration will be used; so for $i = 1,2,\ldots$ define $F^i(x) = \int_0^x F^{i-1}(z)\,dz$ with $F^0(x) = f(x)$, where $f(x)$ is a probability distribution function defined on the closed compact support interval $[0, M]$ where M is finite.

Notions of Distributional Overlap (OV) and Transvariation (TR) and extensions to it (Anderson, Linton and Whang 2012; Gini 1916; Dagum 1968; Anderson, Linton and Thomas 2017) will also be of use in the analysis. Distributional Overlap (OV) measures the extent to which there is commonality in two distributions, for two distributions $f_a(x), f_b(x)$ the overlap is defined as:

$$\mathrm{OV}\left(f_a(x), f_b(x)\right) = \int_0^M \min\left(f_a(x), f_b(x)\right)dx$$

Gini (1916) defined TR, the Transvariation of two distributions $f_a(x)$ and $f_b(x)$ as:

$$\begin{aligned}\mathrm{TR}\left(f_a(x), f_b(x)\right) &= \frac{1}{2}\int_0^M \left|f_a(x) - f_b(x).\right|dx \\ &= \frac{1}{2}\int_0^M \left[\max\left(f_a(x), f_b(x)\right) - \min\left(f_a(x), f_b(x)\right)\right]\end{aligned}$$

Note that:

$$\mathrm{TR}\left(f_a(x), f_b(x)\right) = 1 - \mathrm{OV}\left(f_a(x), f_b(x)\right)$$

The notion of Transvariation may be extended to *i*th order integrals (Anderson, Linton and Thomas 2017) as:

$$\begin{aligned}\mathrm{TR}\left(F_a^i(x), F_b^i(x)\right) &= \frac{1}{2}\int_0^M \left|F_a^i(x) - F_b^i(x)\right|dx \\ &= \frac{1}{2}\int_0^M \left[\max\left(F_a^i(x), F_b^i(x)\right) - \min\left(F_a^i(x), F_b^i(x)\right)\right]\end{aligned}$$

Note that generally:

$$\mathrm{TR}\left(F_a^i(x), F_b^i(x)\right) \geq \frac{1}{2}\left|\int_0^M \left(F_a^i(x) - F_b^i(x)\right) dx\right|$$

With equality prevailing when $f_b()$ stochastically dominates $f_a()$ at the ith order.[6]

For a collection of distributions the concepts of ith order upper (FUE^i) and lower (FLE^i) envelopes and the Multilateral Transvariation (MTR^i) of the collection will be useful and are defined as follows.

For the collection of distributions $f_a(x), f_b(x), \ldots, f_h(x)$:

$$\mathrm{FUE}^i(x) = \max\left(F_a^i(x), F_b^i(x), \ldots F_h^i(x)\right)$$

The upper envelope is a non-negative, non-decreasing and piecewise function

$$\mathrm{FLE}^i(x) = \min\left(F_a^i(x), F_b^i(x), \ldots F_h^i(x)\right)$$

Like the upper envelope, the lower envelope is a non-negative, non-decreasing and piecewise function. Note that $\mathrm{FUE}^i(x)$ is (weakly) dominated at the ith order by all distributions in the collection and $\mathrm{FLE}^i(x)$ (weakly) dominates at the ith order all distributions in the collection. Hence ith order Transvariation (distributional variation at the ith order) is given by:

$$\mathrm{MTR}^i(x) = \int_0^\infty \left(\mathrm{FUE}^i(x) - \mathrm{FLE}^i(x)\right) dx$$

$\mathrm{MTR}^i(x)$ reflects the distributional variation in the collection at the ith level.

[6] Suppose 1 intersection point at z where $0 < z < \infty$ where $F_a(x) \geq F_b(x)$ *for* $x < z$ *and* $F_a(x) < F_b(x)$ *for* $x > z$, then $\int_0^M \left|F_i(x) - F_j(x)\right| dx = \int_0^M \left(F_a(x) - F_b(x)\right) dx - \int_a^M \left(F_a(x) - F_b(x)\right) dx$ $= \int_0^M \left(F_a(x) - F_b(x)\right) dx - 2\int_a^M \left(F_i(x) - F_j(x)\right) dx > \int_0^M \left(F_i(x) - F_j(x)\right) dx$ since $2\int_a^M \left(F_i(x) - F_j(x)\right) dx$ is negative. When dominance prevails there will be no intersection point, $F_a(x) \geq F_b(x)$ for all x and $\mathrm{TR} = 0.5\int_a^M \left(F_a(x) - F_b(x)\right) dx$.

Stochastic Dominance Relations

For probability distributions $f(x)$ defined on [0, M] absence of an intersection between two curves relating to higher order integrals of $f_a(x)$ and $f_b(x)$ means that a dominance relationship prevails between them at that order, more formally:

When $F_a^i(x) \le F_b^i(x)$ with $F_a^i(x) < F_b^i(x)$ for some $x > 0$, $f_a(x)$ is said to stochastically dominate $f_b(x)$ at the *i*th order. In this case, for all $U(x)$[7] with $(-1)^{j+1}(dU(x)/dx) > 0$ $j = 1,\ldots, i$, $f_a(x)$ would be unambiguously preferred to $f_b(x)$, which may be written $f_a(x) \succcurlyeq_i f_b(x)$, in the sense that the expected value of $U(x)$ under $f_a(x)$ is at least as great as it is under $f_b(x)$, that is to say $E_{f_a}(U(x)) - E_{f_b}(U(x)) \ge 0$. Note that $\mathrm{TR}_i(f_a(x), f_b(x)) \ge \left| \int_0^M (F_a^i(x) - F_b^i(x))dx \right|$ with equality holding when $f_a(x) \succcurlyeq_i f_b(x)$ or $f_b(x) \succcurlyeq_i f_a(x)$.

The importance of this result is that all indices or instruments in compliance with the class defined by $(-1)^{j+1}(dU(x)/dx) > 0$ $j = 1,\ldots, i$ would be in agreement. For some intuition for how this might be, consider:

$E_{f_a}(U(x)) - E_{f_a}(U(x)) = \int_0^M U(x)(dF_a - dF_b) \ge 0$, where $U(x)$ has the above properties, integrating by parts i times yields a sequence of non-negative terms plus a term that looks like:

$$(-1)^i \int_0^M \frac{\partial^i U(x)}{\partial x^i} \int_0^M (F_b^{i-1}(x) - F_a^{i-1}(x))dx$$

which will be positive when $F_a^i(x) \le F_b^i(x)$ with $F_a^i(x) < F_b^i(x)$ for some $x > 0$.

[7] Here we think of $U(x)$ as corresponding to some index that is a criterion of x that reflects individual wellbeing, the class of $U(x)$ being entertained is referred to as the preference space and imposing restrictions on U can be interpreted as reducing the preference space.

What Does $f_a(x) \succcurlyeq_i f_b(x)$ *for Different "I" Imply for Societal Preferences?*

Foster and Shorrocks (1988), in discussing the implications of stochastic dominance criteria for poverty orderings, provide an interpretation of the societal preferences coherent with a particular level of ordering. These can be best understood by first noting that the general incomplete moments formula for the *i*th level of integration, $F^i(x) = ((i-1)!)^{-1} \int_0^x (x-y)^{i-1} dF(y)$, attaches increasing weight to the lower part of range of the distribution as *i* increases.

Thus, first order dominance (FOD), which considers all $U(x)$ such that $dU(x)/dx > 0$, requires:

$$F_a^1(x) \leq F_b^1(x) \text{ with } F_a^1(x) < F_b^1(x) \text{ for some } x > 0.$$

This relationship reflects societal preference for more of something without reference to how it is achieved (monotonic Utilitarian or Benthamite preferences) and compares the respective cumulative density functions.

Second order dominance (SOD) admits all $U(x)$ where $dU(x)/dx > 0$, $d^2U(x)/dx^2 < 0$. In admitting an additional restriction on the nature of *U*, it yields the SOD rule:

$$F_a^2(x) \leq F_b^2(x) \text{ with } F_a^2(x) < F_b^2(x) \text{ for some } x > 0.$$

This rule reflects societal preference for more with weak preference for reduced spread (monotonic increasing, equality preferring Daltonian societal preferences) so that, at the margin, for two societies with the same average utility the one with the lowest inequality is preferred. It compares the integrals of the cdfs.

Third order dominance (TOD) admits all $U(x)$ where $dU(x)/dx > 0$, $d^2U(x)/dx^2$ 0 and $d^3U(x)/dx^3 > 0$. By imposing a third restriction on *U*, it yields the TOD rule:

$$F_a^3(x) \leq F_b^3(x) \text{ with } F_a^3(x) < F_b^3(x) \text{ for some } x > 0.$$

It represents an expression of societal preference for more spread with weak preference for reduced spread, especially at the low end of the distribution (monotonic increasing, equality preferring transfer sensitive societal preferences).

The discussion proceeds ad nauseam with successive orders of dominance reflecting successively more refined societal preferences until infinite order dominance is reached. This particular comparison level reflects Rawlsian Societal preferences, which attach infinite weight to the poorest individual. So entertaining increasingly restrictive forms of *U*(.) leads to comparing successively higher order integrals. The general practice in application of stochastic dominance comparisons has been to seek a decision at the lowest possible order and, if there is no decision, move to a higher order, in essence seeking the clarity of a clear distinction by restricting the societal preference space.

An Illustration: Consider all possible bi-lateral first order dominance comparisons of the distributions underlying the Eurozone inequality adjusted income comparisons in Table 3.1 using the Kolmogorov-Smirnov test outlined in Chap. 2. Recall that, letting $\hat{F}_a(x), \hat{F}_b(x)$ be the respective estimates of the cdfs of distributions $f_a(x)$ and $f_b(x)$, stochastic dominance tests can be contrived using $DU\left(\hat{F}_a(x), \hat{F}_b(x)\right) = \sup_x \left(\hat{F}_a(x) - \hat{F}_b(x)\right)$ and $DL\left(\hat{F}_a(x), \hat{F}_b(x)\right) = \left|\inf_x \left(\hat{F}_a(x) - \hat{F}_b(x)\right)\right|$. These values are compared to a critical value $c(n_a n_b \alpha) = \sqrt{-0.5\ln(\alpha)}\left(\frac{n_a + n_b}{n_a n_b}\right)$, where n_a and n_b are the respective sample sizes and α is the chosen size of the test. When $DU > c(n_a n_b \alpha)$ and $DL < c(n_a n_b \alpha)$, $f_b(x)$ is said to dominate $f_a(x)$ and when $DU < c(n_a n_b \alpha)$ and $DL > c(n_a n_b \alpha)$, $f_a(x)$ is said to dominate $f_b(x)$. If both *DU* and *DL* exceed $c(n_a n_b \alpha)$ or if neither exceeds $c(n_a n_b \alpha)$, first order dominance cannot be declared. Comparisons are made with α set to 0.1 and 0.025, in the former case 14, 22, 24 and 17 first order dominance relationships were detected in the respective observation years 2006, 2009, 2012 and 2015 in the latter case 15, 28, 27 and 23 cases were detected. The point is, with a possible 136 comparisons, either there are many similarities in Eurozone income distributions or first order dominance comparisons are not a very sharp instrument. The latter scenario is often the case since the first order dominance criteria encompass all criterion functions that are monotonically increasing in *x*; it is not very selective or restrictive in the space of criteria.

4.3 On Restricting the Criterion Space

Since $F_a^{i+1}(x) - F_b^{i+1}(x) = \int_0^x \left(F_a^i(z) - F_b^i(z)\right)dz$, when $F_a^i(x) \le F_b^i(x)$ with $F_a^i(x) < F_b^i(x)$ for some $x > 0$ then $F_a^{i+1}(x) \le F_b^{i+1}(x)$ with $F_a^{i+1}(x) < F_b^{i+1}(x)$ for some $x > 0$ so that dominance at order i implies dominance at all higher orders $i + m$ for any positive integer m. Hence, it is usually the practice for researchers to look for a dominance relationship at the first order and, if the comparison is inconclusive, then seek a comparison at the next order. The process of exploring progressively higher orders of integration in the search for a clear decision can be rationalized using Lemma 4.1 of Davidson and Duclos (2000). In the present context, the tenor of the Lemma is that, for any two distributions, there will ultimately be an order of integration at which a dominance comparison is decisive.

Lemma 4.1: If $f_a(x) \succcurlyeq_1 f_b(x)$ over all values of x up to some value $w > 0$, with strict dominance over at least part of that range, then for any finite threshold z, $f_a(x) \succcurlyeq_i f_b(x)$ at order i up to z for i values that are sufficiently large.

To understand how the magnitude $\int_0^w \left(dF_b(y) - dF_a(y)\right)$ influences i, it will be helpful to follow the proof of Lemma 4.1. Expressing the relationship in partial moment form, the essence of the proof is to show that, when $F_a^1(x) \le F_b^1(x)$ with $F_a^1(x) < F_b^1(x)$ somewhere for $w > x > 0$, for i values that are sufficiently large, it will be the case that: $\int_0^x \left(1 - \frac{y}{x}\right)^{i-1} \left(dF_b(y) - dF_a(y)\right) \ge 0$ for all $x < M$ with strict equality somewhere. That is to say, $F_a^i(x) \le F_b^i(x)$ for all $x \ge 0$ and $F_a^i(x) < F_b^i(x)$ for some $x \ge 0$. Integrating by parts, the expression in question may be written as:

$$\frac{i-1}{x}\left\{\int_0^w (F_b(y)-F_a(y))\left(1-\frac{y}{x}\right)^{i-2} dy+\int_w^x (F_b(y)-F_a(y))\left(1-\frac{y}{x}\right)^{i-2} dy\right\} \tag{4.1}$$

Since $|F_b(x)-F_a(x)| \leq 1$ for any y and $1- y/x \geq 0$ for all $y \leq x$, the second term can be shown to be bounded, that is, no larger than $\left(1-\frac{w}{x}\right)^{i-1}$; furthermore, the first term can be shown to be at least $\frac{\delta(i-1)}{x}\left(1-\frac{w}{x}\right)^{i-2}$, where $\delta > 0$ reflects the magnitude of the first term (in effect the dominance area). Putting these together, it may be seen that:

$$\int_0^x \left(1-\frac{y}{x}\right)^{i-1}(dF_b(y)-dF_a(y)) \geq \left(1-\frac{w}{x}\right)^{i-2}\left(\frac{\delta(i-1)}{x}-\left(1-\frac{w}{x}\right)\right)$$

which will be positive for all $i > 1 + (z - w)/\delta$ and $x > w$ making the second component positive (first order dominance over $(0, w)$ secures positivity of the first term). Note that since $w < M$, the larger is "δ" the smaller will "i" have to be. Thus, when the transgression area is small relative to the Transvariation and in the top end of the distribution range, fewer successive orders of integration will be necessary in order to yield an absence of ambiguity. Intuitively, in this case clarity, in the sense of absence of ambiguity, does not require extensive restriction of the class of admissible utility functions. However, if the transgression area is large and encroaching the low end of the range (i.e. δ small), absence of ambiguity will only be achieved at a much higher order of integration.

The partial moment form of $F^i(x)$, where $F^i(x)=\frac{1}{(i-1)!}\int_0^x (x-y)^{i-1} dF(y)\, for\, i=1,\ldots,$ also provides some intuition as to what successive orders of integration imply since it can be seen to attach increasing weight to lower values of x in the distribution. This can be mimicked in the data by re-weighting observation x_m by $\left(2\left(1-F\left(x_m\right)\right)\right)^{1/h}$ for some choice of $h > 1$. Calculation of indices based upon such re-weighted data will give an insight into their behavior under greater expressed concern for outcomes at the lower end of the distribution in the choice of index $U(x)$ (see e.g. Anderson et al. 2019).

Clearly, when the two curves, $F_a^i(x)$ and $F_b^i(x)$ intersect, the possibility of a completely unambiguous ordering no longer exists at the *i*th level. An alternative approach to looking at a higher order is to seek a weaker form of "Almost Dominance" following Leshno and Levy (2002). In the context of cumulative density functions or second order dominance relations, Leshno and Levy (2002) exploit the extent to which two curves transgress the dominance condition in developing the notion of "Almost Dominance". Extending Gini's Transvariation of two pdfs to cumulative densities, they consider $\mathrm{TR}_2(f_a(x), f_b(x))$ where

$\mathrm{TR}_2(f_a(x), f_b(x)) = \int_0^\infty |F_b(x) - F_a(x)| dx$

$= \int_0^\infty (\max(F_b(x), F_a(x)) - \min(F_b(x), F_a(x)) dx)$. They define the transgression region $\mathrm{TRG} = \int_0^\infty |F_b(x) - F_a(x)| I[(F_b(x) - F_a(x)) < 0] dx$ where $I[.]$ is an indicator function returning 1 when the argument is true and 0 otherwise and consider θ where:

$$\theta = \frac{\mathrm{TRG}}{\mathrm{TRF}} = \frac{\int_0^\infty |F_b(x) - F_a(x)| I[(F_b(x) - F_a(x)) < 0] dx}{\int_0^\infty |F_b(x) - F_a(x)| dx}$$

If θ is small in some sense, then "Almost Dominance" of $f_a(x)$ over $f_b(x)$ is declared. If it is supposed that the curves cross once and the transgression area is in the upper tail, then the smaller θ is, the larger will be the dominance area in the lower tail. In the context of financial choice, they can be interpreted as ruling out "perverse preferences" (where, e.g. someone would prefer a safe dollar to a 99.9% chance of a million dollars). In terms of the Davidson and Duclos (2000) Lemma, this implies that it would not take a much higher order integral to achieve a definitive solution.

4.4 Stochastic Dominance and Inequality Orderings

In the Introduction the concept of a Lorenz curve, which relates successive portions of a society to the successive portions of the aggregate income that they share, was employed to illustrate the ambiguity problem. If the respective Lorenz curves $L_a(p), L_b(p)$ corresponding to distributions $f_a(x)$ and $f_b(x)$ do not cross, then that "unambiguously" tells us something about the relative inequality of the two societies. Recalling that $\text{GINI} = 2\int_0^1 (p - L(p))dp$ if:

$$L_a(p) \geq L_b(p) \text{ for all } p \in [0,1] \text{ with } L_a(p) > L_b(p) \text{ for some } p$$

Then $f_a(x)$ is said to Lorenz Dominate $f_b(x)$ (written $f_a(x) \succcurlyeq_L f_b(x)$) and it will follow that GINI($(f_b(x))$ > GINI($f_a(x)$) since:

$$2\int_0^1 (p - L_a(p))dp - 2\int_0^1 (p - L_b(p))dp = 2\int_0^1 (L_b(p) - L_a(p))dp > 0$$

An important theorem in Atkinson (1970) proves that if $f_a(x)$ and $f_b(x)$ have equal means then;

$$f_a(x) \succcurlyeq_L f_b(x) <=> E_{f_a}(U(x)) \geq E_{f_b}(U(x)) \text{ for all } U(x) \text{ such that } U'(x) > 0\, U''(x) < 0$$

That is to say for distributions with equal means Lorenz dominance implies and is implied by second order dominance. Shorrocks (1983) extends the notion of the Lorenz curve to that of the Generalized Lorenz Curve [GL(p) = $L(p)\mu$] and then proves that Generalized Lorenz dominance implies and is implied by second order dominance.

4.5 Stochastic Dominance and Poverty Orderings

Atkinson (1987) contributed to poverty analysis using stochastic dominance criteria. In letting $U(x) = -P(x,z)$ where $P(x,z)$ is some poverty index based upon a poverty cut-off point z, then dominance relations can be applied to poverty analysis. Once dominance of a given order is established between $f_a(x)$ and $f_b(x)$ over a range 0,b then it can be asserted that poverty is lesser (greater) for any poverty measure in the corresponding class for any poverty line within the range 0,b. In essence, this alleviates all questions and concerns about specifying the poverty line (which has always been a matter of great debate among poverty analysts).

In this context ith order dominance relates to the following families of poverty measures:

i = 1~ Headcount
i = 2~ Depth of Poverty (e.g. average income distance below the poverty line of the poor)
i = 3~ Intensity of Poverty (e.g. average squared income distance below the poverty line of the poor)

.

$I = \infty$~ Rawlsian measure (e.g. Income distance below the poverty line of the poorest person

Foster and Shorrocks (1988) provide a useful discussion of poverty orderings and the Foster Greer Thorbeke (1984) class of decomposable measures:

$$P_i(f(x) = \int_0^z \left(1 - \frac{x}{z}\right)^{i-1} dF(x)$$

are directly relatable to each of these classes in a very obvious fashion (here z is the poverty cut-off and the integration runs from 0 to z). These ideas are readily extended to multivariate situations (see Duclos, Sahn & Younger 2006).

4.6 Stochastic Dominance and Polarization

The polarization indices discussed in Chap. 3 were based upon a so-called Identification-Alienation nexus wherein a society is presumed to be made up of groups and notions of polarization are fostered jointly by an agent's sense of increasing within-group identity and between-group distance or alienation. The overall distribution of a characteristic (for the sake of argument, let's call it income) is really a mixture of these group distributions and polarization is about the changing nature of these subgroups and their impact on the shape or anatomy of the overall distribution. The anatomy of polarization is best understood by employing ideas of "separation" drawn from the stochastic dominance literature together with that we've already encountered with one addition, the notion of the counter-cumulative density $F^{cc}(x) = \int_x^M f(z)dz$. Standard dominance relationships between distributions $f_a(x)$ and $f_b(x)$ (where $f_a(x)$ dominates $f_b(x)$ at some order) can be thought of as ways of depicting the "right separateness" of $f_a(x)$ from $f_b(x)$ in some particular manner, that is, the "*i*th" integral of $f_a(x)$ ais everywhere to the right of the corresponding *i*th

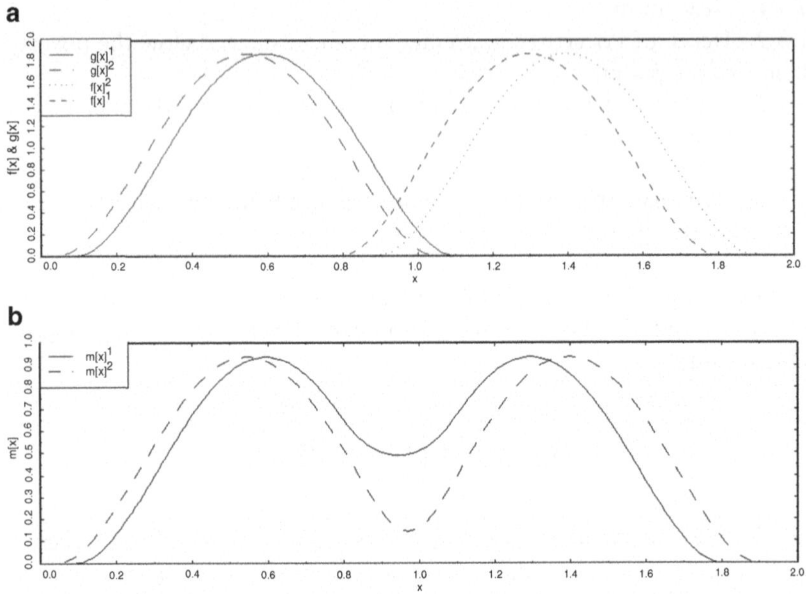

Fig. 4.2 (**a**) Divergence in means between population polarization. (**b**) Divergence in means within population polarization. (Source: Author's calculations)

order integral of $f_b(x)$. In a similar fashion left separateness can be contemplated by considering the counter cumulants[8] so:

"*i*th order" Right Separated => $\int_0^M \left(F_b^{i-1}(x) - F_a^{i-1}(x)\right)dx \geq 0$

"*i*th order" Left Separated => $\int_0^M \left(F_b^{cc,i-1}(x) - F_a^{cc,i-1}(x)\right)dx \geq 0$

These relationships are probably best understood by looking at some pictures. In Fig. 4.2a, b, think of superscript 2 as denoting the second period and superscript 1 as denoting the first period and $f(x)$ and $g(x)$ correspond to the distributions of two subgroups in society; we'll assume each group has the same number of agents. In effect, we are considering the changes in a society over the two periods. If they are directly observed (i.e.

[8] These particular dominance ideas are used in the finance literature in the study of risk loving behavior.

every agent in society has a label telling us which group he or she belongs to), the first figure is what we could observe. If we do not know which group each person belongs to the second figure is all we could observe (essentially the observed distribution is a mixture of the two sub distributions). We'll consider three basic changes, changes in means (holding all else constant), changes in variances (holding all else constant) and changes in skewness (holding all else i.e. means and variances constant). Increasing mean differences which promotes first order right and left separation.

Here $f(x)^2$ would first order dominate $f(x)^1$ and $g(x)^2$ would first order counter dominate $g(x)^1$. Essentially the sub distributions have not changed shape, $g(x)$ has slid leftwards (i.e. left separated) and $f(x)$ has slid rightwards (i.e. right separated). Notice in this case that the overlap of the distributions has diminished over the period and as far as the mixture is concerned, all that is observed is a hollowing out of the middle of the distribution.

Diminishing variances which promote second order left and right separation (Fig. 4.3a, b).

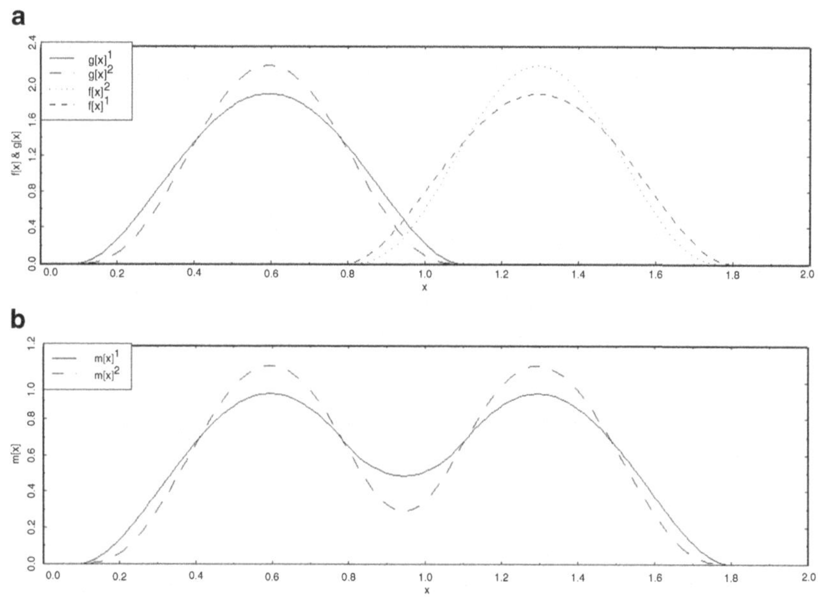

Fig. 4.3 (**a**) Intensified concentration between population polarization. (**b**) Increased concentration within population polarization. (Source: Author's calculations)

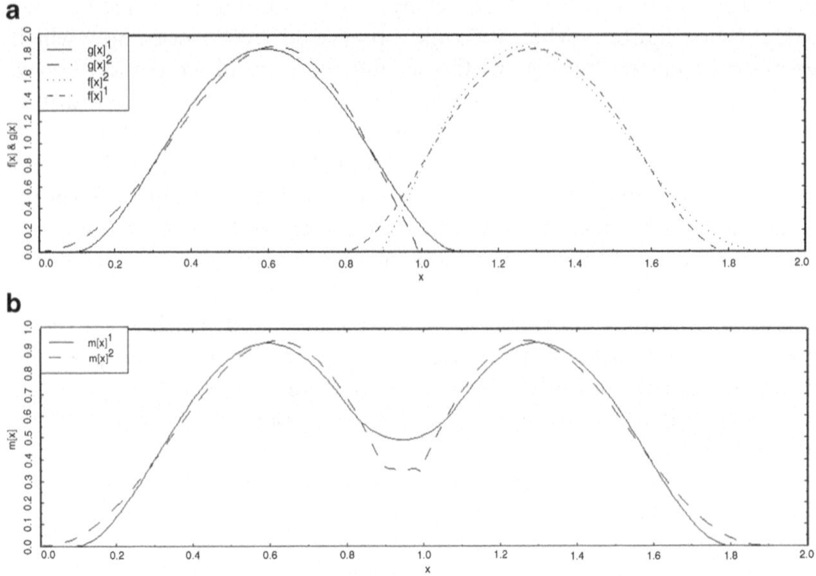

Fig. 4.4 (**a**) Opposite skewness between population polarization. (**b**) Opposite skewness within population polarization. (Source: Author's calculations)

Here $f(x)^2$ would second order dominate $f(x)^1$ and $g(x)^2$ would second order counter dominate $g(x)^1$. Essentially the sub distributions have not changed shape $G(x)$, the cumulative density of $g(x)$, has slid leftwards (i.e. left separated) and $F(x)$, the cumulative density of $f(x)$, has slid rightwards (i.e. right separated). Notice in this case the overlap of the distributions has diminished over the period and as far as the mixture is concerned, all that is observed is a hollowing out of the middle of the distribution.

Increasing left and right skewness which promotes third order left and right separation (Fig. 4.4a, b).

Here $f(x)^2$ would third order dominate $f(x)^1$ and $g(x)^2$ would third order counter dominate $g(x)^1$. Essentially the sub distributions have not changed means or variances but the integral of the integral of $G(x)$, the cumulative density of $g(x)$, has slid leftwards (i.e. left separated) and the integral of the integral of $F(x)$, the cumulative density of $f(x)$, has slid rightwards (i.e. right separated). Notice in this case that the overlap of the distributions has diminished over the period and as far as the mixture is concerned, all that is observed is a hollowing out of the middle of the distribution. This suggests several things as far as motivating the completely ordered polarization indices of Chap. 3 are concerned. Since these various combinations of "separation" influence the degree to which distributions overlap, if the sub distributions are observed we can use an overlap measure as an indicator of potential polarizing states with diminishing overlap being indicative of increased polarization. Alternatively, we could imagine a trapezoid formed by the modal heights of each sub distribution and the distance between their respective modes. Such a trapezoid would increase in area with polarization. An advantage of these measures is great simplification in multivariate problems since it turns out that they are easy to calculate in those circumstances. An additional advantage of the trapezoid measure is that it can be calculated when the sub distributions are not observed, that is, it can be calculated using the peaks of the mixture distribution (it is interesting to note that the Duclos Esteban and ray measure is really the average value of all the trapezoids that can be formed for all pairs of points in a distribution with an average height $f(x)^{\alpha}$).

4.7 The Problem of Ambiguity and Conditions for its Absence

The issue of ambiguity was raised and exemplified in Chap. 3 with the existence of contradictory ordering engendered by indices from the same class in a collection of nation income distributions. Ambiguity would be absent at comparison level "i" if all pertinent ordering instruments are unanimous in ranking the collection of K states at that level. So that a collection of K distributions such that $F_k^i(x) \le F_{k+1}^i(x)$ for all x and $F_k^i(x) < F_{k+1}^i(x)$ for some x, for distributions indexed $k = 1,\ldots,K\text{-}1$, would correspond to an unambiguously ordered collection at the ith order, since all index representations of $U(x)$ with $(-1)^{i+1}(dU(x)/dx) > 0$ yield identical or unanimous rankings of the K states at order i. In this situation, since dominance at order i implies dominance at all higher orders, there would be Unanimity amongst all appropriate ordering instruments at each and all higher orders $j > i$. Furthermore, $F_K^i(x)$ would correspond to the lower envelope of the collection and coincide with $\mathrm{FLE}^i(x)$ (and the highest ranked distribution) and $F_1^i(x)$

would correspond to the upper envelope of the collection and coincide with FUE$^i(x)$ (and lowest ranked distribution) at order "i". Conceptually in this case $\mathrm{TR}(i)=\int_0^\infty \left(F_1^i(x)-F_K^i(x)\right)dx$ is a measure of the degree of distributional variation at the ith order of integration of the K distributions.[9]

The Case of Perfect Segmentation

Perfect segmentation of the distributions generates a complete absence of ambiguity at all levels. K distributions are said to be perfectly segmented (Yitzahki 1994), when the range over which $f_k(x)>0$ is a closed compact mutually exclusive interval for each $f_k(x)$ $k=1,\ldots,K$ so that $f_k(x)=0$ for all $f_j(x)>0$ and $f_j(x)=0$ for all $f_k(x)>0$) for all $k \neq j$. In this case, given ordering by index, $F_k(x) < F_j(x)$ for all x for $k > j$ and $f_k(x) \succcurlyeq_1 f_j(x)$ for all $k>j$ and all i. Indeed, since ith order dominance implies dominance at all higher orders, $f_k(x) \succcurlyeq_i f_j(x)$ for all i. Thus, there will be unanimity and a complete absence of ambiguity at any and every order when the collection is perfectly segmented.[10] Furthermore, in this case it would not be possible to find contradictions through sampling variation.

Note that segmentation is a sufficient but not necessary condition for absence of ambiguity. Suppose there are J indices $U_{j,k}(x)$ indexed $j=1,\ldots,J$ under consideration for the K constituencies $k=1,\ldots,K$ and define the index range for the kth constituency as:

$$\left[U_{Lk}(x),U_{Hk}(x)\right]=min_j\left(U_{1k}(x),U_{2k}(x),\ldots U_{Jk}(x)\right),$$
$$max_j\left(U_{1k}(x),U_{2k}(x),\ldots U_{Jk}(x)\right).$$

Absence of ambiguity is secured when the ranges $\left[U_{Lk}(x),U_{Hk}(x)\right]$ $k=1,\ldots,K$ are mutually exclusive. Since $\left[U_{Lk}(x),U_{Hk}(x)\right]$ will usually be interior to the ranges engendered by the distributions $f_k(x)$ for $k=1,\ldots,K$, perfect segmentation is stronger than is necessary for the absence of ambiguity since mutual exclusivity of these ranges can still prevail in the presence of some overlap in the probability density functions.

[9] For a multi distributional higher order extension of the Gini (1916) transvariation measure, see Anderson, Linton and Thomas (2017).

[10] It is interesting to note that the Gini coefficient is subgroup decomposable under perfect segmentation of subgroups Mookherjee and Shorrocks (1982).

Dealing with Ambiguity When K = 2

Clearly, when any two curves, $F_k^i(x)$ and $F_j^i(x)$ $i \neq j$ intersect, the possibility of a completely unambiguous ordering over the *K* distributions no longer exists at the *i*th level. With respect to a specific two-way comparison, the conventional practice in this case has been either to seek a weaker form of "Almost Dominance" following Leshno and Levy (2002) or to seek a non-intersecting orientation of the curves at some higher order of integration (higher value of "*i*"). Both approaches may be seen as further restricting the class of *U*(*x*) in some fashion, indeed they are related by the magnitude of Leshno and Levy's dominance transgression area. In the context of cumulative density functions or second order dominance relations, Leshno and Levy (2002) exploit the extent to which two curves transgress the dominance condition in developing the notion of "Almost Dominance". Extending Gini's Transvariation of two pdfs to cumulative densities, TRF(2) (= $\int_0^\infty |F_b(x) - F_a(x)|dx$ = $\int_0^\infty (\max(F_b(x), F_a(x)) - \min(F_b(x), F_a(x))dx$), they define TRG, the transgression region, as $\int_0^\infty |F_b(x) - F_a(x)| I\left[(F_b(x) - F_a(x)) < 0\right]dx$ where *I*[.] is an indicator function returning 1 when the argument is true and 0 otherwise and consider θ where:

$$\theta = \frac{\text{TRG}}{\text{TRF}} = \frac{\int_0^\infty |F_b(x) - F_a(x)| I\left[(F_b(x) - F_a(x)) < 0\right]dx}{\int_0^\infty |F_b(x) - F_a(x)|dx}$$

If θ is small in some sense, then "Almost Dominance" of $f_a(x)$ over $f_b(x)$ is declared. If it is supposed that the curves cross once and the transgression area is in the upper tail, then the smaller θ is, the larger will be the dominance area in the lower tail.

Restricting the Preference Space Reduces Ambiguity

Application of the Duclos and Davidson Lemma to all *K* distributions simultaneously would ultimately yield a value i at which there was an absence of ambiguity. In practice, ambiguity is eliminated by successively restricting the parameter space. Alternatively, in the financial decision making literature, Leshno and Levy (2002) modified the comparison process by admitting the idea of "almost dominance" (Zheng (2016) adapts this idea for Lorenz dominance comparisons). They compute θ, the magnitude of the dominance transgression area relative to the overall Transvariation of the two distributions and, if it is smaller than some pre-specified value, "almost dominance" is declared. Clearly θ reflects the ambiguity inherent in the comparison being made in this case and can be construed as a measure of the potential ambiguity or non-robustness inherent in a ranking process (if there were no transgression of the dominance rule all such indicators in a class would be unambiguous or robust in the sense that they would generate the same ranking of states). The approach effectively rules out pathological cases in the class, facilitating a more decisive process in more frequently successfully ranking alternatives.

Ambiguity in Inequality Measures

These notions can be extended to collections of indices of relative inequality the most well-known of which is probably the Gini coefficient. The Gini (G) and Absolute Gini (AG) coefficients[11] given by:

$$G = \frac{1}{E(X)} \int_0^\infty \int_0^\infty f(y) f(x) |x - y| dxdy, \text{ and } AG$$

$$= \int_0^\infty \int_0^\infty f(y) f(x) |x - y| dxdy = E(X) * G$$

$$\text{where } E(X) = \int_0^\infty x f(x) dx \tag{4.2}$$

provide a complete ordering of a collection of such distributions *f*, in the first instance with respect to the average absolute distance between the atoms of a distribution relative to their mean and, in the second instance, with respect to the average absolute distance between those atoms. These statistics can also be respectively related to their associated Lorenz ($L(p)$) and Generalized Lorenz (GL(p)) curves:

[11] The Gini coefficient is due to Gini (1912), the Absolute Gini to Hey and Lambert (1980).

$$L(p)=\frac{\int_0^p F^{-1}(x)dF(x)}{\int_0^1 F^{-1}(x)dF(x)}, \quad \text{and} \quad GL(p)=E(x)\frac{\int_0^p F^{-1}(x)dF(x)}{\int_0^1 F^{-1}(x)dF(x)} \tag{4.3}$$

where $F^{-1}(x)$ is the inverse of $F(x)$, the CDF of $f(x)$

Wherein:

$$G=2\int_0^1 (p-L(p))dp, \text{ and } AG=E(X)2\int_0^1 (p-L(p))dp=E(X)*G \tag{4.4}$$

In the former case, the Gini is twice the area between the Lorenz curve and the 45° line, in the latter case, this quantity is scaled by average income (i.e. the Generalized Lorenz curve is the Lorenz curve scaled by average income). An alternative to the Absolute Gini as a measure of income well-being in the family of indices representing monotonic concave felicity functions is Atkinson's equally distributed income measure (arithmetic mean income less geometric mean income).

Let Lorenz Transvariation (LT) and Generalized Lorenz Transvariation (GLT) be respectively defined as:

$$LT_{a,b}=\int_0^1 |L_a(p)-L_b(p)|dp; \quad \mathrm{GLT}_{a,b}=\int_0^1 |GL_a(p)-GL_b(p)|dp;$$

Conceptually these correspond to the absolute area between two curves and provide a metric for the extent of their difference. Letting $I(z)$ be an indicator function returning 1 when $z > 0$ and 0 otherwise, and where $\int(L_a(p)-L_b(p))dp > 0$, the operational index $\theta(f_a(x), f_b(x))$ in terms of Lorenz and Generalized Lorenz curves employed by Leshno and Levy (2002) is given by:

$$\theta_L(f_a(x), f_b(x))=\frac{\int_0^1 I(L_b(p)-L_a(p))(L_a(p)-L_b(p))dp}{\mathrm{LT}_{a,b}}$$

and (4.5)

$$\theta_{GL}(f_a(x), f_b(x))=\frac{\int_0^1 I(GL_b(p)-GL_a(p))(GL_a(p)-GL_b(p))dp}{\mathrm{GLT}_{a,b}}$$

In essence, when the ratio of the dominance transgression area to the total (Generalized) Lorenz Transvariation (Leo 2017) was small relative to some pre-specified amount, the relationship was deemed to be "almost dominant" at the second order. Leshno and Levy (2002) used the concept to rule out "pathological" or extreme cases of risk averse behavior in portfolio choice, for example, where someone would prefer a certain \$1 over a 99.9% chance of \$1,000,000.

Here the ratio is used as an index of ambiguity inherent in the Gini (Absolute Gini) ordering of $f_a(x)$ and $f_b(x)$ relationship. Noting that $0 \leq \theta \leq 0.5$, an ambiguity index $AI = 2\theta$ provides a sense of how ambiguous the corresponding Gini or Absolute Gini ordering is. The extension of this index to a collection (>2) of distributions is straightforward. Working just with the Generalized Lorenz–Absolute Gini (AG) relationship (extension to Gini and Lorenz is straightforward), consider a collection of K distributions $f_k(x)$ with corresponding Lorenz curves $L_k(p)$ and Gini coefficients G_k $k = 1,\ldots,K$ where, for convenience and without loss of generality, $i > j = \mathrm{AG}_i \geq \mathrm{AG}_j$ for $i,j \in 1,\ldots,K$. Note this implies $\int (GL_j(p) - GL_i p))\,\mathrm{d}p = AG_i - AG_j \geq 0$ for $i > j$. Define GLT(K), the Generalized Lorenz analog of Gini's distributional Transvariation (Gini 1916; Dagum 1968) for a collection of distributions as:

$$\mathrm{GLT}(K) = \int_0^1 \left\{ \begin{matrix} \max\left(GL_1(p), GL_2(p), \ldots, GL_K(p)\right) \\ -\min\left(GL_1(p), GL_2(p), \ldots, GL_K(p)\right) \end{matrix} \right\} dp$$

GLT(K) is a measure of the extent of variation in the collection of Generalized Lorenz curves, as the area between the upper and lower envelopes of the collection of Lorenz curves, Generalized Lorenz analog of the range of a collection of numbers. Then $AI(K)$, the Ambiguity Index for a monotonic non-decreasing concave function ordering of a collection of K distributions, is of the form:

$$\begin{aligned} AI(K) &= \frac{\lambda}{GLT(K)} \sum_{j=2}^{K} \sum_{i=1}^{j} \int_0^1 I\left(GL_i(p) - GL_j(p)\right) \left|GL_j(p) - GL_i(p)\right| dp \\ &= \frac{\lambda}{\mathrm{GLT}(K)} \sum_{j=2}^{K} \sum_{i=1}^{j} \theta_{GL}(i, j) \int_0^1 \left|GL_j(p) - GL_i(p)\right| dp \end{aligned}$$

For some choice of $\lambda > 0$, $AI(K)$ measures magnitude of the Generalized Lorenz Dominance Transgressions in the collection relative to the Generalized Lorenz Transvariation. Natural values for λ are 1, whereby AI(K) corresponds to the cumulated Generalized Lorenz Dominance transgressions relative to GLT(K), $1/(K-1)!$, whereby $AI(K)$ corresponds to the average Lorenz Dominance transgression value relative to LT(K) over all pairwise comparisons and $1/K^*$ where K^* is the number of instances in which $I(L_i(p) - L_j(p))$ is non-zero whereby AI(K) corresponds to the average Lorenz Dominance transgression value relative to $LT(K)$ over all pairwise comparisons that exhibited transgressions. In each of these cases when the collection of Lorenz curves do not intersect at all $AI(K) = 0$ and the respective Gini's are unambiguously ordered, when they intersect there is potential ambiguity in the ordering and $AI(K) > 0$.

Suppose the third variant of Υ will be used with the interpretation that $AI(K)$ is the average value of the transgression area when there is one. Thinking about it from an inferential perspective for the moment, if one wished to test the hypothesis that any ordering in the class was unambiguous and our critical value was based upon an average value of 1% of overall Transvariation for all transgressions, then a version of the central limit theorem would give us $AI(K) \sim a\ N(0.01, 0.0099/K)$ yielding a simple upper tailed test of size α with a critical value $C = 0.01 + \sqrt{(0.0099/K)}Z_{1-\alpha}$ for example.

Finally, to measure the extent of discord in the ranking of a state across the indices the standard deviation of a states rank generated by each index will be averaged over the states, clearly when there is complete accord this average will be 0, when there is much discord the average will be large.

4.8 Determination of Ambiguity Groupings: Non-Ambiguity Cuts and Groups

Frequently, especially for low values of i, there will not be unanimity of ranking in a collection; however, these ideas can be extended to the ranking of a particular alternative or subgroups of alternatives. Intuitively if, at a given order, an alternative is strictly dominated by all alternatives above it, and strictly dominates all alternatives below it, it will be unambiguously ranked at that order and all higher orders since there will always be the same group of alternatives ranked above it and the same group of alternatives ranked below it no matter which index in the appropriate class is chosen. Such an alternative can also be thought of as partitioning the collection at that order into two groups wherein ambiguity may exist within each group but there will be no pairwise ambiguity between any between pairing of an alternative from each group. In such a circumstance, the lower envelope of the dominated group would be dominated by the upper envelope of the dominating group at the appropriate order. Indeed, even in the absence of the particular alternative the upper and lower groups could be deemed "partitionable" since an artificial partitioning alternative can be constructed as a linear combination of the two envelopes. This idea can be used to determine non-ambiguity groupings or sets of distributions between which there is no ambiguity in ordering. To do so the concepts of subgroup *i*th order upper (FUE^i) and lower (FLE^i) envelopes and Transvariation (TR^i) are employed.

Suppose that, in the collection of $k = 1,\ldots,K$ alternatives, there exists a $k^* \in (1, K)$ such that:

$$\begin{aligned}&\text{FUE}^i_{k^*}(x)\left\{= \max\left(F^i_1(x), F^i_2(x),\ldots F^i_{k^*}(x)\right)\right\} \leq \\ &\text{FLE}^i_{k^*+1}(x)\left\{= \min\left(F^i_{k^*+1}(x), F^i_{k^*+2}(x),\ldots F^i_K(x)\right)\right\}\end{aligned} \quad (4.6)$$

with strict inequality somewhere (in effect the upper envelope of the 1 to k^* grouping stochastically dominates the lower envelope of the $k^* + 1$ grouping). Then it will be the case that:

$$F^i_a(x) \leq F^i_b(x) \text{ and } F^i_a(x) < F^i_b(x) \text{ for some } x > 0 \text{ for all } a \in [1,\ldots,k^*] \text{ and } b \in [k^*+1,\ldots,K]$$

That is to say, any distribution indexed 1 to k^* will dominate at the *i*th order any distribution indexed $k^* + 1$ to K. Indeed a fictitious partitioning alternative $F^{i*}(x)$ can be envisaged as some linear combination of the upper envelope of the dominating group and the lower envelope of the dominated group so that: $F^{i*}\left(x, k^*, \alpha\right) = \alpha\text{FUE}^i_{k^*}(x) + (1-\alpha)\text{FLE}^i_{k^*+1}(x)$ for $\alpha \in [0,1]$

Interpreting ambiguity as an expression of uncertainty these ideas can be used to form ordered groups where there is certainty with respect to between-group rankings or classes but uncertainty about within-group rankings. Thus, given the right orientation of distributions, poor, middle and high income groups could be determined. As corollary, if [4.6] can be established for $k^* = 1,\ldots,K\text{-}1$, then the collection of distributions is perfectly partitionable or segmented at the *i*th order of integration and there will be no ambiguity of indices appropriate for order *i* and above.

4.9 Tools for Ordering Groups and Quantifying their Differences

The forgoing ideas lead Anderson, Post and Whang (2019), Anderson and Leo (2017) and Anderson, Linton, Pittau, Whang and Zelli (2019) to develop new measures (indices) for ranking or ordering the wellbeing of a collection of groups or states (The Utopia-Dystopia Index) and for measuring the extent of distributional discrepancy between groups (the Distributional Gini and Multilateral Transvariation coefficients). Both types of measures can be exploited at higher orders of comparison reflecting higher levels of criterion function restrictiveness.

Ordering Groups, the Utopia-Dystopia Index

Suppose K groups labeled $k = 1,\ldots,K$ are to be ordered or ranked with respect to each groups collective "goodness" in terms of X where goodness is measured by some unknown formula $U(x)$. Each group contains items or individuals. They could be members of a particular Nation, Region, Class, the participants in a clinical trial subjected to a particular treatment, the history of monthly returns of a portfolio manager and so on. In the kth group, X is distributed over its members according to a known (or at least estimable) probability density function $f_k(x) k = 1,\ldots,K$. Ideally, if the correct formula for $U(x)$ was known, the correct ranking of the collection of groups would be straightforward, but generally it is not. The nature of $U(x)$ is important. If x relates to incomes, it may have to reflect an aversion to inequality in x, if it relates to asset returns $U(.)$ may have to reflect an aversion to downside risk and if it refers to blood pressure reduction in a clinical trial extreme values both high and low may be a matter of concern. Unfortunately all that is known about the family of measures $U(x)$ is that $(-1)^{j+1}(d^jU(x)/dx^j) > 0$ for $j = 1, 2,\ldots i$, for some i, when $U(x)$ comes from the ith family so defined it will be written as $U(x) \in \Psi_i$.

The Utopia-Dystopia index relies upon the notion that when:

$$F_a^i(x) \leq F_b^i(x) \text{ with } F_a^i(x) < F_b^i(x) \text{ for some } x > 0$$

the area between the two functions $\int_0^M \left(F_b^i(x) - F_a^i(x)\right)\mathrm{dx}$ represents a sense of distance between the two states that relates to "Goodness" when $U(x) \in \Psi_i$ in that the larger is the area the further apart are the two states.

The theory of stochastic dominance implies that this area reflects the magnitude of the difference $E_{f_a}(U(x)) - E_{f_b}(U(x))$ when $U(x) \in \Psi_i$.

The Upper Envelope of the collection of distributions at the *i*th order of integration is a function $\text{UEF}^i(x) = \max(F_1^i(x), F_2^i(x), \ldots, F_K^i(x))$, it is piecewise continuous and represents the worst possible set of outcomes across the collection, the worst case scenario as it were, what could be referred to as "Dystopia". If there were a distribution that was dominated at the *i*th order by all other distributions in the collection it would be equal to UEF$^i(x)$. As it stands UEF$^i(x)$ is dominated at order "*i*" by all distributions in the collection and $\int_0^M (\text{UEF}^i(x) - F_k^i(x))dx$ is a measure of how much better state "*k*" is than the worst case scenario. Similarly, the Lower Envelope $\text{LEF}^i(x) = \min(F_1^i(x), F_2^i(x), \ldots, F_K^i(x))$ is a piecewise continuous function representing the best possible state in the collection, the "Utopian" state. If there was a distribution that dominated at the *i*th order all other distributions in the collection, it would be equal to LEF$^i(x)$.

K times the *i*th order Multilateral Transvariation of the collection is given by:

$$\int_0^M (\text{UEF}^i(x) - \text{LEF}^i(x))dx$$

and represents the maximal variation of the collection of distributions at the *i*th order. It follows that an index $I_k(F_1^i(x), F_2^i(x), \ldots, F_K^i(x))$ for ranking the distributions at the *i*th order can be constructed where:

$$0 \le I_k^i(F_1^i(x), F_2^i(x), \ldots, F_K^i(x)) = \frac{\int_0^M (UEF^i(x) - F_k^i(x))dx}{\int_0^M (UEF^i(x) - LEF^i(x))dx} \le 1$$

The ratio $I_k^i(F_1^i(x), F_2^i(x), \ldots, F_K^i(x))$ is the proportion of the area between Utopia and Dystopia that is covered by the area between the *k*th outcome distribution and Dystopia providing a very natural measure of how "Good" state *k* is with respect to $U(x) \in \Psi_i$.

$\text{UEF}^i(x)$ and $\text{LEF}^i(x)$ are piecewise continuous functions representing the upper and lower envelopes respectively of the collection of functions $F_k^i(x) k = 1, \ldots, K$. Thinking about the first order relationships where $i = 1$ and recalling the fact that $E(X) = \int_0^M (1 - F(x))dx$ suggests that

$I_k^1\left(F_1^i(x), F_2^i(x),\ldots, F_K^i(x)\right)$ can be interpreted as the mean of X under $f_k(x)$ less the mean of X under the worst case scenario if the distributions were convoluted divided by the mean of X under the best case scenario less the mean of X under the worst case scenario if all the distributions were convoluted.

An interesting feature of the index is that $I_k(.)$ does not necessarily return values of 1 and 0 for the highest and lowest ranked groups respectively, reflecting the possibility that the best and the worst state are not unarguably so. However if a state is universally dominated by or dominates all other states in the collection then $I_k^i(.)$ would return the value 0 or 1 respectively.

To facilitate statistical inference, Anderson, Post and Whang 2018 provide derivations of the limit distribution for the empirical counterpart of the Utopia Index for a general class of dynamic processes. Generally, the indices are functions of asymptotic Gaussian (i.e. normal) processes the standard errors for which require bootstrapping. The paper proposes consistent and feasible procedures based on resampling techniques in the spirit of Linton, Maasoumi and Whang (2005), Scaillet and Topaloglou (2010) and Arvanitis, Hallam, Post and Topaloglou (2018). This framework also allows for statistical inference about standard Almost Stochastic Dominance relations which arise as special cases of the analysis.

Measures of Discrepancies Between Distributions

Anderson, Linton and Whang (2019) developed two measures of the extent to which distributions differ, a Multilateral Transvariation measure and a Gini-like coefficient DISGINI (Distributional GINI coefficient). Both are based on Gini's work on Transvariation and the average relative mean difference of objects commonly known as the Gini Coefficient (Gini 1912, 1916). Recall that Gini's Transvariation measure between distributions $f_i(x)$ and $f_j(x)$ and its relationship to statistical overlap[12] OV_{ij} is given by:

$$\mathrm{GT}_{i,j} = \frac{1}{2}\int_0^\infty \left|f_i(x) - f_j(x)\right| dx = \frac{1}{2}\int_0^\infty \begin{bmatrix} \max\left(f_i(x), f_j(x)\right) \\ -\min\left(f_i(x), f_j(x)\right) \end{bmatrix} dx = 1 - OV_{i,j}$$

[12] $\mathrm{OV}(i,j) = \int_0^\infty \min\left(f_i(x), f_j(x)\right)dx$ (Anderson, Linton and Whang 2012).

And the Gini coefficient of K subgroup means where subgroups have relative sizes w_k $k = 1,\ldots,K$ is given as:

$$\frac{1}{\sum_{k=1}^{K} w_k \mu_k} \sum_{i=1}^{K} \sum_{j=1}^{K} w_i w_j \left|\mu_i - \mu_j\right|$$

Multilateral Transvariation

Generalizing the Transvariation to K distributions indexed $k = 1,\ldots,K$ (Anderson et al. 2019) suggest contemplating a multilateral measure MGT where:

$$\text{MGT} = \frac{1}{\text{K}} \int_0^\infty \left[\max\left(f_1(x), f_2(x), \ldots, f_K(x)\right) - \min\left(f_1(x), f_2(x), \ldots, f_K(x)\right)\right] dx \tag{4.7}$$

When the distributions have mutually exclusive support, MGT = 1; when the distributions are identical, MGT = 0. A subgroup relative size weighted version of MGT would have the form:

$$\text{MGTW} = \int_0^\infty \begin{bmatrix} \max\left(w_1 f_1(x), w_2 f_2(x), \ldots, w_K f_K(x)\right) \\ -\min\left(w_1 f_1(x), w_2 f_2(x), \ldots, w_K f_K(x)\right) \end{bmatrix} dx$$

For inference purposes, the sampling distributions of the above can be shown to be asymptotically normal with computable standard errors (see Anderson et al. 2019).

A Distributional Gini Coefficient

The coefficient DISGINI, is modeled as an analog of the Gini coefficient for relative differences in group means representing the inequality of a collection of probability distribution functions using Transvariations. Suppose the distributions are drawn from a collection of groups whose relative sizes are w_k $k = 1,\ldots,K$ (note, a version which does not reflect relative group sizes is easily computed by setting the w_ks to $1/K$). Following the above expression, consider a weighted sum of the Transvariations:

$$\text{DISGINI} = \frac{1}{\varphi}\sum_{i=1}^{K}\sum_{j=1}^{K}0.5\int_{0}^{\infty}\frac{w_i w_j\left|f_i(x)-f_j(x)\right|}{E(f(x))}dx = \frac{1}{\varphi}\sum_{i=1}^{K}\sum_{j=1}^{K}\frac{w_i w_j GT_{i,j}}{E(f(x))} \quad (4.8)$$

Given an appropriate choice for φ and using the relationship between Transvariation and statistical overlap, DISGINI can be shown to be:

$$\text{DISGINI} = \frac{1}{(2K-2)}\sum_{i=1}^{K}\sum_{j=1}^{K}w_i w_j\left(1-OV_{ij}\right) \quad (4.9)$$

where $0 \leq \text{DISGINI} \leq 1$. When distributions are perfectly segmented and there is no commonality ($OV_{ij}=0$ all i,j) and DISGINI = 1, when all distributions are identical DISGINI = 0. For inference purposes, the sampling distributions of the above can be shown to be asymptotically normal with computable standard errors (see Anderson, Linton and Whang 2019).

Multivariate Considerations

An interesting feature of DISGINI is that it can handle multivariate distributions of discrete or continuous forms (or mixtures of both). Simply write [4.8] as:

$$\text{DISGINI} = \frac{1}{\varphi}\sum_{i=1}^{K}\sum_{j=1}^{K}\frac{w_i w_j GT_{i,j}}{E(f(x))}$$
$$= \frac{0.5}{\varphi}\sum_{i=1}^{K}\sum_{j=1}^{K}\int_{0}^{\infty}\int_{0}^{\infty}\int_{0}^{\infty}\frac{w_i w_j\left|f_i(x,y,z)-f_j(x,y,z)\right|}{E(f(x,y,z))}dxdydz \quad (4.10)$$

Formula (4.9) then follows directly.

Inference for Multilateral Transvariation and Distributional Gini Coefficients

The derivation of the asymptotic variances for the Multilateral Transvariation and Distributional Gini Coefficients is derived in the appendix of Anderson et al. (2019); it is repeated here for completeness.

Multilateral Transvariation

Suppose $f_k(x)$ to be K continuous distributions indexed k = 1,…,K defined on closed and bounded support [a, b] with independent random samples from the kth population X_{kt} t = 1,…,T, yielding kernel estimates:

$$\widehat{f_k}(x) = \frac{1}{T}\sum_{i=1}^{T} K_b\left(x - X_{k,t}\right) \tag{4.11}$$

where K is a (potentially d dimensioned multivariate) Kernel with $K_b(.) = K(./b)/b^d$ where b is a bandwidth sequence. The estimated K distribution unweighted Transvariation index MGT is of the form:

$$\hat{\theta}_{MGT} = \frac{\left\{\int_a^b \max\left(\widehat{f_1}(x), \widehat{f_2}(x), \ldots, \widehat{f_K}(x)\right) - \int_a^b \min\left(\widehat{f_1}(x), \widehat{f_2}(x), \ldots, \widehat{f_K}(x)\right)\right\}}{g_{KT}(K)}$$

$$= \hat{\theta}_{KTU} - \hat{\theta}_{KTL} \tag{4.12}$$

Where

$$\hat{\theta}_{KTU} = \frac{\left\{\int_a^b \max\left(\widehat{f_1}(x), \widehat{f_2}(x), \ldots, \widehat{f_K}(x)\right)\right\}}{g_{KT}(K)} \text{ and}$$

$$\hat{\theta}_{KTL} = \frac{\left\{\int_a^b \min\left(\widehat{f_1}(x), \widehat{f_2}(x), \ldots, \widehat{f_K}(x)\right)\right\}}{g_{KT}(K)}$$

Where $g_{KT}(K)$ is a known linear function of K, the number of distributions in question. Considering [4.12], assume for simplicity that the contact set is of measure 0 and let the sets $CK_{i,*}$ and $CK^{i,*}$ be defined as:

$$CK_{i,*} = \left\{x : f_i(x) < f_j(x)\right\} \text{and} CK^{i,*} = \left\{x : f_i(x) > f_j(x)\right\} \text{ for all } j = 1,\ldots,K, j \neq i$$

Let $p_{kU} = P\left(X_k \in CK^{k,*}\right)$ and $p_{kL} = P\left(X_k \in CK_{i,*}\right)$ noting that $CK_{i,*} \cap CK^{i,*} = \emptyset$ so that $p_{kU} > 0 \Rightarrow p_{kL} = 0$ and $p_{kL} > 0 \Rightarrow p_{kU} = 0$ furthermore $p_{kUL} = P\left(X_k \in CK^{k,*} \cap CK_{i,*}\right) = 0$. Then:

$$\left(\hat{\theta}_{KTU} - \theta_{KTU}\right) = \frac{1}{g_{KT}(K)}\sum_{k=1}^{K}\int_{CK^{k,*}}\left(\widehat{f_k}(x) - E\left(\widehat{f_k}(x)\right)\right)dx + r = \frac{1}{g_{KT}(K)}\sum_{k=1}^{K}\left(\widehat{p_{kU}} - p_{kU}\right)$$

$$+ r \approx \frac{1}{g_{KT}(K)}\sum_{k=1}^{K}\frac{1}{T_k}\sum_{h=1}^{T_k}\left(1\left(X_{kh} \in CK^{k,*}\right) - E\left(1\left(X_{kh} \in CK^{k,*}\right)\right)\right) + r$$

For notational convenience, assume $T_k = T$ for all k and independent sampling over $k = 1,\ldots,K$.

$$\mathrm{AVAR}\left(\hat{\theta}_{\mathrm{KTU}}\right) = \frac{1}{T}\sum_{k=1}^{K} p_{kU}\left(1 - p_{kU}\right) \text{where } p_{kU} = P\left(X_k \in CK^{k,*}\right)$$

which can be estimated as:

$$\frac{1}{T}\sum_{k=1}^{K}\widehat{p_{kU}}\left(1 - \widehat{p_{kU}}\right)$$

Similarly:

$$\left(\hat{\theta}_{KTL} - \theta_{KTL}\right) = \frac{1}{g_{KT}(K)}\sum_{k=1}^{K}\int_{CK_{i,*}}\left(\widehat{f_k}(x) - E\left(\widehat{f_k}(x)\right)\right)dx + r = \frac{1}{g_{KT}(K)}\sum_{k=1}^{K}\left(\widehat{p_{kL}} - p_{kL}\right)$$

$$+ r \approx \frac{1}{g_{KT}(K)}\sum_{k=1}^{K}\frac{1}{T_k}\sum_{h=1}^{T_k}\left(1\left(X_{kh} \in CK_{i,*}\right) - E\left(1\left(X_{kh} \in CK_{i,*}\right)\right)\right) + r$$

And:

$$\mathrm{AVAR}\left(\hat{\theta}_{KTL}\right) = \frac{1}{T}\sum_{k=1}^{K} p_{kL}\left(1 - p_{kL}\right) \text{where } p_{kL} = P\left(X_k \in CK_{i,*}\right)$$

which can be estimated as:

$$\frac{1}{T}\sum_{k=1}^{K}\widehat{p_{kL}}\left(1 - \widehat{p_{kL}}\right)$$

Then:

$$\hat{\theta}_{KT}-\theta_{KT}\approx\frac{1}{Tg_{KT}(K)}\sum_{k=1}^{K}\sum_{h=1}^{T_k}\left(1\left(X_{kh}\in CK^{k,*}\right)-E\left(1\left(X_{kh}\in CK^{k,*}\right)\right)\right)$$
$$-\left(1\left(X_{kh}\in CK_{i,*}\right)-E\left(1\left(X_{kh}\in CK_{i,*}\right)\right)\right)$$

Typically $\text{AVAR}\left(\hat{\theta}_{KT}\right)=\frac{1}{T}\sum_{k=1}^{K}\left\{p_{kU}\left(1-p_{kU}\right)+p_{kL}\left(1-p_{kL}\right)\right\}+2COV\left(\hat{\theta}_{KTU},\hat{\theta}_{KTL}\right)$

Where $\text{COV}\left(\hat{\theta}_{KTU},\hat{\theta}_{KTL}\right)=\sum_{kU=1}^{K}\sum_{\substack{kL=1\\KU\neq KL}}^{K}\left(p_{kUL}-p_{kU}p_{kL}\right)$. However since $p_{kU}>0=>p_{kL}=0$ and $p_{kL}>0=>p_{kU}=0$ furthermore $p_{kUL}=P\left(X_k\in CK^{k,*}\cap CK_{i,*}\right)=0$, $\text{COV}\left(\hat{\theta}_{KTU},\hat{\theta}_{KTL}\right)=0$. Thus:

$$\text{AVAR}\left(\hat{\theta}_{KT}\right)=\frac{1}{T}\sum_{k=1}^{K}\left\{p_{kU}\left(1-p_{kU}\right)+p_{kL}\left(1-p_{kL}\right)\right\}$$

which can be estimated as:

$$\frac{1}{T}\sum_{k=1}^{K}\left\{\widehat{p_{kU}}\left(1-\widehat{p_{kU}}\right)+\widehat{p_{kL}}\left(1-\widehat{p_{kL}}\right)\right\}$$

The distributional properties of MGTW, the weighted version of MGT, can be derived as above by working with $w_k\widehat{f_k}(x)$ in place of $\widehat{f_k}(x)$ and modifying $g_{KT}(K)$ accordingly as in [4.12].

The Distributional Gini

The Distributional Gini Index over *K* distributions is of the form:

$$\hat{\theta}_{DG}=\frac{1}{g_{DG}(K)}\sum_{i=1}^{K}\sum_{j=1}^{K}w_iw_j\left\{1-\int_a^b\min\left(\widehat{f_i}(x),\widehat{f_j}(x)\right)dx\right\}\tag{4.13}$$

where $g_{DG}(K)$ is a known function of *K* and the w_i's are also assumed known. This may be written as:

$$\hat{\theta}_{DG} = \frac{1}{g_{DG}(K)}\left(1K^2 - \sum_{i=1}^{K}\sum_{j=1}^{K} w_i w_j \left\{\int_a^b \min\left(\widehat{f}_i(x), \widehat{f}_j(x)\right)\right\} dx\right)$$

So, for the distributional properties of $\hat{\theta}_{DG}$ attention can be focussed upon:

$$\theta_{OV} = \sum_{i=1}^{K}\sum_{j=1}^{K} w_i w_j \left\{\int_a^b \min\left(\widehat{f}_i(x), \widehat{f}_j(x)\right) dx\right\} = \sum_{i=1}^{K}\sum_{j=1}^{K} w_i w_j \left\{\hat{\theta}_{i,j}\right\} \quad (4.14)$$

where $\widehat{f}_k(x)$ are defined as in [4.11]. Considering the $\hat{\theta}_{i,j}$, for simplicity assume independent samples of T observations and that the contact sets are of measure 0. Define the sets $C_{i,j}\ i, j = 1,\ldots,K\ i \neq j$ as:

$$C_{i,j} = \left\{x : f_i(x) < f_j(x)\right\}$$

Then:

$$\left(\hat{\theta}_{i,j} - \theta_{i,j}\right) = \int_{C_{i,j}} \left(\widehat{f}_i(x) - E\left(\widehat{f}_i(x)\right)\right) dx + \int_{C_{j,i}} \left(\widehat{f}_j(x) - E\left(\widehat{f}_j(x)\right)\right) dx + r$$

$$\approx \frac{1}{T}\sum_{h=1}^{T}\left(1\left(X_{ih} \in C_{i,j}\right) - E\left(1\left(X_{ih} \in C_{i,j}\right)\right)\right) + \left(1\left(X_{jh} \in C_{j,i}\right) - E\left(1\left(X_{jh} \in C_{j,i}\right)\right)\right) + r'$$

where $r \sim O_p\left(b^s\right)$ and thus:

$$\hat{\theta}_{OV} = \sum_{i=1}^{K}\sum_{j=1}^{K} w_i w_j \left(\hat{\theta}_{i,j} - \theta_{i,j}\right) = \sum_{i=1}^{K}\sum_{j=1}^{K} w_i w_j \begin{pmatrix} \int_{C_{i,j}} \left(\widehat{f}_i(x) - E\left(\widehat{f}_i(x)\right)\right) dx \\ + \int_{C_{j,i}} \left(\widehat{f}_j(x) - E\left(\widehat{f}_j(x)\right)\right) dx \end{pmatrix} + r''$$

Turning to its asymptotic variation, define:

$$p_{i:ij} = P\left(X_i \in C_{i,j}\right) \text{and}\ p_{ij} = P\left(X_i \in C_{i,j} \cap X_j \in C_{j,i}\right)$$

Then generally, $\text{AVAR}\left(\hat{\theta}_{i,j}\right) = \frac{1}{T}\left(p_{i:ij}\left(1 - p_{i:ij}\right) + p_{j:ji}\left(1 - p_{j:ji}\right) + 2\left(p_{ij} - p_{i:ij}p_{j:ji}\right)\right)$ which may simplify with independent sampling. However even if X_i and X_i are independent $\hat{\theta}_{i,j}$ and $\hat{\theta}_{k,l}$ will be dependent if they have one subscript in common so that $ACOV\left(\hat{\theta}_{i,j}, \hat{\theta}_{k,l}\right) \neq 0$ when there is a commonality in subscripts. All such terms need to be considered so that a threefold summation is required involving probabilities of sets of the form:

$$C_{i,j} \cap C_{i,k} = \left\{x : f_i(x) < \min\left(f_j(x), f_k(x)\right)\right\}$$

Ultimately:

$$\begin{aligned}\text{AVAR}\left(\hat{\theta}_{OV}\right) &= \sum_{i=1}^{K}\sum_{j<k} w_i^2 w_j^2 \left(Pr\left(X_i \in C_{ij}\right) - Pr\left(X_i \in C_{ij}\right)^2\right) \\ &\quad + 2\sum_{i=1}^{K}\sum_{j>i}\sum_{k>j>i} w_i^2 w_j w_k \begin{pmatrix} Pr\left(X_i \in C_{ij} \cap C_{ik}\right) \\ -Pr\left(X_i \in C_{ij}\right)\Pr\left(X_i \in C_{ik}\right)\end{pmatrix}\end{aligned}$$

which may be estimated as:

$$\sum_{i=1}^{K} w_i^2 \sum_{j>i} w_j^2 V\left(1\left(X_i \in C_{ij}\right)\right) + 2\sum_{i=1}^{K} w_i^2 \sum\sum w_j w_k COV\left(1\left(X_i \in C_{ij}\right), 1\left(X_i \in C_{ik}\right)\right)$$

References

Anderson, G., & Leo, T. W. (2017). *On Providing a Complete Ordering of Non-Combinable Alternative Prospects.* University of Toronto Discussion Paper.

Anderson, G., Linton, O., & Thomas, J. (2017). Similarity, Dissimilarity and Exceptionality: Generalizing Gini's Transvariation to Measure "Differentness" in Many Distributions. *Metron. 75*(2) 161–180.

Anderson, G. J., Linton, O., & Whang, Y.-J. (2012). Nonparametric Estimation and Inference About the Overlap of Two Distributions. *Journal of Econometrics, 171*(1), 1–23.

Anderson, G., Linton, O., Pittau, M. G., Whang, Y.-J., & Zelli, R. (2019). *Segmentation or Convergence in European Household Income Distributions? New Tools for Analyzing Multilateral Differentness in Collections of Distributions.* Toronto: University of Toronto. Mimeo.

Anderson, G., Post, T., & Whang, Y.-J. (2019). Somewhere Between Utopia and Dystopia: Choosing From Multiple Incomparable Prospects. *Forthcoming Journal of Business and Economic Statistics.*

Arvanitis, S., Hallam, M., Post, T., & Topaloglou, N. (2018). Stochastic Spanning. *Journal of Business Economics and Statistics.* Forthcoming.

Atkinson, A. B. (1970). On the Measurement of Inequality. *Journal of Economic Theory, 2*(3), 244–263.

Atkinson, A. (1983). *Social Justice and Public Policy.* Boston Mass: MIT Press.

Atkinson, A. B. (1987). On the Measurement of Poverty. *Econometrica, 55*, 749–764.

Atkinson, A., & Bourguingnon, F. (1987). Income Distribution and Differences in Needs. In Feiwel (Ed.), *Arrow and Foundations of the Theory of Economic Policy.* London: Macmillan.

Dagum, C. (1968) *Nonparametric and Gaussian Bivariate Transvariation Theory: Its Application to Economics.* Econometric Research Program, Princeton University, Research Memorandum No. 99.

Davidson, R., & Duclos, J.-Y. (2000). Statistical Inference for Stochastic Dominance and for the Measurement of Poverty and Inequality. *Econometrica, 68*(6), 1435–1464.

Davies, J., & Hoy, M. (1994). The Normative Significance of Using Third-Degree Stochastic Dominance in Comparing Income Distributions. *Journal of Economic Theory, 64*, 520–530.

Davies, J., & Hoy, M. (1995). Making Inequality Comparisons When Lorenz Curves Intersect. *American Economic Review, 85*, 980–986.

Duclos, J.-Y., Sahn, D. E., & Younger, S. D. (2006). Robust Multidimensional Poverty Comparisons. *Economic Journal, 116*(9), 43–968.

Foster, J., & Shorrocks, A. (1988). Poverty Orderings. *Econometrica, 56*, 173–177.

Gini, C. (1912). Variabilità e mutabilità. Reprinted in Pizetti, E., & Salvemini, T. (Eds.) (1955). *Memorie di metodologica statistica.* Rome: Libreria Eredi Virgilio Veschi.

Gini, C. (1916). Il Concetto di Transvariazione e le sue Prime Applicazioni. In C. Gini (Ed.), *Transvariazione. Libreria Goliardica* (pp. 1–55).

Hadar, J., & Russell, W. R. (1969). Rules for Ordering Uncertain Prospects. *Amer. Econom. Rev., 59*, 25–34.

Hanoch, G., & Levy, H. (1969). The Efficiency Analysis of Choices Involving Risk. *Review of Economic Studies, 36*, 335–346.

Hey, J. D. AND *P.* J. Lambert (1980): "Relative Deprivation and the Gini Coefficient: Comment," Quarterly Journal of Economics, 95, 567–573.

Lambert, P. J., & Ok, E. A. (1999). On Evaluating Social Welfare by Sequential Generalized Lorenz Dominance. *Economics Letters, 63*, 45–53.

Leo, T. W. (2017). On the Asymptotic Distribution of (Generalized) Lorenz Transvariation Measures. *METRON, 75*(2), 195–213.

Leshno, M., & Levy, H. (2002). Preferred by "All" and Preferred by "Most" Decision Makers: Almost Stochastic Dominance. *Management Science, 48*(8), 1074–1085.
Levy, H. (1998). *Stochastic Dominance Investment Decision Making Under Uncertainty.* Boston: Kluwer Academic Publishers.
Linton, O., Maasoumi, E., & Whang, Y. J. (2005). Consistent Testing for Stochastic Dominance Under General Sampling Schemes. *Review of Economic Studies, 72*(3), 735–765.
Linton, O., Post, T., & Whang, Y.-J. (2014). Testing for the Stochastic Dominance Efficiency of a Given Portfolio. *The Econometrics Journal, 17*, S59–S74.
Mookherjee, D., & Shorrocks, A. (1982). A Decomposition Analysis of the Trend in UK Income Inequality. *Economic Journal, 92*(368), 886–902.
Rothschild, M., & Stiglitz, J. E. (1970). Increasing Risk: I. A Definition. *Journal of Economic Theory, 2*, 225–243.
Scaillet, O., & Topaloglou, N. (2010). Testing for Stochastic Dominance Efficiency. *Journal of Business Economics and Statistics, 28*(1), 169–180.
Shorrocks, A. F. (1983). Ranking Income Distribution. *Economica, 50*(197), 3–17.
Yitzahki, S. (1994). Economic Distance and Overlapping of Distributions. *Journal of Econometrics, 61*, 147–159.
Zheng, B. (2016). *Almost Lorenz Dominance.* University of Colorado, Denver, Discussion Paper.

CHAPTER 5

Comparing Latent Subgroups

The preceding chapters have relied upon the groups under comparison being identified, in the sense that every data element has been unequivocally drawn from an identified group. Often groups are less well defined and are in effect latent; this chapter addresses the issue of determining the number, size and distributional shape of latent subgroups using semi-parametric mixture distribution techniques. After an Introduction which provides a rational for modeling latent distributions using semi-parametric mixtures, Sect. 5.2 lays out the basic semi-parametric mixture distribution model; and, in that context, the probability of class membership for an individual with a given characteristic is developed in Sect. 5.3. Estimation of the model is discussed in Sect. 5.4 and methods for determining the number of classes are discussed in Sect. 5.5. Sect. 5.6 develops some ideas for studying factors relating to class membership in terms of the correlates of class membership probabilities. Section 5.7 briefly extends the ideas for comparing subgroups in the previous chapters to latent subgroups and Sect. 5.8 reports an example.

5.1 Introduction

Thus far, interest has focused on populations with identifiable subgroups where observed individuals clearly and uniquely belong to particular subgroups. Boundaries between subgroups are clearly defined in terms of observed variables making group membership delineation straightfor-

G. Anderson, *Multilateral Wellbeing Comparison in a Many Dimensioned World*, Global Perspectives on Wealth and Distribution,
https://doi.org/10.1007/978-3-030-21130-1_5

ward. This follows the long established practice of classifying agents within a society into well-defined groups in order to measure and study their wellbeing or behavior. Invariably this involves clearly specifying boundaries for class inclusion and exclusion purposes. To the extent that the class frontiers have been a matter of arbitrary choice on the part of the researcher, they have been a matter of much concern and dispute (Exactly how should a poverty line be defined? What range of incomes constitutes "middle class income?).[1] Clearly, such choices can often be invidious with untoward consequences for analysis.

Yet sometimes the subgroups in a society are not so well defined or identified using available information. For example, suppose a household's class membership is jointly determined by the family backgrounds of the adults in the household (race, heritage, resources etc.), their education levels, occupations and geographical locations but all that is observed is the household income. It will invariably be the case that households with the same incomes could come from different classes, that is to say in terms of incomes, classes overlap, in essence the classes are latent, not directly discernable in terms of the information available. The observable household income distribution becomes a mixture of the unobservable sub distributions.

In Chaps. 1 and 3, in order to facilitate analysis, $U(x)$, the household or individual wellbeing measure with respect to income x, was assumed homogeneous across agents[2] (going forward the object of interest within a group be it household or individual will be referred to as an agent). Since the function was assumed monotonic increasing in x, ordering agents in terms of the observable x was equivalent to ordering agents in terms of unobservable $U(.)$ and studying the distribution of X was in essence the same as studying the distribution of the unobservable $U(.)$. Objects like

[1] Examples of disputed boundaries are not hard to find; determining the poor has probably been the most contentious (e.g. Sen 1982; Foster 1998). Things are not different when the focus of the analysis is on the middle or rich class (Atkinson and Brandolini 2013; Banerjee and Duflo 2008; Easterly 2001; Saez and Veall 2005). The most recent disputation as to the value of this type of classification argues that "wellness" is in general a many dimensioned concept so that income of itself is but a reflection of societal wellness (Stiglitz et al. 2010). Sen and others (e.g. papers in Grusky and Kanbur, 2006; Kakwani and Silber 2008; Nussbaum, 1997 2011; Alkire and Foster 2011) have forcibly argued that limitations to individual's functionings and capabilities should be considered the determining factors in her/his poorness or wellness, again implying that an individual's income will only partially reflect her/his poverty status.

[2] Indeed, this is generally assumed in practice in elementary wellbeing measurement.

average income, the variation in incomes income quantiles would reflect, though not necessarily be the same as, the corresponding concepts with respect to *U*(.).

But suppose the homogeneity assumption was false and society was in fact heterogeneous with respect to *U*(.) such that there were K types of agent labeled $k = 1,\ldots,K$ with unobserved income wellbeing measures $U_k(x)$ that were monotonic increasing in *x*. If one knew which type an agent belonged to, then ordering within type k with respect to observable *x* would be equivalent to ordering with respect to unobservable $U_k(x)$ and studying the distribution of observable *X* within type k, denote it $f_k(x)$, would be equivalent to studying the distribution of $U_k(x)$. Given w_k, the proportions of the societies agents in type k, the societal income distribution $f(x)$ could be generated and estimated as a mixture of observable income distributions:

$$f(x) = \sum_{k=1}^{K} w_k f_k(x) \tag{5.1}$$

However, its equivalence with the unobservable income wellbeing distribution $g(U(x)) = g\left(\sum_{k=1}^{K} w_k U_k(x)\right)$ would be broken since generally $U_k(x) \neq U_j(x)$ for $j \neq k$.

When agent type is not identified and the w_k are unknown, distributions like [5.1] can still be estimated, provided information is available on the parametric structure of the $f_k(x)$'s using semi-parametric techniques. Indeed, suppose information on the things that determine agent type (e.g. social class, occupation, race, location etc.) is available in the vector z following Anderson et al. (2016), the estimation process can be further refined by semi-parametric estimation of distributions of the form:

$$f(x|z) = \sum_{k=1}^{K} w_k(z) f_k(x|z) \tag{5.2}$$

Here in the estimation process class membership probability $w_k(z)$ is like a random variable in its own right.

Essentially the randomness of the class membership indicators is a direct consequence of unobserved heterogeneity. If all the characteristics that determine an agent's class are fully observed, then agent class allocation is a well-defined process and 0–1 class indicators can be calculated rather than their probabilities. Unfortunately, the longer the list of characteristics that determine class, the boundary set in any one of them inevitably becomes more blurred when other characteristics are not observed, intensifying the arbitrary nature of the process (Alkire and Foster 2011; Anderson et al. 2011). Furthermore, many of those determining characteristics, the freedoms an individual enjoys, the capabilities they possess (as opposed to the extent to which they exercise those capabilities) and the security they experience in their actions are fundamentally unobservable. Nonetheless, if these unobservable characteristics limit or bound an individual's observable actions and if members within each class face similar limits to those actions, which in turn differ from the limits faced by other classes, it may be possible to discern individual behavior common to a class in their observable actions.

When agents from the same group suffer similar circumstances, their observable actions will follow similar patterns or sequences and this similarity can be relied upon to suggest the nature of the outcome distribution of the group. In the economics field there is an extensive literature regarding the modeling of such sequences in consumption and income as stochastic processes which have implications for the distribution of outcomes. This follows a theoretical and applied statistics literature on the size distribution of a vector x that is the consequence of a stochastic process (see for example Gabaix 1999, Reed 2001 and more generally Cox 2017). Very often, the size distribution turns out to be multivariate normal or log normal—Gibrat's law is a classic example of such theorems (see Sutton 1997, for a discussion). The power of these laws, like all central limit theorems, is that a (log) normal distribution prevails in the limit almost regardless of the underlying distribution of the stochastic shocks though the mean and variance of the distribution do depend on the parameters governing the process. The choice of normality or log normality under Gibrat's Law depends on the assumed nature of the process of x. Suppose that the functionings and capabilities set that characterize a particular class (denote it "j") also determine the parameters that govern the stochastic process of an observable vector variable x for that class. Then, to the extent that the functionings and capabilities of different classes impose different limits on the actions of their members, x at time t will have a particular multivariate distribution $f_j(x)$ that is distinguishable from the corresponding distribution of $f_h(x)$ for class $j \neq h$. Furthermore, the distribution of x in the population will be a mixture of these subclass distributions where the mixing weights are the proportions of society that are members of the respective classes. If these sub distributions and their respective weights can be estimated, much can be said about the behavior and state of wellbeing of classes without resorting to debates about defining boundaries.

This chapter deals with this problem. Here techniques are proposed for grouping agents without defining boundaries: an agent's category is partially determined on the basis of its location in the distribution of observables. It is partial in the sense that only the probability of category membership—a random class indicator function—is developed, and usually it is not 0 or 1. However, this will not impede analysis of behavior or the ordering of classes. It turns out that, while it is not possible to uniquely determine a households' class membership, with the aid of some assumptions, the number of classes, the shapes of their distributions and the probability that a household is in a particular class can be computed and that is often all that is required for analysis. Data driven empirical Bayesian semi-parametric methods facilitate estimation of a mixture of the various sub distributions and their respective weights. The technique can be used in a variety of situations; here it will be illustrated in the context of developing a household income distribution.

5.2 Semi-Parametric Mixture Distributions

Finite mixture models have featured in many fields where heterogeneity of individual types, data contamination, misclassification and dynamic regime switching are known issues (Eckstein and Wolpin (1990); Keane and Wolpin (1997), Kim and Nelson (1999), Lewbel (2007); Chen et al. (2011)). Here they will be used to classify agents on the basis of their outcome variable x, while the discussion will be carried out in terms of an income or consumption variable, the analysis can be readily adapted to accommodate other types of variates. Initially suppose a collection of K latent subgroups corresponding to the socioeconomic classes indexed $k = 1,\ldots,K$ with respective income distributions $f_k(x, \varphi_k)$ (where φ_k is a vector of parameters of the kth distribution) with associated cumulative densities $F_k(x, \varphi_k)$ and corresponding means and population shares μ_k and w_k, the overall income distribution $f(x)$, cumulative distribution $F(x)$ and mean income μ may be written as:

$$f(x) = \sum_{k=1}^{K} w_k f_k(x, \varphi_k)$$

$$F(x) = \sum_{k=1}^{K} w_k F_k(x, \varphi_k)$$

$$\mu = \sum_{k=1}^{K} w_k \mu_k$$

$$\sum_{k=1}^{K} w_k = 1 \tag{5.3}$$

Some assumptions regarding the nature of the distributions $f_k(x, \varphi_k)$ $k = 1,\ldots,K$ are necessary in order to estimate [5.3]; the stochastic process theory and some economics in terms of the Permanent Income Hypothesis will be of help here. The idea is that households with common or similar socioeconomic backgrounds, education status, preferences and demographics will have similar processes driving their permanent and transitory income and consumption outcomes. Following the microeconomic literature that builds on Modigliani and Brumberg (1954) and Friedman (1957), agents from a particular class are assumed to maximize the present value of their lifetime utility, $\int_0^T U_k(C_t) e^{-r_k^* t} dt$ subject to the present value of their lifetime wealth $\int_0^T x_t e^{-rt} dt$ where $U_k(.)$ is an instantaneous consumption utility function for the *k*th class, x_t is income in period *t*, r_k^* is the rate of time preference for the *k*th class and *r* is the market lending rate. Browning and Lusardi (1996) showed that, taken with assumptions of an across class constant relative risk aversion parameter γ, and "no bequest" preferences, this leads to a consumption smoothing model of the form $C_t = e^{g_k t} C_0$. This implies a one period consumption process with a growth rate $g_k = \frac{r - r_k}{\gamma}$, such that a one period process will be of the form $C_t = e^{g_k} C_{t-1}$ which may be associated with a corresponding proportionate permanent income process for each class of the form: $x_t = (1 + \delta_{kt}) x_{t-1}$ where δ_{kt} is a random variable, small relative to 1, with mean δ_k and variance σ_k^2. This equation follows Gibrat's Law of proportionate effects

(Gibrat 1931) wherein he showed[3] that for a collection of agents whose incomes followed such a process after T periods with an initial value x_{k0} their income distribution would be of the form:

$$ln\,x_{kT} \sim N\left(\left(ln\,x_{k0} + T\left(\delta_k + 0.5\sigma_k^2\right)\right), T\sigma_k^2\right) = N\left(\mu_k, \sigma_k^2\right)$$

Classical economic models of income (Friedman 1957; Hall 1978) use these ideas to predict increasingly unequal income distributions (Battistin et al. 2009; Blundell and Preston 1998; Browning and Lusardi 1996; Anderson 2012).

In more general situations, the assumption of normality may be thought to be too restrictive, since in principle any functional form can be taken into account. However, this is not an overly strong assumption since any continuous distribution can be approximated to some desired degree of accuracy by an appropriate finite Gaussian mixture (Rossi 2014). Furthermore, it can be rationalized on three grounds. Firstly, since so many things can be construed as the consequence of an aggregation of random events, normality is a very natural choice for a variety of phenomena because of the central limit theorem. Secondly, mixtures of normal distributions form a much more general class; in fact, any absolutely continuous distribution can be approximated by a finite mixture of normal distributions with arbitrary precision (Marron and Wand 1992). Thirdly, a mixture model of normal distributions seems to capture better than other functional forms the idea of a polarized economy where relatively homogeneous groups of households are clustered around their expected incomes. This is not to say that other distributions cannot be entertained for a given problem; but as a general rule, normality works well and is a tried and tested approach to the problem.

5.3 The Probability of Class Membership of an Agent with an Income *X*

It is possible, given estimates of a mixture distribution, to calculate the probability that a particular agent with income *x* is in a particular class, and these class membership probabilities can be useful in studying class membership patterns.

[3]The law is basically a central limit theorem (see Chap. 2) using the idea that averages of things will be normally distributed in the limit.

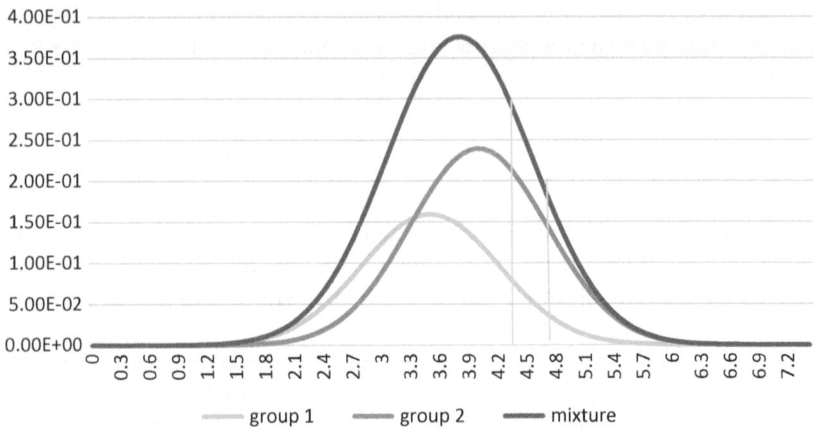

Fig. 5.1 A 40–60 mixture and the subgroup components. (Source: Author's calculations)

In a general mixture with J classes denominated $j = 1,\ldots,J$, the probability that an agent with income x_i is in class j is given by:

$$P(i,j) = \frac{w_j f(x_i,\mu_j,\sigma_j)}{\sum_{j=1}^{J} w_j f(x_i,\mu_j,\sigma_j)} \tag{5.4}$$

Here it is assumed that $f(x_i,\mu_j,\sigma_j) = \frac{1}{\sqrt{2\pi}\sigma} e^{-\frac{(x_i-\mu_j)^2}{2\sigma^2}}$ and w_j is the proportion of the population in class j.

This can be understood by viewing a simple 60–40 mixture of two normal distributions in Fig. 5.1. Suppose an agent has an income in the region of 4.5 $\pm\delta$ identified by the two vertical lines in the figure. The chance that the agent is from group 1 is the area in that interval under the group 1 curve between the lines divided by the area in that same interval under the mixture curve. Now imagine δ tends toward zero so the vertical lines move toward each other, in the limit the probability of an agent with an income of 4.5 will be the ratio of the height of the blue curve at 4.5 divided by the height of the green curve at 4.5. In a similar fashion the probability that an agent is in group 2 will be the height of the group 2 curve divided by the height of the mixture curve at $x = 4.5$. Furthermore, since the height of the green curve is the sum of the heights of the blue and red curves at any given value of x, this will always be a number between 0 and 1, that is a probability number.

For the model in [5.4], there will be J probabilities for each value of x, which can be used to examine correlates of class membership. However, it should be noted that the probabilities always sum to 1 so relationships to the correlates should be studied in the context of a J-1 system of equations which will be discussed later.

Sometimes interest is focused on the chance that a particular collection of individuals is in a particular class. For example, in a four latent class model of household incomes in the Eurozone, Anderson et al. (2018) were interested in the probabilities that particular nations in the Eurozone were in particular income classes. For the kth collection of agents (where $k = 1,\ldots,K$) with n_k observations x_i $i = 1,\ldots,n_k$ the probability that collection k is in class j is given by:

$$\theta_{jk} = \frac{1}{n_k}\sum_{i=1}^{n_k} P(i,j) \text{ for } j = 1,\ldots,J$$

This turns out to be particularly useful when studying transitional patterns, indeed given correlates of collection or class k, z_k for $k = 1,\ldots,K$, the estimates so generated can be employed in studying determinants of class membership with equations of the form:

$$\theta_{jk} = g\left(\beta_k, z_k\right).$$

However, all of these things hinge on having available estimates of the underlying mixture distribution.

5.4 Estimating the Model

Given K components, there are 3K-1 unknown parameters in a mixture of normal (means, variances and proportions of each component with K-1 independent proportions), which are estimated by maximum likelihood (ML) via the expectation-maximization (EM) algorithm (Dempster et al. 1977). Starting from an initial set of parameters for the normal distributions each data point is assigned the current posterior probabilities—the E step. Next (the M-step), the maximum likelihood estimates of the parameters of the normal distributions are computed using the assigned weights (proportions) then the parameters of the normal distributions are used to produce a new set of weights. The sequence of alternate E and M steps continues until a satisfactory degree of convergence occurs to the ML estimates. It is well known that the likelihood function of normal mixtures is unbounded and the global maximizer does not exist (McLachlan and Peel 2000). Therefore, the maximum likelihood estimator should be the root of the likelihood equation corresponding to the largest of the local maxima located. The solution usually adopted is to apply a range of starting solutions for the iterations. Usually the model is repeatedly fitted using a variety of initial values based upon separate models for outcomes based upon K means (Kaufman and Rousseeuw 1990).

5.5 Determining the Number of Classes

The number of components can be assessed by using the Bayesian information criterion (BIC). Since BIC adds a term in the log likelihood it penalizes the complexity of the model, and in this context is particularly helpful in finding a parsimonious parametrization of the model. Although regularity conditions do not hold for mixture models, Keribin (2000) showed that BIC is consistent for choosing the number of components in a mixture.

K, the number of components in the model can be evaluated using their maximum penalized likelihood following Leroux (1992) and Keribin (2000) to determine the optimal number of classes within each pooled series. Keribin (2000) proposed the penalty of,

$$A = \frac{K}{2}\sqrt{\frac{\ln(n)^{\alpha}}{n}}$$

where $\alpha = 1,\ldots, 5$. Keribin (2000) noted from simulations of a simple mixture model that the penalty when $\alpha = 1$ was sufficient to avert underestimation for the case of a bimodal two component mixture distribution, and $\alpha = 1; 2$ for a uni-modal two component mixture distribution as the sample size increases past $n = 1000$.

Selection of *K* for a mixture distribution can also be performed by minimizing the proximity of the mixture distribution, to a kernel estimate of the distribution, $f_{krn}(x)$, using two versions of Gini's Transvariation Coefficient (Gini 1916), which measures the dissimilarity of two distributions, modified by a penalty factor. Following arguments in Akaike (1972), the penalty is the number of coefficients in the mixture times $2/n$ where n is the sample size. The two versions (unweighted and "importance weighted") of the of Gini's Transvariation Coefficient, GT and GTIM, relate to half the integral of absolute differences between two probability distribution functions (Anderson et. al. 2017).

$$\mathrm{GT} = 0.5\int \left| f\left(x\right) - f_{\mathrm{ker}}\left(x\right) \right| dx$$

$$\mathrm{GTIM} = 0.5\int \left| f\left(x\right) - f_{\mathrm{ker}}\left(x\right) \right| f_{\mathrm{ker}}\left(x\right)^{-0.5} dx$$

In particular, GT relates to the overlap measure, $\theta = \int \min\left(\hat{f}\left(x\right), f_{\mathrm{kern}}\left(x\right)\right)dx$ where GT = 1 − θ. Anderson et al. (2012) showed the overlap estimator to be asymptotically normally distributed with a known mean and variance which facilitates inference.

Gini's Transvariation Coefficient can be seen as cumulating the absolute difference between the functions over the whole real line, whereas the GTIM version can be seen as cumulating the "importance" weighted absolute difference. It can be seen as weighting the difference of $f(x)$ from the "target" $f_{\mathrm{krn}}(x)$ by some monotonic function of the "target" function, so that a given difference from a small target plays a bigger role in the calculation than the same order of difference in a correspondingly larger target. In essence, the differences are weighted with respect to some reference distribution.

5.6 Studying the Probability of Class Membership

Often the determinants of class membership are of interest, an agents' propensity for belonging to a particular group is an issue of interest. In this case, the w_k s in [5.3], which can be interpreted as class membership probabilities need to be modeled. Suppose z_i is a vector of circumstances or observable characteristics of agent i (who has outcome x_i) that contribute to determine the agent's membership in class k. Note that the covariates z_i are not determinants of the outcome directly but only indirectly through class membership. Effectively, each class membership refers to a latent outcome class which is conditional on the covariates. Therefore, the effects β_k of the observable characteristics z are related to the probabilities of belonging to a certain component j and may be written in the following form:

$$w_{ik} = P\left(I\left(C_i = k\right) = 1 \middle| Z\right) = g\left(\beta_k, z_i\right)$$

$$\sum_{k=1}^{K} w_{ik} = 1$$

$$0 \le w_{ik} \le 1; i = 1,.., N\, k = 1,.., K$$

In this system, the link function $g(.)$ will have to satisfy the appropriate constraints; a natural solution would be to use a logistic transform, but a crucial issue is that C_i values are not observed, and so the classic multinomial logistic regression model cannot be directly inserted. The model can be summarized as:

$$f(x_i) = \sum_{k=1}^{K} w_{ik} f_k(x_i, \varphi_k)$$

$$ln\left(\frac{w_k}{w_1}\right) = z_i' \beta_k \quad k = 2,.., K$$

which may be equivalently represented as:

$$f(x_i) = \sum_{k=1}^{K} \frac{e^{x_i \beta_k}}{\sum_{j=1}^{K} e^{x_j \beta_k}} f_k(x_i, \varphi_k)$$

5.7 Comparing the Subgroups

Once the mixture distribution has been estimated, dominance relations between the subgroups (classes) can be examined parametrically in a straightforward fashion; for example, for $X \sim N(\mu_X, \sigma_X^2)\, and\, Y \sim N(\mu_Y, \sigma_Y^2)$ it will be the case that $\mu_X > \mu_Y\, and\, \sigma_X^2 \le \sigma_Y^2, <=> X \succcurlyeq_1 Y$ and $\mu_X = \mu_Y\, and\, \sigma_X^2 < \sigma_Y^2, <=> X \succcurlyeq_2 Y$. Similarly, the parametric distributions and their weights can be employed in Distributional Gini and Multilateral Transvariation formulae.

5.8 An Example: The Eurozone Income Distribution

Anderson, Pittau, Zelli and Thomas (2018) were interested in viewing the collection of Eurozone nations as an entity in itself in order to understand its household income class structure and the relationships of the constituent nations to that class structure. At question was the cohesiveness of the community of nations. Motivated by the fact that any absolutely continuous distribution can be approximated by a finite mixture of normals with arbitrary precision (Marron and Wand 1992), they assumed that the overall income distribution in the Eurozone can be described by a mixture of normal distributions. The unknown mixture parameters (means, variances and proportions of each component) are estimated by maximum likelihood (ML) as per Sect. 5.4. The model was fitted repeatedly using a variety of initial values and the results were fairly stable with respect to the starting values in the sense that the same maximum for the likelihood or a value very close to it was invariably obtained.

For comparison, the number of components was assessed by using the Bayesian information criterion (BIC) or a version of the Akaike information criterion (AIC) with a parameter penalty factor. (The formula for the Bayesian information criterion (BIC) is similar to the formula for AIC, but with a different penalty for the number of parameters. With AIC the penalty is $2k$, whereas with BIC the penalty is $\ln(n)k$.) In addition, the consistent Akaike information criterion (CAIC) and the AIC with a parameter penalty factor of three (AIC3), which is proved to perform well in a mixture context (Andrews and Currim 2003), were computed. Given sample size of between 141,000 and 154,000 observations per year, all the criteria yield similar results with the parameter penalty factor having little effect. Indeed, all picked four- or five-component mixtures as the "best" parsimonious model for all the years. As may be seen the results of the five criteria are very similar favoring a four-component mixture in 2006 and five-component mixtures thereafter. However, this is where mixture modeling becomes somewhat more of an art than a science since on closer inspection the addition of the fifth component appeared to contribute very little to the modeling exercise. It represented a very small portion of the population (less than 1%) with a considerable overlap of the fourth component and did not seem to affect components 1–3 at all. Table 5.1 lists the results.

The four components can be interpreted as "low"(L), "lower-middle"(LM), "upper-middle"(UM) and "high"(H) income groups. Their parametric structure is reported in Table 5.2. Roughly speaking the low and high income groups have grown over the period with the lower-middle diminishing and the upper-middle growing. Mean incomes have generally grown for all groups over the period with growth rates of 1.80%, 1.45%, 1.72% and 1.80%, respectively with a slight downturn for the

Table 5.1 Determining the number of components

Year	*Number of components*	*Loglikelihood*	*BIC*	*AIC*	*CAIC*	*AIC3*
2006	1	−470,056	940,136	940,114	940,138	940,138
	2	−466,189	932,437	932,383	932,442	932,393
	3	−465,139	930,373	930,286	930,381	930,302
	4	−464,693	929,516	929,397	929,527	929,419
	5	−464,695	929,556	929,404	929,570	929,432
2009	1	−510,880	1,021,784	1,021,762	1,021,786	1,021,766
	2	−500,152	1,000,363	1,000,309	1,000,368	1,000,319
	3	−498,302	996,699	996,612	996,707	996,628
	4	−497,977	996,084	995,965	996,095	995,987
	5	−497,864	995,894	995,742	995,908	995,770
2012	1	−528,245	1,056,514	1,056,492	1,056,516	1,056,496
	2	−517,724	1,035,507	1,035,453	1,035,512	1,035,463
	3	−516,046	1,032,187	1,032,100	1,032,195	1,032,116
	4	−515,655	1,031,441	1,031,321	1,031,452	1,031,343
	5	−515,636	1,031,438	1,031,286	1,031,452	1,031,314
2015	1	−562,189	1,124,402	1,124,380	1,124,404	1,124,384
	2	−552,080	1,104,220	1,104,165	1,104,225	1,104,175
	3	−550,175	1,100,445	1,100,358	1,100,453	1,100,374
	4	−549,761	1,099,653	1,099,533	1,099,664	1,099,555
	5	−549,701	1,099,569	1,099,416	1,099,583	1,099,444

Source: Anderson et al. (2018)

Table 5.2 Subgroup parameters and mixing coefficients

Year	*2006*			*2009*			*2012*			*2015*		
Class	μ	σ	w	μ	σ	w	μ	σ	w	μ	σ	w
Low (L)	6.77	2.50	0.15	7.84	2.68	0.16	8.21	2.98	0.19	7.99	3.14	0.18
Lower-middle (LM)	12.95	3.90	0.49	13.75	3.99	0.35	14.54	4.26	0.38	14.83	4.66	0.36
Upper-middle (UM)	20.88	5.92	0.33	21.30	5.90	0.39	23.08	6.47	0.37	24.47	7.17	0.40
High (H)	36.27	4.01	0.03	36.11	7.29	0.10	39.52	6.36	0.06	42.85	5.98	0.06

Source: Anderson et al. (2018)

lowest income group in 2015. Similarly, within-group income variation has grown over the period much in line with the predictions of Gibrat's Law.

The authors go on to use the model to explore polarization and inequality characteristics of the Eurozone using the parameters of the mixture distribution which revealed increasing inequality and polarization over the period.

References

Akaike, H. (1972). *Information Theory and an Extension of the Maximum Likelihood Principle.* Proceedings of the 2nd International Symposium on Information Theory to Problems of Control and Information Theory, Budapest, 267–281.

Alkire, S., & Foster, J. E. (2011). Counting and Multidimensional Poverty Measurement. *Journal of Public Economics, 95*, 476–487.

Anderson, G. J. (2012). *Boats and Tides and 'Trickle Down' Theories: What Economists Presume About Wellbeing When They Employ Stochastic Process Theory in Modeling Behavior* (Economics Discussion Paper No. 2012–28). Available at SSRN: https://ssrn.com/abstract=2087933 or https://doi.org/10.2139/ssrn.2087933

Anderson, G. J., Crawford, I., & Leicester, A. (2011). Welfare Rankings From Multivariate Data, a Nonparametric Approach. *Journal of Public Economics, 95*, 247–252.

Anderson, G., Linton, O., & Whang, Y.-J. (2012). Nonparametric estimation and inference about the overlap of two distributions. *Journal of Econometrics, 171*(1), 1–23.

Anderson, G., Linton, O., & Thomas, J. (2017). Similarity, Dissimilarity and Exceptionality: Generalizing Gini's Transvariation to Measure 'Differentness' in Many Distributions. *Metron, 75*, 161–180.

Anderson G. J., Pittau, M. G., Zelli, R., & J. Thomas. (2018). Income Inequality, Cohesiveness and Commonality in the Euro Area: A Semi-parametric Boundary-free Analysis. *Econometrics, 6*(2), 15. https://doi.org/10.3390/econometrics6020015

Anderson, G. J., Farcomeni, A., Pittau, M. G., & Zelli, R. (2016). A New Approach to Measuring and Studying the Characteristics of Class Membership: Examining Poverty, Inequality and Polarization in Urban China. *Journal of Econometrics, 191*(2), 348–359.

Andrews, R. A., & Currim, I. S. (2003). A Comparison of Segment Retention Criteria for Finite Mixture Logit's Models. *Journal of Marketing Research, XL*, 235–243.

Atkinson, A. B., & Brandolini, A. (2013). On the Identification of the Middle Class. In J. C. Gornick & M. Jaantti (Eds.), *Income Inequality* (pp. 77–100). Stanford: Stanford University Press.

Banerjee, A. V., & Duflo, E. (2008). What is middle class about the middle classes around the world? *Journal of Economic Perspectives, 22*(2), 3–28.

Battistin, E., Blundell, R., & Lewbel, A. (2009). Why Is Consumption More LogNormal Than Income? Gibrat's Law Revisited. *Journal of Political Economy, 117*(6), 1140–1154.

Blundell, R., & Preston, I. (1998). Consumption Inequality and Income Uncertainty. *The Quarterly Journal of Economics, 113*(2), 603–640.

Browning, M., & Lusardi, A. (1996). Household Saving: Micro Theories and Micro Facts. *Journal of Economic Literature, 34*(4), 1797–1855.

Chen, X., Hong, H., & Nekipelov, D. (2011). Nonlinear Models of Measurement Errors. *Journal of Economic Literature, 49*, 901–937.

Cox, D. R. (2017). *Stochastic Process Theory.* New York: Routledge.

Dempster, A. P., Laird, N. M., & Rubin, D. B. (1977). Maximum Likelihood from Incomplete Data via EM Algorithm. *Journal of the Royal Statistical Society, B, 69*, 1–38.

Eckstein, Z., & Wolpin, K. (1990). Estimating a Market Equilibrium Search Model from Panel Data on Individuals. *Econometrica, 58*, 783–808.

Easterly, W. (2001). The Middle Class Consensus and Economic Development. *Journal of Economic Growth, 6*(4), 317–335.

Foster, J. (1998). Absolute Versus Relative Poverty. *The American Economic Review, 88*(2), 335–341.

Friedman, M. (1957). *A Theory of the Consumption Function.* Princeton: Princeton University Press.

Gabaix, X. (1999). Zipf's Law for Cities an Explanation. *Quarterly Journal of Economics, 111*, 739–767.

Gibrat, R. (1931). *Les Inegalites Economiques.* Paris: Librairie du Recueil Sirey.

Gini, C. (1916). Il Concetto di Transvariazione e le sue Prime Applicazioni. In C. Gini (Ed.), Transvariazione. Libreria Goliardica (pp. 1–55).

Grusky, D. B., & Kanbur, R. (2006). *Poverty and Inequality: Studies in Social Inequality.* Stanford: Stanford University Press.

Hall, R. E. (1978). Stochastic Implications of the Life Cycle-Permanent Income Hypothesis: Theory and Evidence. *Journal of Political Economy, 86*(6), 971–987.

Kaufman, L., & Rousseeuw, P. J. (1990). *Finding Groups in Data: An Introduction to Cluster Analysis.* New York: Wiley.

Keane, M., & Wolpin, K. (1997). The Career Decisions of Young Men. *Journal of Political Economy, 105*, 473–522.

Keribin, S. (2000). Consistent Estimation of the Order of Mixture Model. *Sankhya, 62*, 49–66.

Kakwani, N., & Silber, J. (2008). *Quantitative Approaches to Multidimensional Poverty Measurement.* London: Palgrave Macmillan.

Kim, C. J., & Nelson, C. (1999). *State-Space Models with Regime-Switching: Classical and Gibbs-Sampling Approaches with Applications.* Cambridge: MIT Press.

Leroux, B. G. (1992). Maximum Likelihood Estimation for Hidden Markov Models. *Stochastic Processes and their Applications, 40*, 127–143.

Lewbel, A. (2007). Estimation of Average Treatment Effects with Misclassification. *Econometrica, 75*, 537–551.

Marron, J. S., & Wand, M. P. (1992). Exact Mean Integrated Squarred Error. *Annals of Statistics, 20*, 712–736.

McLachlan, G., & Peel, D. (2000). *Finite Mixture Models.* New York: Wiley.

Modigliani, F., & Brumberg, R. (1954). Utility Analysis and the Consumption Function: An Interpretation of Cross Section Data. In K. K. Kurihara (Ed.), *Post Keynesian Economics* (pp. 388–436). London: Routledge.

Nussbaum, M. C. (1997). Capabilities and Human Rights. *Fordham Law Review, 66*, 273–300.

Nussbaum, M. C. (2011). *Creating Capabilities: The Human Development Approach.* Cambridge, MA: Harvard University Press.

Reed, W. J. (2001). The Pareto, Zipf and Other Power Laws. *Economics Letters, 74*, 15–19.

Rossi, P. E. (2014). *Bayesian Non and Semi-Parametric Methods and Applications.* Princeton/Oxford: Princeton University Press.

Saez, E., & Veall, M. R. (2005). The Evolution of High Incomes in Northern America: Lessons from Canadian evidence. *American Economic Review, 95*(3), 831–849.

Sen, A. (1982). *Choice, Welfare and Measurement.* Cambridge, MA: MIT Press.

Stiglitz, J. E., Sen A., & J.P. Fitoussi (2010). *Mis-measuring Our Lives: Why GDP Doesn't Add Up.* The Report of the Commission on the Measurement of Economic Performance and Social Progress. New York/London: The New Press

Sutton, J. (1997). Gibrat's Legacy. *Journal of Economic Literature, 35*(1), 40–59.

CHAPTER 6

Ambiguity, Comparability, Segmentation and All That

We have seen that when assessing differences and similarities or ordering a collection of groups, be they identified or latent, the orientation of their respective distributions can engender ambiguity and comparability problems in the context of a particular criterion function. This chapter offers an analysis of this problem in comparing the household income distributions of 18 Eurozone nations. Section 6.2 outlines some criteria for the absence of ambiguity with respect to a particular criterion function and the manner in which the problem has been dealt with in the bilateral comparison case is discussed in Sect. 6.3. It turns out that the potential for ambiguity in a collection of distributions can be measured and two "ambiguity indices" are proposed in Sect. 6.4. While these ideas have been applied to problems with indices of wellbeing levels they can equally be applied to measures of inequality, Sect. 6.5 discusses this issue. The concept of partitioning a collection of groups into sets within which there may be some ambiguity but between which there is no ambiguity is explored in Sect. 6.6 and all of these ideas are exemplified in the Eurozone application in Sect. 6.7.

6.1 Introduction

At the end of Chap. 3, a peremptory comparison of Eurozone nations with respect to a variety of measures of income wellbeing levels revealed how a collection of ranking measures (indices) designed with the same objective can yield conflicting or ambiguous orderings. Using some of the

G. Anderson, *Multilateral Wellbeing Comparison in a Many Dimensioned World*, Global Perspectives on Wealth and Distribution,
https://doi.org/10.1007/978-3-030-21130-1_6

ideas discussed in Chap. 4, with the Eurozone comparisons as an exemplar, this chapter explores the issue in more detail. Measures of the potential for ambiguity will be introduced together with tools for partitioning groups and measuring distributional dissonance in both identifiable and latent groupings.

At the heart of the multilateral comparison problem is the notion that a family of perfectly reasonable, theoretically justifiable (and hence equally appropriate) comparison instruments will very often yield conflicting results. This is entirely a consequence of the particular orientation of the subgroup distributions of the characteristic under comparison. It is not simply a matter of statistical uncertainty engendered by sampling variability; the problem would exist even if the subgroup distributions were known with certainty. Rather it is a consequence of the particular juxtaposition and shape differences of the distributions in question and as such it is an uncertainty that is inherent in the structure of the problem, an uncertainty that more information or data cannot resolve. It would be useful to have a measure of the extent to which such "structural uncertainty" or structural ambiguity is a problem.

One simple conclusion to be drawn from Chap. 4's discussion of partial orderings is that, if a collection of groups under comparison are perfectly segmented, there will be no ambiguity or lack of coherency in any collection of relevant indicators of household wellbeing levels at any order of comparison. This is so since each and every pair of groups will have a first order dominance relationship and, as was demonstrated in Chap. 2, first order dominance implies dominance at all higher comparison orders. Perfect segmentation implies that none of the distributions overlap so that for two ordered groups A and B, where A has higher overall level of wellbeing, all of the agents in society A will have more than the richest agent in society B. This most extreme form of separation between groups rarely emerges in practice; however, it is often the case that a first order or second dominance relationship prevails between nations and, if this can be established between the groups under comparison, it can be exploited as a partitioning device in classifying or partitioning nations into poor, middle and high income classes.

Before embarking on the analysis, some detail about the exemplar used in this chapter is necessary. In order to study the latent income class structure in the Eurozone group of countries Anderson, Pittau, Zelli, and Thomas (2018b) chose four temporally equi-spaced waves of data: 2006, 2009, 2012 and 2015 drawn from the cross-sectional component of The European

Union Survey on Income and Living Conditions (EU-SILC). EU-SILC is a collection of annual national surveys of socio-economic conditions of individuals and households in European Union countries. The Eurozone area, a subset of the Union, is defined as those countries that are currently using the Euro. Since data for Malta are only available from the 2008 wave, this country was excluded from analysis leaving 18 Eurozone countries. Household Income in those countries is total household net disposable income obtained by aggregating of all income sources from all household members net of direct taxes and social contributions. All observations are weighted by cross-sectional weights and income is Purchasing Power Parity (PPP) adjusted. Assuming cohabitation generates economies of scale in consumption and therefore needs do not grow proportionally with household size, incomes are age and size-adjusted using the so-called modified-OECD equivalence scale which assigns a value of 1 to the household head, of 0.5 to each additional adult member aged 14 and above and of 0.3 to each child aged below 14. Gaussian kernel estimates of the distributions are employed throughout. So the example used throughout this chapter will be household income wellbeing in 18 Eurozone nations, and the objective is to order the 18 nations (or a collection of latent subgroups to be determined later) with respect to some income wellbeing measure.

To get a sense of the problem in terms of the example we will be using, Fig. 6.1 presents the mutually coherent scaled diagrams of the Gaussian kernel estimated probability density functions for the 18 Eurozone nations for the 2012 wave. As is evident, the distributions are anatomically very different; they clearly overlap and present much opportunity for ambiguity. All distributions are right skewed to some degree, but that is about all they have in common.

A sensible formulation of an ambiguity measure or index should record 0 when there is no potential for ambiguity so a clear idea of when there will be no ambiguity in comparing a collection of groups would be a good starting point. To fix ideas assume there are K groups, (in the exemplar they are the 18 nations in the Eurozone) indexed $k = 1,\ldots, K$ under comparison. Each has an income probability density function (pdf) $f_k(x)$, a corresponding cumulative distribution function (cdf) $F_k(x)$ and a mean income $E_{f_k}(x)$ which is denoted $\mu_k\left(=\int x f_k(x)dx\right)$ where, for convenience the distributions are organized so that, $k > j \Rightarrow \mu_k \geq \mu_j$. For notational purposes denote the Overlap of two pdfs $f_k(x)$ and $f_j(x)$ as $OV_{k,j}\left(=\int \min\left(f_k(x), f_j(x)\right)dx\right)$, the corresponding Transvariation as $TR_{k,j}\left(=0.5\int\left|f_k(x)-f_j(x)\right|dx\right)$ and higher order (ith order) Transvariations

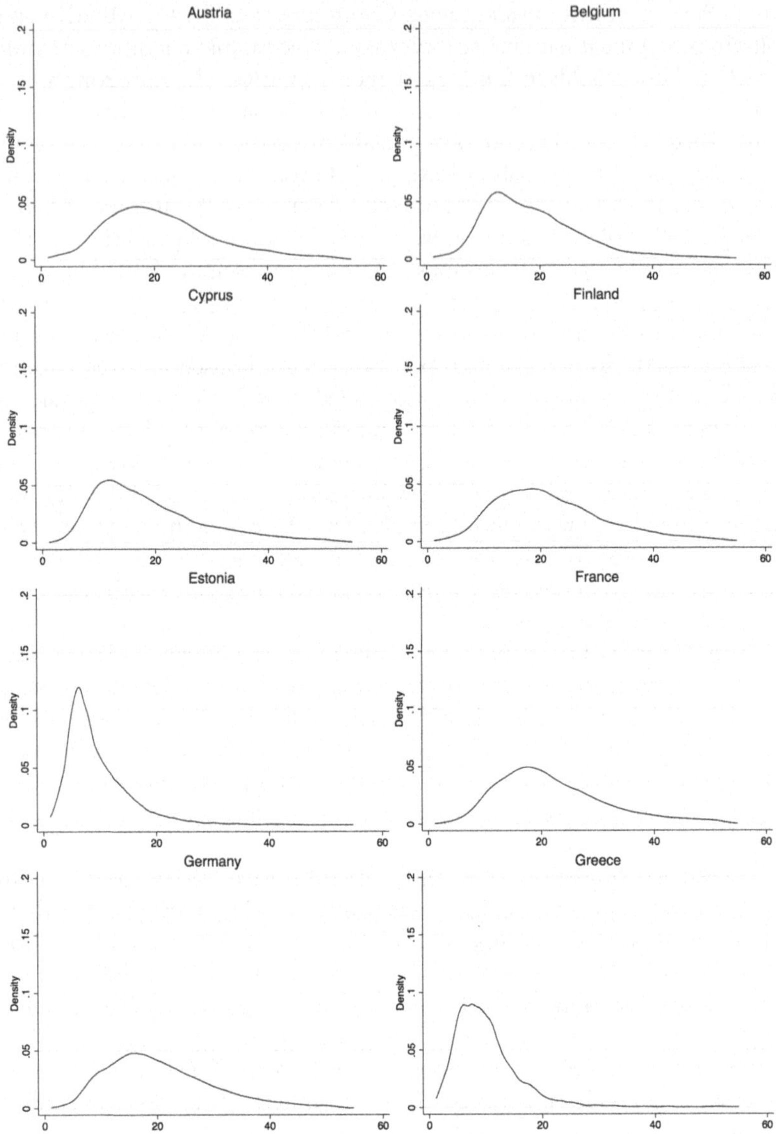

Fig. 6.1 National probability density functions 2012. (Source: Anderson et al. 2018b)

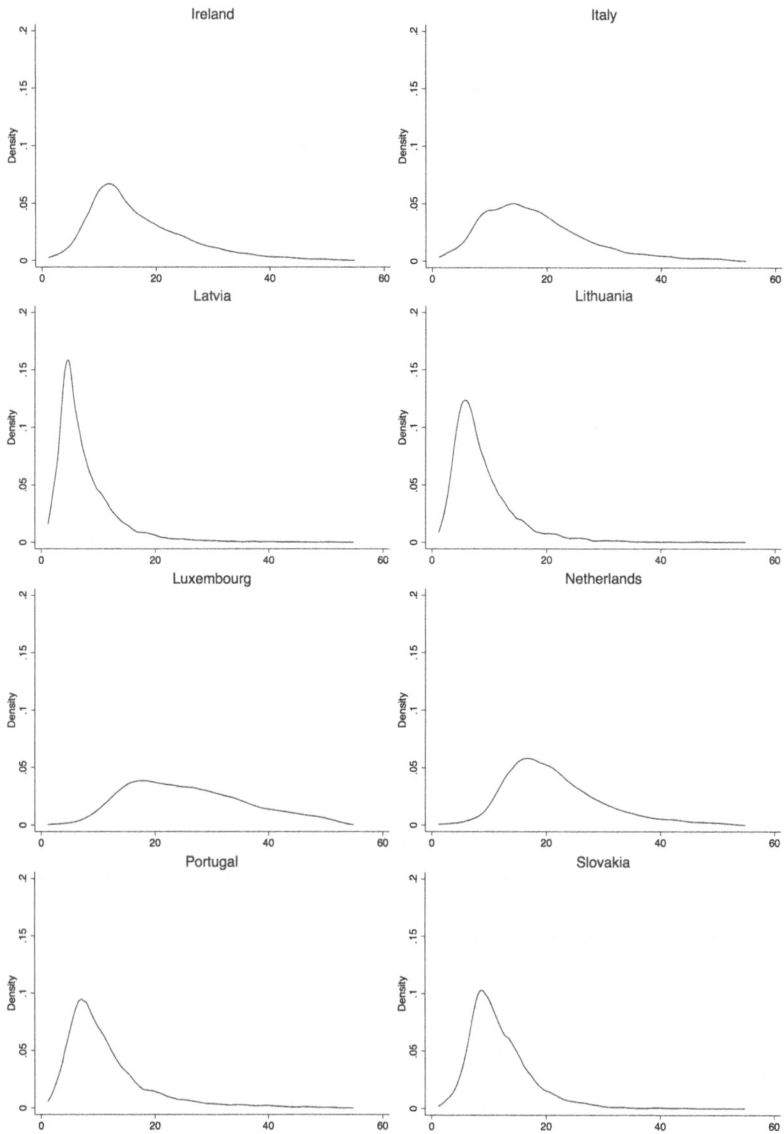

Fig. 6.1 (continued)

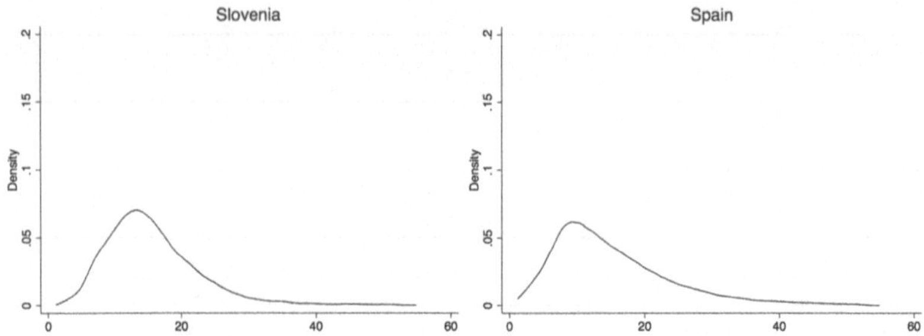

Fig. 6.1 (continued)

as $TR^{i}_{k,j}\left(=0.5\int\left|F^{i}_{k}(x)-F^{i}_{j}(x)\right|dx\right)\text{for } i=1,2,\ldots$. Note that generally $\int\left|F^{i}_{k}(x)-F^{i}_{j}(x)\right|dx \geq \left|\int\left(F^{i}_{k}(x)-F^{i}_{j}(x)\right)dx\right|$ with dominance at the *i*th order prevailing when equality prevails since there will be no dominance transgression (the curves do not cross) in the sense of Leshno–Levy (2002). With regard to the collection of distributions, concepts of the *i*th order upper (FUE^{i}) and lower (FLE^{i}) envelopes of the collection will be needed. These are piecewise continuous functions defined as $\text{FUE}^{i}(x)=\max\left(F^{i}_{1}(x),F^{i}_{2}(x),..F^{i}_{K}(x)\right)$ and $\text{FLE}^{i}(x)=\min\left(F^{i}_{1}(x),F^{i}_{2}(x),..F^{i}_{K}(x)\right)$ respectively.

6.2 An "Absence of Ambiguity" Criteria

The Case of Complete Segmentation

K distributions are said to be completely segmented (Yitzahki 1994), when the range over which $f_k(x)>0$ is a closed compact mutually exclusive interval for each $f_k(x)$ $k=1,\ldots,K$ so that $f_k(x)=0$ for all $f_j(x)>0$ and $f_j(x)=0$ for all $f_k(x)>0$) for all $k \neq j$. In this case, given the distributions are ordered by index, $F_k(x) < F_j(x)$ for all x for $k > j$ so that $f_k(x)\pm_1 f_j(x)$ for all $k > j$ and all i. Indeed, since *i*th order dominance implies dominance at all higher orders, $f_k(x)\pm_i f_j(x)$ for all i. Thus, there will be unanimity and a complete absence of ambiguity at any and every order when the collection is perfectly segmented.[1] Furthermore, in

[1] It is interesting to note that the Gini coefficient is subgroup decomposable under perfect segmentation of subgroups Mookherjee and Shorrocks (1982).

this case it would not be possible to find contradictions through sampling variation. Indeed any randomly selected element from each of the distributions would yield an appropriate ordering for any monotonic increasing wellbeing measure.

Perfect segmentation over the collection of distributions requires $OV_{k,j} = 0$ for all $k, j = 1,\ldots,K \;\; j \neq k$, it would guarantee absence of ambiguity in all indices measuring the level of wellbeing over the group. It is a sufficient, but not a necessary condition and so it is perhaps an extreme requirement. Intuitively suppose there are J indices $U_{j,k}(x)$ indexed $j = 1,\ldots, J$ (all normalized to be between 0 and 1) under consideration for the K constituencies $k = 1,\ldots, K$ and define the index range for the kth constituency as:

$$\left[U_{Lk}(x), U_{Hk}(x)\right] = \min_j\left(U_{1k}(x), U_{2k}(x),..U_{Jk}(x)\right), \max_j\left(U_{1k}(x), U_{2k}(x),..U_{Jk}(x)\right).$$

Absence of ambiguity is secured when the ranges $\left[U_{Lk}(x), U_{Hk}(x)\right]$ $k = 1,\ldots, K$ are mutually exclusive. Since $\left[U_{Lk}(x), U_{Hk}(x)\right]$ will usually be interior to the ranges engendered by the distributions $f_k(x)$ for $k = 1,\ldots, K$, perfect segmentation is stronger than is necessary for the absence of ambiguity since mutual exclusivity of the $U()$ index ranges can still prevail in the presence of some overlap in the probability density functions (this can be visualized in Figs. 2.1, 2.2, 2.3 and 2.4 in Chap. 2 which show, in the case of Poisson and normal distributions, substantially overlapping pdfs whose corresponding cdfs obey a first order dominance relation).

The stochastic dominance conditions outlined in Chap. 4 can be used to demonstrate that all indices $U(x)$, where $U(x)$ is such that $(-1)^{j+1}(dU(x)/dx) > 0$ $j = 1,\ldots, i$, would cohere (i.e. not conflict) when ith order dominance prevails, which suggests a dominance based criterion for the absence of ambiguity at the ith comparison level.

Definition Ambiguity is absent at dominance order comparison level "i" if all pertinent ordering instruments $U(x)$, such that $(-1)^{j+1}(dU(x)/dx) > 0$ $j = 1,\ldots, i$, are unanimous in ranking the collection of K states at that level.

A collection of K distributions such that $F_k^i(x) \leq F_{k+1}^i(x)$ for all x and $F_k^i(x) < F_{k+1}^i(x)$ for some x, for distributions indexed $k = 1,\ldots, K$-1, corresponds to an unambiguously ordered collection at the ith order, since all index representations of $U(x)$ with

$(-1)^{i+1}(dU(x)/dx) > 0$ yield identical or unanimous rankings of the K states at order i. Indeed, in this situation, since dominance at order i implies dominance at all higher orders, there would be unanimity among all appropriate ordering instruments at each and all higher order comparison levels $h > i$. Thus a condition for the absence of ambiguity at the ith comparison level would be:

$$\int\left|F_k^i(x)-F_j^i(x)\right|dx=\left|\int\left(F_k^i(x)-F_j^i(x)\right)dx\right| \text{for all } k,j=1,\ldots,K\ k\neq j$$

In this event $F_K^i(x)$ would correspond to the lower envelope of the collection and coincide with $\mathrm{FLE}^i(x)$ (and the highest ranked distribution) and $F_1^i(x)$ would correspond to the upper envelope of the collection and coincide with $\mathrm{FUE}^i(x)$ (and lowest ranked distribution) at order "i". Conceptually in this case $TR(i)=\int_0^\infty\left(F_1^i(x)-F_K^i(x)\right)dx$, which is a measure of the area between the highest and lowest curves in the collection, presents a metric of the degree of distributional variation at the ith order of integration of the K distributions[2] which forms a basis for the Dystopia-Utopia indices (Anderson et al. 2018b).

In formulating a measure of ambiguity, some insight can be gleaned by seeing how it has been dealt with in simple two-way comparisons.

6.3 Dealing with Ambiguity within Two Groups

Clearly, when any two curves, $F_k^i(x)$ and $F_j^i(x)$ $i\neq j$ intersect, the possibility of a completely unambiguous ordering over the K distributions no longer exists at the ith level. With respect to a specific two-way comparison, the conventional practice in this case has been either to seek a weaker form of "Almost Dominance" following Leshno and Levy (2002) or to seek a non-intersecting orientation of the curves at some higher order of integration (higher value of "i"). Both approaches may be seen as further restricting the class of $U(x)$ in some fashion, indeed they are related by the magnitude of Leshno and Levy's dominance transgression area. In the context of cumulative density functions or second order

[2] A multi distributional higher order extension of the Gini (1916) Transvariation measure, see Anderson, Linton, and Thomas (2017), Anderson, Linton, and Whang (2019).

dominance relations, Leshno and Levy (2002) exploit the extent to which two curves transgress the dominance condition in developing the notion of "Almost Dominance". In contemplating the "almost dominance" of distribution A over distribution B, they extend Gini's Transvariation of two pdfs to their corresponding cumulative densities, TRF(2) $\left(=\int_0^\infty \left|F_b(x)-F_a(x)\right|dx=\int_0^\infty (\max\left(F_b(x),F_a(x)\right)-\min\left(F_b(x),F_a(x)\right)dx\right)$ and define the transgression region TRG $(=\int_0^\infty \left|F_b(x)-F_a(x)\right| I\left[\left(F_b(x)-F_a(x)\right)<0\right])dx$ where $I[.]$ is an indicator function returning 1 when the argument is true and 0 otherwise and consider θ where:

$$\theta=\frac{\text{TRG}}{\text{TRF}}=\frac{\int_0^\infty \left|F_b(x)-F_a(x)\right| I\left[\left(F_b(x)-F_a(x)\right)<0\right]dx}{\int_0^\infty \left|F_b(x)-F_a(x)\right|dx} \tag{6.1}$$

Intuitively θ is the proportion of the Transvariation which is contrary to the dominance condition. If θ is small in some sense, then "Almost Dominance" of $f_a(x)$ over $f_b(x)$ is declared. If it is supposed that the curves cross once and the transgression area is in the upper tail, then the smaller θ is, the larger will be the dominance area in the lower tail relative to the Transvariation area. The Leshno–Levy claim is that perverse or extreme preferences are being ruled out, so for example in the case of risk aversion, preferences that would have an agent prefer a certain \$1 to a 99.9999% chance of \$1,000,000 are being eliminated.

Restricting the Preference Space Reduces Ambiguity

Seeking clarity at some higher order of integration can be rationalized using Davidson and Duclos (2000) Lemma 1 which was discussed in Chap. 4. In this context, the tenor of the Lemma is that, for any given collection of distributions, there will ultimately be an order of integration at which all available ordering instruments at that level would cohere and as such, ambiguity would be absent. The Davidson–Duclos analysis just considers the comparison of two distributions $f_a(x)$ and $f_b(x)$ each defined on the set of positive numbers but the analysis can be readily extended to many, that is, more than two distributions defined on the set of real numbers. They suppose that $f_a(x)$ first order dominates $f_b(x)$ over values of x on the interval $0 < x < w$ with strict dominance over part of that range and then demonstrate that, for any finite threshold $z > w$, $f_a(x)$ will dominate $f_b(x)$ at some order i over the range $0 < x < z$ for an i value that is sufficiently large.

6.4 Two Ambiguity Indices

It will be helpful to calibrate the potential for ambiguity in ordering a collection of distributions as an indicator of the clarity or reliability with which a particular ordering of the collection can be viewed. Here two indices are considered, the first, a Leshno–Levy dominance transgression based index, calibrates the extent of ambiguity on the unit interval with 0 representing absence of ambiguity and 1 corresponding to complete ambiguity. The second, TRAM, a Transvariation based Ambiguity index calibrates the absence of ambiguity on the unit interval where 1 indicates the complete absence of ambiguity.

A Leshno–Levy Based Index

Recall, for notational convenience, the distributions are ordered by their indices, in such a situation when there is no clear dominance, Leshno and Levy (2002) work with θ_{kj}, the ratio of the second order dominance transgression area to the total second order Transvariation which may be written as:

$$\theta_{kj}^{1} = \frac{\int_{0}^{\infty} \left|F_j(x) - F_k(x)\right| I\left[\left(F_j(x) - F_k(x)\right) < 0\right] dx}{\int_{0}^{\infty} \left|F_j(x) - F_k(x)\right| dx}$$

If it is small, $f_k(x)$ is said to "almost" dominate $f_j(x)$ at the second order. When the collection of K distributions is such that $F_k^1(x) \le F_{k+1}^1(x)$ for all x and $F_k^1(x) < F_{k+1}^1(x)$ for some x, for $k = 1,\ldots, K\text{-}1$ then $\theta_{kj} = 0$ for all pairs k,j where $k > j$ because $\int_{0}^{\infty} \left|F_j(x) - F_k(x)\right| I\left[\left(F_j(x) - F_k(x)\right) < 0\right] dx = 0$ for all such pairs. In the context of the multiplicity of K distributions, a measure of overall distributional variation (Anderson et al. 2017) is given by:

$$\mathrm{MTV}(1) = \int_0^\infty \left\{ \max\left(F_1(x), F_2(x), \ldots F_K(x)\right) - \min\left(F_1(x), F_2(x), \ldots F_K(x)\right) \right\} dx$$

And $AI(1)$, a measure of potential ambiguity at the first order in the collection is:

$$AI(1) = \frac{\sum_{j=2}^{K} \sum_{k=1}^{j} \int_0^\infty \left| F_j(x) - F_k(x) \right| I\left[\left(F_j(x) - F_k(x) \right) < 0 \right] dx}{\int_0^\infty \left\{ \max\left(F_1(x), F_2(x), \ldots F_K(x)\right) - \min\left(F_1(x), F_2(x), \ldots F_K(x)\right) \right\}}.$$

which has the interpretation of the aggregation of all first order dominance transgressions divided by the aggregate Transvariation of the collection of distributions. Alternatively, it is a weighted sum of all possible θ_{ij} where the weights are the corresponding *ij* Transvariation divided by overall Transvariation. This may be generalized to the *i*th order of integration wherein a measure of overall distributional variation at the *i*th level of integration is given by:

$$\mathrm{MTV}(i) = \int_0^\infty \left\{ \max\left(F_1^i(x), F_2^i(x), \ldots F_K^i(x)\right) - \min\left(F_1^i(x), F_2^i(x), \ldots F_1^i(x)\right) \right\} dx$$

And $AI(i)$, a measure of potential ambiguity at the *i*th order in the collection is:

$$AI(i) = \frac{\sum_{j=2}^{K} \sum_{k=1}^{j} \int_0^\infty \left| F_j^i(x) - F_k^i(x) \right| I\left[\left(F_j^i(x) - F_k^i(x) \right) < 0 \right] dx}{\int_0^\infty \left\{ \max\left(F_1^i(x), F_2^i(x), \ldots F_K^i(x)\right) - \min\left(F_1^i(x), F_2^i(x), \ldots F_K^i(x)\right) \right\} dx}$$
$$= \sum_{j=2}^{K} \sum_{k=1}^{j} \theta_{jk}^i w_{jk}.$$

where:

$$w_{jk} = \frac{\int_0^\infty \left| F_j^i(x) - F_k^i(x) \right| dx}{\int_0^\infty \left\{ \max\left(F_1^i(x), F_2^i(x), \ldots F_K^i(x)\right) - \min\left(F_1^i(x), F_2^i(x), \ldots F_K^i(x)\right) \right\} dx}$$

Note the weights w_{jk} generally sum to more than 1 when functions intersect but they can be normalized if desired; however, $AI(i)$ will be 0 when there are no contradictions and will increase as the magnitude of transgressions increase. The index has the interpretation of the aggregation of all ith order dominance transgressions divided by the aggregate Transvariation of the collection of distributions. Naturally, these measures could be extended to the analysis of sub-collection envelopes as in Eq. (6.1) above.

A Transvariation Based Index

Alternatively, following the relationship between the ith level Transvariation of $f_a(x)$ and $f_b(x)$ and half the difference in their ith order integrals (see Eq. (6.1)), it may be shown that when ith order dominance prevails between $f_{k+1}(x)$ and $f_k(x)$ for $k = 1,\ldots, K\text{-}1$ such that:

$$F_{k+1}^i(x) \leq F_k^i(x) \text{ for all } x \text{ with strict inequality somewhere}$$

Then:

$$\int_0^M \left(\max\left(F_1^i(x), F_2^i(x), \ldots, F_K^i(x)\right) - \min\left(F_1^i(x), F_2^i(x), \ldots, F_K^i(x)\right)\right) dx$$

$$= \sum_{k=1}^{K-1} \int_0^M \left(F_k^i(x) - F_{k+1}^i(x)\right) dx$$

Letting $F_0^i(x) = \max\left(F_1^i(x), F_2^i(x), \ldots, F_K^i(x)\right)$ and $F_{K+1}^i(x) = \min\left(F_1^i(x), F_2^i(x), \ldots, F_K^i(x)\right)$, an index, TRAM, of the form:

$$\text{TRAM} = \frac{1}{K-1} \frac{\sum_{k=1}^{K-1} \left| \int_0^M \left(F_k^i(x) - F_{k+1}^i(x)\right) dx \right|}{\sum_{k=1}^{K-1} \int_0^M \left| F_k^i(x) - F_{k+1}^i(x) \right| dx}$$

suggests itself.

Note that $0 \leq \text{TRAM} \leq 1$ will reach a maximum of 1 when $f_{k+1}(x)$ stochastically dominates $f_k(x)$ at the ith order and there is an absence of ambiguity.

6.5 Ambiguity in Inequality Measures

These notions can be extended to collections of indices of relative inequality, the most well-known of which is probably the Gini coefficient. The Gini (G) and Absolute Gini (AG) coefficients[3] given by:

$$G = \frac{1}{E(X)}\int_0^\infty\int_0^\infty f(y)f(x)\,|\,x-y\,|\,dxdy, \text{ and } AG = \int_0^\infty\int_0^\infty f(y)f(x)\,|\,x-y\,|\,dxdy = E(X)^*G$$

$$\text{where } E(X) = \int_0^\infty xf(x)dx \tag{6.2}$$

provide a complete ordering of a collection of such distributions *f*, in the first instance with respect to the average absolute distance between the atoms of a distribution relative to their mean and, in the second instance, with respect to the average absolute distance between those atoms. These statistics can also be respectively related to their associated Lorenz ($L(p)$) and Generalized Lorenz ($GL(p)$) curves:

$$L(p) = \frac{\int_0^p F^{-1}(x)dF(x)}{\int_0^1 F^{-1}(x)dF(x)}, \quad \text{and} \quad GL(p) = E(x)\frac{\int_0^p F^{-1}(x)dF(x)}{\int_0^1 F^{-1}(x)dF(x)}$$

$$\text{where } F^{-1}(x) \text{ is the inverse of } F(x), \text{ the CDF of } f(x) \tag{6.3}$$

Wherein:

$$G = 2\int_0^1 (p - L(p))dp, \quad \text{and} \quad AG = E(X)2\int_0^1 (p - L(p))dp = E(X)^*G \tag{6.4}$$

In the former case, the Gini is twice the area between the Lorenz curve and the 45° line, in the latter case this quantity is scaled by average income (i.e. the Generalized Lorenz curve is the Lorenz curve scaled by average

[3] The Gini coefficient is due to Gini (1912); the Absolute Gini is due to Hey and Lambert (1980).

income). An alternative to the Absolute Gini as a measure of income well-being in the family of indices representing monotonic concave felicity functions is Atkinson's equally distributed income measure (arithmetic mean income less geometric mean income).

Let Lorenz Transvariation (LT) and Generalized Lorenz Transvariation (GLT) be respectively defined as:

$$LT_{a,b} = \int_0^1 \left| L_a(p) - L_b(p) \right| dp; \quad \mathrm{GLT}_{a,b} = \int_0^1 \left| GL_a(p) - GL_b(p) \right| dp;$$

Conceptually these correspond to the absolute area between two curves and provide a metric for the extent of their difference. Letting $I(z)$ be an indicator function returning 1 when $z > 0$ and 0 otherwise, and where $\int (L_a(p) - L_b(p)) dp > 0$, the operational index $\theta(f_a(x), f_b(x))$ in terms of Lorenz and Generalized Lorenz curves employed by Leshno and Levy (2002) is given by:

$$\theta_L(f_a(x), f_b(x)) = \frac{\int_0^1 I(L_b(p) - L_a(p))(L_a(p) - L_b(p)) dp}{LT_{a,b}}$$

and

$$\theta_{GL}(f_a(x), f_b(x)) = \frac{\int_0^1 I(GL_b(p) - GL_a(p))(GL_a(p) - GL_b(p)) dp}{GLT_{a,b}} \tag{6.5}$$

In essence when the ratio of the dominance transgression area to the total (Generalized) Lorenz Transvariation (Leo 2017) was small relative to some pre-specified amount, the relationship was deemed to be "almost dominant" at the second order. Leshno and Levy (2002) used the concept to rule out "pathological" cases of risk averse behavior in portfolio choice, for example, where someone would prefer a certain \$1 over a 99.9% chance of \$1,000,000.

Here the ratio is used as an index of ambiguity inherent in the Gini (Absolute Gini) ordering of $f_a(x)$ and $f_b(x)$ relationship. Noting that $0 \le \theta \le 0.5$, an ambiguity index $AI = 2\theta$ provides a sense of how ambiguous the corresponding Gini or Absolute Gini ordering is. The extension of this index to a collection (>2) of distributions is straightforward. Working just with the Generalized Lorenz–Absolute Gini (AG) relationship (extension to Gini and Lorenz is straightforward), consider a collection of K distributions $f_k(x)$ with corresponding Lorenz curves $L_k(p)$ and Gini coefficients G_k $k = 1,\ldots, K$ where, for convenience and without loss of generality, $i > j \Rightarrow AG_i \geq AG_j$ for $i,j \in 1,\ldots, K$. Note that this implies $\int\left(GL_j(p)-GL_ip\right)dp = AG_i - AG_j \geq 0$ for $i > j$. Define GLT(K), the Generalized Lorenz analog of Gini's distributional Transvariation (Gini 1916, Dagum 1968) for a collection of distributions as:

$$\mathrm{GLT}(K)=\int_0^1\{\max\left(GL_1(p),GL_2(p),\ldots,GL_K(p)\right)$$
$$-\min\left(GL_1(p),GL_2(p),\ldots,GL_K(p)\right)\}\,dp$$

GLT(K) is a measure of the extent of variation in the collection of Generalized Lorenz curves, as the area between the upper and lower envelopes of the collection of Lorenz Curves, Generalized Lorenz analog of the range of a collection of numbers. Then $AI(K)$, the ambiguity index for a monotonic non-decreasing concave function ordering of a collection of K distributions, is of the form:

$$AI(K)=\frac{\lambda}{\mathrm{GLT}(K)}\sum_{j=2}^{K}\sum_{i=1}^{j}\int_0^1 I\left(GL_i(p)-GL_j(p)\right)\left|GL_j(p)-GL_i(p)\right|dp$$
$$=\frac{\lambda}{\mathrm{GLT}(K)}\sum_{j=2}^{K}\sum_{i=1}^{j}\theta_{GL}(i,j)\int_0^1\left|GL_j(p)-GL_i(p)\right|dp$$

For some choice of $\lambda > 0$, $AI(K)$ measures magnitude of the Generalized Lorenz Dominance Transgressions in the collection relative to the Generalized Lorenz Transvariation. Natural values for λ are 1, whereby $AI(K)$ corresponds to the cumulated Generalized Lorenz Dominance transgressions relative to GLT(K), $1/(K\text{-}1)!$, whereby $AI(K)$ corresponds to the average Lorenz Dominance transgression value relative to $LT(K)$ over all pairwise comparisons and $1/K^*$ where K^* is the number of instances in which $I\left(L_i(p)-L_j(p)\right)$ is non-zero whereby $AI(K)$ corresponds to the average Lorenz Dominance transgression value relative to $LT(K)$ over all pairwise comparisons that exhibited transgressions. In each of these cases when the collection of Lorenz curves do not intersect at all $AI(K) = 0$ and the respective Gini's are unambiguously ordered, when they intersect there is potential ambiguity in the ordering and $AI(K) > 0$.

Suppose the third variant of Υ will be used with the interpretation that $AI(K)$ is the average value of the transgression area when there is one. Thinking about it from an inferential perspective for the moment, if one wished to test the hypothesis that any ordering in the class was unambiguous and our critical value was based upon an average value of 1% of overall Transvariation for all transgressions, then a version of the central limit theorem would give us $AI(K) \sim a\ N(0.01, 0.0099/K)$ yielding a simple upper tailed test of size α with a critical value $C = 0.01 + \sqrt{(0.0099/K)}Z_{1-\alpha}$ for example.

Finally, to measure the extent of discord in the ranking of a state across the indices the standard deviation of a states rank generated by each index will be averaged over the states, clearly when there is complete accord this average will be 0, when there is much discord the average will be large.

Assessing the Extent of Incoherent Ranking

An indication of the actual variability in ordering a collection of K distributions using a variety of J indicators can be obtained by summing over nations the standard deviation of each nation's ranking across ranking instruments in a given class. Let R_{kj} be nation k's rank for the jth ranking instrument for $k = 1,\ldots, K$ nations and $j = 1,\ldots, J$ instruments, then a Ranking Variation Index (RVI), an index of the variability in ranking, is given by:

$$\mathrm{RVI} = \frac{1}{K}\sum_{k=1}^{K}\sqrt{\sum_{j=1}^{J}\frac{\left(R_{kj} - \frac{\sum_{j=1}^{J} R_{kj}}{J}\right)^2}{J-1}}$$

6.6 Determination of Ambiguity Groupings: Unambiguous Cuts and Groups

Frequently, especially for low values of i, there will not be unanimity of ranking in a collection; however, these ideas can be extended to the ranking of a particular alternative or subgroups of alternatives. Intuitively if, at a given order, an alternative is strictly dominated by all alternatives above it, and strictly dominates all alternatives below it, it will be unambiguously ranked at that order and all higher orders since there will always be the same group of alternatives ranked above it and the same group of alternatives ranked below it no matter which index in the appropriate class is chosen. Such an alternative provides a very natural dividing line between groupings since all members of the lower group will be unambiguously ranked below all members of the upper group. Indeed such an alternative need not exist in order to successfully distinguish the groups; all that is needed is to show that the lower envelope of the lower group is stochastically dominated by the upper envelope of the higher group to establish a partition between the groups.

Such an approach can also be thought of as partitioning the collection at that order into two groups wherein ambiguity may exist within each group but there will be no pairwise ambiguity between any between pairing of an alternative from each group. In such a circumstance, the lower envelope of the dominated group would be dominated by the upper envelope of the dominating group at the appropriate order. Indeed, even in the absence of the particular alternative the upper and lower groups could be deemed "partitionable" since an artificial partitioning alternative can be constructed as a linear combination of the two envelopes. This idea can be used to determine non-ambiguity groupings or sets of distributions between which there is no ambiguity in ordering. To do so the concepts of subgroup *i*th order upper (FUE^i) and lower (FLE^i) envelopes and Transvariation (TR^i) are employed.

Suppose that, in the collection of $k = 1,\ldots, K$ alternatives, there exists a $k^* \in (1, K)$ such that:

$$\begin{aligned}&\text{FLE}^i_{k^*}(x)\left\{= \min\left(F^i_1(x), F^i_2(x),\ldots F^i_{k^*}(x)\right)\right\} \geq \\ &\text{FUE}^i_{k^*+1}(x)\left\{= \max\left(F^i_{k^*+1}(x), F^i_{k^*+2}(x),\ldots F^i_K(x)\right)\right\}\end{aligned} \tag{6.6}$$

with strict inequality somewhere (in effect the upper envelope of the $k^* + 1$ grouping stochastically dominates the lower envelope of the k^* grouping). Then it will be the case that:

$$F^i_a(x) \geq F^i_b(x) \text{ and } F^i_a(x) > F^i_b(x) \text{ for some } x > 0 \text{ for all } a \in \left[1,\ldots,k^*\right] \text{ and } b \in \left[k^*+1,\ldots,K\right]$$

That is to say, any distribution indexed 1 to k^* will be dominated at the ith order by any distribution indexed $k^* + 1$ to K. Indeed a fictitious partitioning alternative $F^{i*}(x)$ can be envisaged as some linear combination of the upper envelope of the dominating group and the lower envelope of the dominated group so that: $F^{i*}(x,k^*,\alpha)=\alpha\text{FUE}^i_{k^*}(x)+(1-\alpha)\text{FLE}^i_{k^*+1}(x)$ for $\alpha\in[0,1]$.

Interpreting ambiguity as an expression of uncertainty these ideas can be used to form ordered groups where there is certainty with respect to between-group rankings or classes but uncertainty about within-group rankings. Thus given the right orientation of distributions, poor, middle and high income groups could be determined. As a corollary, if (6.6) can be established for $k^* = 1,\ldots, K\text{-}1$, then the collection of distributions is perfectly partitionable or segmented at the ith order of integration and there will be no ambiguity of indices appropriate for order i and above.

6.7 An Empirical Application

The Data

To illustrate the application of these ideas, the evolution of Eurozone national income distributions are compared over time. Four temporally equi-spaced waves: 2006, 2009, 2012 and 2015 were chosen from the cross-sectional component of The European Union Survey on Income and Living Conditions, a collection of annual national surveys of socio-economic conditions of individuals and households in EU countries (the Eurozone is defined as those countries that are currently using the euro). Since data for Malta are only available from the 2008 wave, this country is excluded from analysis leaving 18 Eurozone countries. Income is the total household net disposable income obtained by aggregation of all income sources from all household members net of direct taxes and social contributions. All observations are weighted by cross-sectional weights and income is PPP adjusted. Assuming cohabitation generates economies of scale in consumption and therefore needs do not grow proportionally with household size, incomes are age and size-adjusted using the so-called modified-OECD equivalence scale which assigns a value of 1 to the household head, of 0.5 to each additional adult member aged 14 and above and of 0.3 to each child aged below 14. Gaussian kernel estimates of the distributions are employed throughout. To get an impression of the inherently different shapes and locations of the income distributions in the Eurozone, kernel estimates of the pdfs are graphed in Fig. 6.1.

Exploring the Impact of Ambiguity

Using data on 18 Eurozone countries over four observation years, six second order income wellbeing indices are compared: five drawn from Blackorby and Donaldson (1978) and the second order Utopia index drawn from Anderson, Post, and Whang (2018). Blackorby and Donaldson (1978) developed implicit income wellbeing indices underlying four income inequality measures (Gini, Thiel's Entropy, Coefficient of Variation and Atkinson) which are outlined in Table 3.1 in Chap. 3. Atkinson's index has an inequality aversion parameter "*r*" which for present purposes was set at 0.5 and 0.0. The Utopia index (Anderson et al. 2019)

$$U(k)=\frac{\int_a^b\left\{\max\left(F_1(x),F_2(x)\ldots,F_K(x)\right)-F_k(x)\right\}dx}{\int_a^b\left\{\max\left(F_1(x),F_2(x)\ldots,F_K(x)\right)-\min\left(F_1(x),F_2(x)\ldots,F_K(x)\right)\right\}dx}$$

was also included as a second order measure though it does not have a companion inequality measure. In contrast to inequality adjusted wellbeing indices, the Utopia Index considers all feasible outcome distributions and all welfare indices that are monotonically increasing and concave in income. Seven relative inequality measures were compared. Figure 6.1 presents mutually coherent scaled diagrams of the probability density functions for the 18 nations. As is evident, the distributions are anatomically very different; they clearly overlap and present much opportunity for ambiguity.

Table 6.1 reports the ambiguity indices for the four observation years at one, two and three orders of integration. Notice the dramatic reduction in ambiguity as the order of comparison increases. There is a suggestion that overall the potential for ambiguity declined substantially between 2006 and 2009 but grew steadily thereafter. Table 6.2 reports the wellbeing ranks and Rank Variation Indices for the corresponding years. There was no doubt a structural break existed between 2006 and 2009 given the financial crisis of 2007–2008 which may have something to do with this, witness the dramatic declines of Belgium and Germany relative to France and Finland for example. More importantly, it confirms the notion that the potential for ambiguity diminishes with the order of integration. With the exception of 2006, the actual lack of coherence in

Table 6.1 Ambiguity indices for distributions

	2006	*2009*	*2012*	*2015*
Leshno–Levy				
First order	0.2811	0.2091	0.2059	0.2405
Second order	0.2199	0.0889	0.1026	0.1277
Third order	0.0094	0.0036	0.0042	0.0056
TRAM Indices				
First order	0.7345	0.7554	0.7138	0.6761
Second order	0.9846	0.9944	0.9327	0.7921
Third order	0.9965	0.9965	0.9984	0.8912

Source: Anderson and Thomas (2019)

the indices measured by the sum of standard deviations of nation ranks increased as expected in accord with the ambiguity indices.

As the partial moment representation of $F^i(x)$ suggests, higher order integration attaches more weight to values of x at the low end of the range of x; thus, following Tukey's "Rootgram" approach (Tukey 1977), the effect of higher order integrals can be mimicked by sample weighting observations at the bottom end of the distribution by re-weighting $f(x_m)$ by $\left(2\left(1-F\left(x_m\right)\right)\right)^{1/h}$ with $h = 2$ which can be shown to preserve its probability density nature. Note that the corresponding low end adjusted inequality statistics which mimic higher than second order comparisons had uniformly lower aggregate standard deviation statistics signifying a greater deal of coherency and lack of ambiguity as is to be expected (Table 6.3).

A similar analysis can be pursued for unit free relative inequality measures in terms of their corresponding Lorenz curves. In this case, seven alternative measures are contemplated (refer to Table 3.1 for details)—A: Gini; B: Theils entropic measure; C: The Coefficient of Variation; D: Atkinson (r = 0.25); E: Atkinson (r = 0.75); F: Inter-quartile Range/Median; and G: Inter-quartile Range/Median. Details of the corresponding ambiguity index computations, its components and the Gini coefficient range are reported in Table 6.4 and the inequality index rankings and their average standard deviations are reported in Table 6.5. Note that in this case the ambiguity index diminishes systematically over the period and, as expected, so does the average standard deviation of the rankings.

Table 6.2 Inequality adjusted income wellbeing index ranks

	2006						*2009*						*2012*						*2015*					
Nation	*A*	*B*	*C*	*D*	*E*	*F*	*A*	*B*	*C*	*D*	*E*	*F*	*A*	*B*	*C*	*D*	*E*	*F*	*A*	*B*	*C*	*D*	*E*	*F*
Austria	3	3	3	3	3	3	5	5	5	5	5	5	5	5	5	5	5	5	4	5	4	4	5	4
Belgium	5	5	5	5	5	5	8	7	8	8	8	9	7	7	8	8	7	8	7	6	7	7	7	7
Cyprus	8	8	7	8	8	7	7	8	7	7	7	7	8	8	7	7	8	7	10	11	10	10	11	10
Germany	4	4	4	4	4	4	6	6	6	6	6	6	6	6	6	6	6	6	6	7	6	6	6	6
Estonia	15	16	15	15	15	15	16	16	16	16	16	16	16	16	16	16	16	16	14	14	13	13	14	13
Greece	13	13	13	13	13	13	13	13	13	13	13	13	15	14	15	15	15	15	17	16	18	17	17	18
Spain	12	12	12	12	12	12	12	12	11	12	12	11	12	12	12	12	12	12	12	13	12	12	12	12
Finland	7	7	8	7	7	9	4	4	4	4	4	4	4	4	3	3	4	3	3	3	3	3	3	3
France	6	6	6	6	6	6	3	3	3	3	3	3	3	3	2	2	3	2	2	2	2	2	2	2
Ireland	9	9	9	9	9	8	9	9	9	9	9	8	10	11	10	10	10	10	8	9	8	8	8	8
Italy	10	10	10	10	10	10	10	11	10	10	10	10	9	9	9	9	9	9	9	8	9	9	9	9
Lithuania	16	17	16	16	17	16	17	17	17	17	17	17	17	17	17	17	17	17	16	17	16	16	16	16
Luxembourg	1	1	1	1	1	1	1	1	1	1	1	1	1	1	1	1	1	1	1	1	1	1	1	1
Latvia	18	18	18	18	18	18	18	18	18	18	18	18	18	18	18	18	18	18	18	18	17	18	18	17
Netherlands	2	2	2	2	2	2	2	2	2	2	2	2	2	2	4	4	2	4	5	4	5	5	4	5
Portugal	14	14	14	14	14	14	14	15	14	14	14	14	14	15	14	14	14	14	15	15	14	15	15	14
Slovenia	11	11	11	11	11	11	11	10	12	11	11	12	11	10	11	11	11	11	11	10	11	11	10	11
Slovakia	17	15	17	17	16	17	15	14	15	15	15	15	13	13	13	13	13	13	13	12	15	14	13	15
RVI			0.1957						0.2190						0.2733						0.4477			

Source: Anderson and Thomas (2019)

Table 6.3 Inequality adjusted income wellbeing indices under transformed distributions

Low end adjusted	*2006*						*2009*						*2012*						*2015*					
Nation	*A*	*B*	*C*	*D*	*E*	*F*	*A*	*B*	*C*	*D*	*E*	*F*	*A*	*B*	*C*	*D*	*E*	*F*	*A*	*B*	*C*	*D*	*E*	*F*
Austria	3	3	3	3	3	3	5	5	5	5	5	5	5	5	5	5	5	5	4	5	4	4	5	5
Belgium	5	5	5	5	5	5	8	7	8	8	7	8	7	7	8	7	7	7	7	6	7	7	7	7
Cyprus	8	8	8	8	8	8	7	8	7	7	8	7	8	8	7	8	8	8	10	11	10	10	11	10
Germany	4	4	4	4	4	4	6	6	6	6	6	6	6	6	6	6	6	6	6	7	6	6	6	6
Estonia	15	15	15	15	15	15	16	16	16	16	16	16	16	16	16	16	16	16	14	14	13	14	14	14
Greece	13	13	13	13	13	13	13	13	13	13	13	13	15	15	15	15	15	15	17	17	17	17	17	17
Spain	12	12	12	12	12	12	12	12	12	12	12	12	12	12	12	12	12	12	12	13	12	12	12	12
Finland	7	7	7	7	7	7	4	4	4	4	4	4	4	4	3	3	4	4	3	3	3	3	3	3
France	6	6	6	6	6	6	3	3	3	3	3	3	3	3	2	2	3	3	2	1	2	2	2	2
Ireland	9	9	9	9	9	9	9	9	9	9	9	9	10	11	10	10	10	10	8	8	8	8	8	8
Italy	10	10	10	10	10	10	10	11	10	10	10	10	9	9	9	9	9	9	9	9	9	9	9	9
Lithuania	16	17	16	16	17	16	17	17	17	17	17	17	17	17	17	17	17	17	16	16	16	16	16	16
Luxembourg	1	1	1	1	1	1	1	1	1	1	1	1	1	1	1	1	1	1	1	2	1	1	1	1
Latvia	18	18	18	18	18	18	18	18	18	18	18	18	18	18	18	18	18	18	18	18	18	18	18	18
Netherlands	2	2	2	2	2	2	2	2	2	2	2	2	2	2	4	4	2	2	5	4	5	5	4	4
Portugal	14	14	14	14	14	14	14	15	14	14	14	14	14	14	14	14	14	14	15	15	15	15	15	15
Slovenia	11	11	11	11	11	11	11	10	11	11	11	11	11	10	11	11	11	11	11	10	11	11	10	11
Slovakia	17	16	17	17	16	17	15	14	15	15	15	15	13	13	13	13	13	13	13	12	14	13	13	13
RVI			0.0574						0.1481						0.2054						0.2895			

Source: Anderson and Thomas (2019)

Table 6.4 Ambiguity indices for Lorenz curves

	2006	*2009*	*2012*	*2015*
Relative inequality ambiguity index	0.6757	0.4551	0.4786	0.3636
Gini coefficient range (max–min)	0.1560	0.1548	0.1215	0.1280
Total Lorenz Transvariation (Leo 2017)	0.0795	0.0778	0.0625	0.0669
Aggregate Lorenz Transgression (Zheng 2016)	0.0537	0.0354	0.0299	0.0243

Source: Anderson and Thomas (2019)

Partition Analysis

Using data from the 18 Eurozone countries over four observation years, cumulative and integrated cumulative densities are pairwise compared by ordering nations by their average household income. Each country is compared with the nation with next highest average income using θ_c and θ_{ic}, the analogs of Leshno–Levy relative magnitude of the transgression region for cumulative and integrated cumulative analyses. In this context H_0: $\theta = 0$ against $\theta > 0$ can be construed as tests of dominance at the corresponding order of integration. Table 6.6 reports the number of $\theta = 0$ cases out of the 17 pairwise comparison of empirical kernel estimates of nation distributions. It should be emphasized that this is not a statistical test; it is simply the number of instances where the curves do not cross for two nations with proximate average incomes. For such pairs ranking by indices appropriate to that order would be unambiguous and coherent.

Of course these are simple pairwise comparisons and do not reflect partitions of the whole collections. To explore possible partitions, the collection of nations with average incomes less than or equal to nation *k*s is treated as a "lower" group ($LG(k)$) and the collection with average incomes above nation *k*s is treated as the "upper" group ($UG(k)$). $\mathrm{FUE}^{i}_{UG(k)}(x)$ and $\mathrm{FLE}^{i}_{LG(k)}(x)$ are compared and θ^i for this pair computed under the presumption that FUE dominates FLE. If $\theta^i = 0$, a partition is established. Again, it should be emphasized that this is not a statistical test; very low values of θ^i could be insignificantly different from 0 (see Anderson et al. 2018b for possible tests). Using an arbitrary partition criterion for the Leshno–Levy index between envelopes of <0.0002 as insignificant, Tables 6.7 and 6.8 report the comparisons.

Note the poor ability to determine "partitionable" groups, especially in 2009 and 2015, in this most general case (all indicators monotonic non-decreasing in x). If all measures in a given year were 0 then the 18 nations

Table 6.5 Inequality index rankings

	2006							2009							2012							2015						
Nation	*A*	*B*	*C*	*D*	*E*	*F*	*G*	*A*	*B*	*C*	*D*	*E*	*F*	*G*	*A*	*B*	*C*	*D*	*E*	*F*	*G*	*A*	*B*	*C*	*D*	*E*	*F*	*G*
Austria	2	3	3	2	2	4	4	6	5	5	7	6	4	4	8	8	7	9	8	5	5	6	6	6	6	6	5	5
Belgium	5	5	5	5	5	9	8	7	6	6	6	5	9	8	7	6	6	7	7	8	7	8	7	7	8	7	8	8
Cyprus	11	10	9	10	10	11	13	11	11	11	11	11	12	15	11	11	12	10	11	13	16	12	12	12	11	12	14	14
Germany	6	6	6	7	6	5	5	9	9	8	9	9	6	6	9	9	8	8	9	9	9	9	9	9	9	9	9	9
Estonia	14	15	15	14	15	12	11	14	14	15	13	14	13	13	14	15	15	14	14	16	15	15	15	15	15	15	17	17
Greece	15	14	14	15	14	15	15	13	13	13	14	13	11	11	13	13	13	13	13	10	10	13	13	14	13	13	11	11
Spain	13	13	13	13	13	13	16	15	15	14	15	15	15	17	16	14	14	16	15	17	18	14	14	13	14	14	15	16
Finland	9	8	8	8	8	6	7	8	7	7	8	8	7	7	6	5	4	6	5	7	6	5	5	4	5	5	6	6
France	7	7	7	6	7	7	6	5	4	4	5	4	5	5	4	3	3	4	4	4	4	3	2	1	2	2	4	4
Ireland	12	12	11	11	12	17	17	10	10	10	10	10	14	16	10	10	10	11	10	12	11	10	10	11	10	10	12	13
Italy	10	10	10	12	11	10	10	12	12	12	12	12	10	10	12	12	11	12	12	11	14	11	11	10	12	11	10	10
Lithuania	16	16	16	16	16	14	12	16	16	16	16	16	17	14	15	16	16	15	16	14	13	17	17	17	17	17	16	15
Luxembourg	3	2	2	4	3	8	9	3	2	2	2	2	8	9	2	2	2	2	2	6	8	4	4	3	4	4	7	7
Latvia	18	18	18	18	18	18	18	18	18	18	18	18	18	18	18	18	18	18	18	18	17	18	18	18	18	18	18	18
Netherlands	1	1	1	1	1	1	2	1	1	1	1	1	1	2	1	1	1	1	1	1	1	1	1	2	1	1	2	2
Portugal	17	17	17	17	17	16	14	17	17	17	17	17	16	12	17	17	17	17	17	15	12	16	16	16	16	16	13	12
Slovenia	4	4	4	4	4	3	3	2	3	3	3	3	2	3	3	4	5	3	3	2	2	7	8	8	7	8	3	3
Slovakia	8	9	12	9	9	2	1	4	8	9	4	7	3	1	5	7	9	5	6	3	3	2	3	5	3	3	1	1
RVI				1.296							1.244							1.161							0.964			

Source: Anderson and Thomas (2019)

Table 6.6 Separating cut counts

	2006	*2009*	*2012*	*2015*
First order comparison	3	4	4	3
Second order comparison (additional, first order dominance implies second order dominance)	+5	+6	+5	+6

Source: Anderson and Thomas (2019)

Table 6.7 First order comparison of relative transgression area for $\mathrm{FUE}^{1}_{UG(k)}(x) - \mathrm{FLE}^{1}_{LG(k)}(x) \le 0$

MeanRank 1 low	*2006*		*2009*		*2012*		*2015*	
	Id	*contra*	*Id*	*contra*	*Id*	*contra*	*Id*	*contra*
1	14	0.3303	14	0.7685	**14**	**0.0000**	6	0.4710
2	18	0.6008	12	0.5774	**12**	**0.0000**	14	0.2717
3	12	0.0052	5	0.5872	5	0.1055	12	0.3220
4	**5**	**0.0000**	18	0.0595	**6**	**0.0000**	18	0.5134
5	16	0.0579	16	0.0370	16	0.3543	16	0.7372
6	6	0.1650	6	0.0125	18	0.0402	5	0.2482
7	7	0.4810	17	0.4991	7	0.4242	7	0.0005
8	17	0.0635	7	0.1499	17	0.0806	17	0.2436
9	11	0.2818	11	0.4635	10	0.0639	3	0.0861
10	8	0.8169	2	0.6360	11	0.4560	11	0.5349
11	10	0.9760	10	0.3547	2	0.5122	10	0.0126
12	3	0.7873	3	0.1627	3	0.1010	2	0.1464
13	9	0.8737	4	0.2616	4	0.3785	4	0.2358
14	2	0.1002	1	0.0858	1	0.7743	15	0.2888
15	4	0.0996	8	0.0062	15	0.7370	1	0.0069
16	1	0.0252	9	0.3945	8	0.8636	8	0.4333
17	15	0.0254	15	0.0086	**9**	**0.0000**	9	0.1206
18	13	0.0254	13	0.0086	**13**	**0.0000**	13	0.1206

Source: Anderson and Thomas (2019)

Key: Austria (1) Belgium (2) Cyprus (3) Germany (4) Estonia (5) Greece (6) Spain (7) Finland (8) France (9) Ireland (10) Italy (11) Lithuania (12) Luxembourg (13) Latvia (14) Netherlands (15) Portugal (16) Slovenia (17) Slovakia (18). Elements in bold are partition points

would be unambiguously ranked in that year for all first order indices but there are only five such partitions over the four comparison years. Looking at the more restrictive class ($i = 2$) in Table 6.8 affords a greater degree of discrimination.

Table 6.8 Second order comparison of relative transgression area for $\text{FUE}^2_{UG(k)}(x) - \text{FLE}^2_{LG(k)}(x) \leq 0$

Rank of mean (1= low)	*2006*		*2009*		*2012*		*2015*	
	Id	*contra*	*Id*	*contra*	*Id*	*contra*	*Id*	*contra*
1	**14**	**0.0000**	**14**	**0.0000**	**14**	**0.0000**	6	0.3508
2	18	0.0666	**12**	**0.0000**	**12**	**0.0000**	**14**	**0.0000**
3	**12**	**0.0001**	**5**	**0.0001**	5	0.0003	**12**	**0.0000**
4	**5**	**0.0000**	18	0.0046	**6**	**0.0000**	18	0.4500
5	**16**	**0.0000**	**16**	**0.0001**	**16**	**0.0000**	16	0.4115
6	**6**	**0.0000**	**6**	**0.0000**	18	0.0025	5	0.0332
7	**7**	**0.0000**	17	0.9543	7	0.0003	**7**	**0.0000**
8	17	0.0063	7	0.0152	17	0.0107	17	0.1312
9	11	0.0003	11	0.0007	10	0.0089	3	0.0115
10	8	0.9037	2	0.9732	11	0.0008	11	0.3064
11	10	0.6230	10	0.1069	2	0.5519	**10**	**0.0000**
12	3	0.0031	3	0.0034	3	0.0012	2	0.0331
13	9	0.0242	4	0.0069	4	0.0047	4	0.0012
14	2	0.0018	1	0.0018	**1**	**0.0002**	15	0.1846
15	4	0.0005	**8**	**0.0000**	15	0.4509	1	0.0011
16	**1**	**0.0000**	**9**	**0.0000**	8	0.6681	8	0.0014
17	15	0.0048	15	0.0013	**9**	**0.0000**	9	0.0705
18	13	0.0048	13	0.0013	**13**	**0.0000**	13	0.0705

Source: Anderson and Thomas (2019)

Key: Austria (1) Belgium (2) Cyprus (3) Germany (4) Estonia (5) Greece (6) Spain (7) Finland (8) France (9) Ireland (10) Italy (11) Lithuania (12) Luxembourg (13) Latvia (14) Netherlands (15) Portugal (16) Slovenia (17) Slovakia (18). Elements in bold are partition points; note that there are several partition points in the lower groups

Considering the class of monotonically increasing concave indicators affords much more discrimination and better determination of classes, now there are 24 possible partitions and an obvious reduction in ambiguity. Broadly speaking this suggests that three partition classes can be determined by the 7th and 16th ranked distributions in 2006, the 6th and 15th ranked in 2009, the 5th and 14th in 2012 and the 7th and 10th in 2015. Hence, the resultant middle class can be seen as narrowing over the observation years. There also appears to be an absence of ambiguity in the poor nation group so determined with very little separation in the higher and middle groups.

6.8 Conclusions

When indices are used to rank a collection of societal groupings with regard to some aspect of those communities, it is often the case that alternative, equally appropriate, indices are available and frequently they report conflicting orderings. This ambiguity need not be a consequence of sampling variability; it could well be an inherent property of the juxtaposition of the societal distributions of the aspect of interest, engendering "unmeasurable" uncertainty as to the ordering even in the presence of full information (when the distributions are known with certainty).

Here the nature of this ambiguity has been studied and found to depend upon the nature of separation that prevails between the respective distributions that are being compared, the greater the separation the lesser the potential for ambiguity. Furthermore, the more restrictive are the societal preferences that the indicators reflect, the less pervasive will ambiguity be. The analysis also suggests a method for partitioning nations into ambiguity groupings wherein, while there will be no ambiguity in between-group comparisons there may be ambiguity in within-group comparisons. Two ambiguity indices have been developed and applied to a collection of 18 Eurozone national household income distributions over the years 2006, 2009, 2012 and 2015; they both indicate a decline and then an increase in the presence of ambiguity in the rankings. Some well-known inequality averse income wellbeing indicators and inequality indicators were examined which clearly exhibited contradictory rankings.

References

Anderson, G., Linton, O., & Thomas, J. (2017). Similarity, Dissimilarity and Exceptionality: Generalizing Gini's Transvariation to Measure "Differentness" in Many Distributions. *Metron, 75*, 161–180.

Anderson, G. J., & Thomas, J. (2019). *Structural Ambiguity in Wellbeing Indices.* Toronto: University of Toronto. Mimeo.

Anderson, G., Post, T., & Whang, Y.-J. (2019). Somewhere Between Utopia and Dystopia: Choosing From Multiple Incomparable Prospects. *Forthcoming Journal of Business and Economic Statistics.*

Anderson, G., Pittau, G., Zelli, R., & Thomas, J. (2018b). Income Inequality, Cohesiveness and Commonality in the Euro Area: A Semi-Parametric Boundary-free Analysis. *Econometrics, 6*(2), 15. https://doi.org/10.3390/econometrics6020015.

Anderson, G. J., Linton, O., & Whang, Y.-J. (2019). *Measuring Differentness in Collections of Distributions: Multilateral Transvariation and the Distributional Gini Coefficient*. Mimeo University of Toronto.

Blackorby, C., & Donaldson, D. (1978). Measures of Relative Equality and Their Meaning in Terms of Social Welfare. *Journal of Economic Theory, 18*, 59–80.

Dagum, C. (1968). *Nonparametric and Gaussian Bivariate Transvariation Theory: Its Application to Economics*. Econometric Research Program, Princeton University, Research Memorandum n. 99.

Davidson, R., & Duclos, J.-Y. (2000). Statistical Inference for Stochastic Dominance and for the Measurement of Poverty and Inequality. *Econometrica, 68*(6), 1435–1464.

Gini, C. (1912). *Variabilità e mutabilità*. Reprinted in Pizetti, E., & Salvemini, T. (Eds.). (1955). *Memorie di metodologica statistica*. Rome: Libreria Eredi Virgilio Veschi.

Gini, C. (1916). Il Concetto di Transvariazione e le sue Prime Applicazioni. In *Transvariazione*, ed. C. Gini. Libreria Goliardica, (1{55).

Hey, J. D., & Lambert, P. J. (1980). Relative Deprivation and the Gini Coefficient: Comment. *Quarterly Journal of Economics, 95*, 567–573.

Leo, T. W. (2017). On the Asymptotic Distribution of (Generalized) Lorenz Transvariation Measures. *Metron, 75*(2), 195–213.

Leshno, M., & Levy, H. (2002). Preferred by "All" and Preferred by "Most" Decision Makers: Almost Stochastic Dominance. *Management Science, 48*(8), 1074–1085.

Mookherjee, D., & Shorrocks, A. (1982). A Decomposition Analysis of the Trend in UK Income Inequality. *Economic Journal, 92*(368), 886–902.

Tukey, J. W. (1977). *Exploratory Data Analysis*. Reading: Addison-Wesley.

Yitzahki, S. (1994). Economic Distance and Overlapping of Distributions. *Journal of Econometrics, 61*, 147–159.

Zheng, B. (2016). *Almost Lorenz Dominance* (University of Colorado, Denver, Discussion Paper).

CHAPTER 7

Some Applications

7.1 Introduction

In this chapter, five very diverse examples of multilateral comparisons from a variety of situations are presented. The first, drawn from Anderson and Thomas (2019) is a comparison of income distributions drawn across Aboriginal–non-Aboriginal, gender and urban–rural lines, highlights the polarization–inequality distinction in revealing a society that is becoming more unequal overall yet more similar across its various divides. The second, drawn from Anderson et al. (2018), is an examination of equality of opportunity in the German education system illustrating a multidimensional application of multilateral comparison techniques. An application evaluating portfolio manager performance drawn from Anderson, Post and Whang (2018) is the subject matter of the third example and an analysis of crop yields in Sub Saharan East Africa irrigation schemes is reported in the fourth example. The fifth example is an illustration of how the techniques can be used in a multivariate dynamic setting looking at the progress of the Human Development Index for 164 nations.

G. Anderson, *Multilateral Wellbeing Comparison in a Many Dimensioned World*, Global Perspectives on Wealth and Distribution,
https://doi.org/10.1007/978-3-030-21130-1_7

7.2 An Example of Canadian Unidimensional Income Distribution Analysis

There is little or no chance that there would be complete income equality in a society or any of its subgroups; if there were, the income distribution would be degenerate and collapse to a point which would be the average value of income. However, it may be expected that the subgroups in a society may have similar income levels and perhaps be equal in their unequalness. This can be examined by comparing the income distributions of the various subgroups in a society which is what Anderson and Thomas (2019) did—some of the results of which are reported here.

There has been concern that the well documented increase in Canadian income inequality (Green et al. 2016; Fortin et al. 2012) has not been equally shared among its various Aboriginal–non-Aboriginal, urban–rural and gender divides or constituencies. Aboriginal peoples have, on average, lower incomes than non-Aboriginals and similar urban–rural and male–female dichotomies have prompted Canadian parliamentarians from all sides to argue that the nation faces a moral imperative to close such gaps (Anderson and Thomas 2019).

Based upon Gibrat's law (Gibrat 1931), theoretical stochastic process models of income predict increasing inequality among collections of individuals whose income processes are similar (Friedman 1957; Hall 1978; Battistin et al. 2009; Blundell and Preston 1998; Browning and Lusardi 1996). On the other hand, the growth and convergence literature (Hahn and Matthews 1964; Durlauf 1996; Galor 1996; Quah 1996a, b, 1997; Solow 1956) argues that with absent trade barriers and with the free factor flows, constituency distributions should converge, that is, become more similar. However, increasing overall inequality neither implies nor is implied by increasing inequality between constituencies since, with process heterogeneity over groups, it is quite possible for overall inequality to increase and between-group inequality to diminish simultaneously. In effect, constituencies can either diverge or segment with their respective distributions ceasing to overlap, or they can become more alike with increasingly overlapping distributions (which is the reason polarization and inequality measures are distinct and can go in opposite directions). The matter is in essence an empirical question which can be approached with the Distributional Gini coefficient (DISGINI) coefficient since it can be used as a convergence/segmentation index (when all constituencies converge it takes the value 0, when all subgroup distributions are segmented its value will be 1).

Data from Statistics Canada's National Household Survey (NHS) public use microdata files for 2001, 2006 and 2011 are employed to construct kernel estimates of personal before tax income distributions for the observation years 2000, 2005 and 2010 for males and females in five categories: Urban Non-Aboriginal, Rural Non-Aboriginal, Metis, Inuit and North American Indian yielding ten constituencies. For this data set, Anderson and Thomas (2019) report that overall inequality increased over the period with a Gini coefficient 0.4624 in 2001 rising to 0.4967 in 2011; with the exception of Rural Non-Aboriginal Females and Metis Females, Gini coefficients for all constituencies rose. Table 7.1 reports the estimates of weighted and unweighted versions of the multilateral version of Ginis Transvariation, MGT, and the Distributional Gini coefficient, DISGINI, with Tables 7.2 and 7.3 reporting the corresponding significance tests.

Unweighted and weighted versions of both MGT and DISGINI yield contradictory results, with the former recording significant convergence over the period while the latter recording significant divergence. Clearly, weighting matters here in diluting the impact of Aboriginal community distributions relative to non-Aboriginal distributions, leading one to be somewhat circumspect in declaring success in closing Aboriginal–non-Aboriginal, urban–rural and gender gaps. In essence, if a representative agent view of the world is taken the designated constituencies are diverging whereas when weighted by their importance in the overall population, they are not.

Table 7.1 Multilateral Transvariations and Distributional Ginis

	Multilateral Transvariation (std error)		*Distributional Gini (std error)*	
	Unweighted	*Weighted*	*Equally weighted*	*Weighted*
2001	0.08665	0.03683	0.06716	0.07713
	(0.00173)	(0.00076)	(0.00104)	(0.00106)
2006	0.08764	0.03902	0.06642	0.08575
	(0.00167)	(0.00076)	(0.00101)	(0.00107)
2009	0.08297	0.03849	0.05984	0.07946
	(0.00162)	(0.00073)	(0.00095)	(0.00102)

Source: Authors own calculations

Table 7.2 Multilateral Transvariation differences

Weighted	*2001–2006*	*2001–2011*	*2006–2011*
Difference	−0.00219	−0.00166	0.00053
Standard error	0.00004	0.00004	0.00004
$P(\text{Diff} \leq 0)$	1.00000	1.00000	0.00000
Unweighted	*2001–2006*	*2001–2011*	*2006–2011*
Difference	−0.00099	0.00368	0.00467
Standard error	0.00009	0.00009	0.00008
$P(\text{Diff} \leq 0)$	1.00000	0.00000	0.00000

Source: Authors own calculations

Table 7.3 Weighted and unweighted overlap measures and Distributional Ginis

2003 (Weights L 0.3425 M 0.3534 H 0.3041)	*Unidimensional comparison*		*Multidimensional comparison*	
OV_{LM} (standard error)	0.43887	(0.01569)	0.91111	(0.00900)
OV_{LH} (standard error)	0.41664	(0.01559)	0.88404	(0.01012)
OV_{MH} (standard error)	0.61504	(0.01539)	0.23242	(0.01336)
Weighted DISGINI (standard error)	0.34010	(0.00849)	0.20675	(0.00701)
Unweighted DISGINI (standard error)	0.33988	(0.00849)	0.21609	(0.00708)
2009 (Weights L 0.2698 M 0.3817 H 0.3485)	*Unidimensional comparison*		*Multidimensional comparison*	
OV_{LM} (standard error)	0.49056	(0.01581)	0.90323	(0.00935)
OV_{LH} (standard error)	0.35088	(0.01509)	0.91258	(0.00893)
OV_{MH} (standard error)	0.71453	(0.01428)	0.98301	(0.00409)
Weighted Gini (standard Error)	0.30295	(0.00832)	0.04190	(0.00567)
Unweighted Gini (standard error)	0.32090	(0.00835)	0.04471	(0.00588)

7.3 A Multidimensional Equal Opportunity Example: German Educational Attainment

Comparing distributions from a univariate perspective is common in the Equal Opportunity literature (see e.g. Lefranc et al. 2009) though it is usually performed in order to see whether or not there is equality of opportunity. Atkinson (2012) and Sen (2009) have argued that it is unlikely that the transcendental state of equality of opportunity would ever prevail; rather, we should seek to measure progress toward such a state. Here, based on Anderson, Pittau, Zelli, and Fruehauf (2019b), an example in a multivariate paradigm is reported that yields an index of the extent to which Equality of Opportunity prevails, which can be employed to examine the extent to which progress toward the Equal Opportunity imperative has been made.

In the Equal Opportunity/Social Mobility literature, the focus of attention is the degree of variability in circumstance conditioned outcome distributions. The ultimate policy objective in equalizing opportunities or securing social mobility is that such circumstance conditioned outcome distributions should be identical (or parties should be appropriately compensated). Progress toward such a goal can be measured by the extent to which the variability in such distributions has been reduced, the question is, how unequal are the circumstance conditioned outcome distributions? DISGINI is an appropriate tool for examining this.[1]

The results of the first Program for International Student Assessment (PISA) in 2003 were a disappointment for Germany and raised concerns about the extent to which a child's circumstances limited his/her academic outcomes (child academic achievements were strongly correlated with parental economic and academic success; children of immigrant workers in the Gastarbeiter Program faced extraordinary challenges because German was their second language). This prompted the government to embark upon a €4 billion, five-year plan to reform the schooling system with the objective of equalizing educational opportunities. The plan involved substantive changes in curricula, teaching, testing and tracking methods in addition to changes affecting their parental circumstance, all of which were introduced in a piecemeal fashion throughout Germany over the period. Unfortunately, the nature of the reforms meant that student capability/achievement measures before and after the implementation, though cardinally comparable within year would not be comparable between years because test scores before and after the many interventions would not retain cardinal equivalence.

Anderson et al. (2018) used a sample of German students aged 15 in 2003 (before the reforms had been implemented) and 2009 (after the reforms had taken effect) drawn from the PISA data files to construct an achievement index ACH for students who have completed exams in Math

[1] Shorrocks (1978) seeks indices mobility (equality of opportunity) indices M for square transition matrices which possess four primary properties of normalization ($0 \leq M \leq 1$), Monotonicity (increasing with independence), Immobility ($M = 0$ when dependence is complete) and Perfect Mobility ($M = 1$ independence is complete) DISGINI can be shown to satisfy these requirements for any square or non-square transition matrix.

($X1$), Reading ($X2$) and Science ($X3$). Because the evaluation methodology differed across disciplines and over time, a student's overall achievement index in each year was based upon the average of their maximum mark standardized subject scores, that is, ACH(i), the overall achievement score for person i—whose achievement score in the Jth discipline is XJ_i—is given by:

$$ACH(i) = \frac{1}{3}\left(\frac{X1_i}{Max(X1)} + \frac{X2_i}{Max(X2)} + \frac{X3_i}{Max(X3)}\right)$$

Semi-parametric mixture methods were then employed to determine the structure of achievement groupings before and after the interventions (and indeed the structure had changed) and child outcome/parental circumstance relationships before and after the reforms were compared to see if achievement groups were converging in terms of change in the transition matrix structure during the 2003–2009 period.

A question arises as to whether the grade aggregation process affected the evaluation of progress toward an Equal Opportunity goal. In truth, what matters for equality of opportunity is whether the circumstance conditioned multidimensional achievement distributions are becoming more similar. The circumstance conditioned unidimensional achievement distributions contrived in Anderson et al. (2018) by aggregating each student's marks across disciplines may well conceal similarities or differences in the trivariate marks distributions.

Using Gaussian kernel estimates of the multivariate achievement scores distribution and univariate aggregated achievement scores distribution of students in each circumstance group, overlap and standard errors based upon Anderson, Linton and Wang (2012) were calculated together with the corresponding weighted and unweighted DISGINI Coefficient and Standard Errors. These are reported in Table 7.3.

Both sets of results indicate a significant drop in distributional inequality over the period (asymptotic t statistics of 3.125 and more) indicating some significant movement toward equality of opportunity, more so in the multivariate analysis. There the similarity ends; generally, the circumstance conditioned univariate distributions overlap much less than the corresponding multivariate distributions and thus yield higher inequality coefficients. Under marks aggregation the middle and upper circumstance groups exhibit the most commonality in both periods whereas in the multivariate analysis they appear to have little in common in 2003 but a great deal in common in 2009, a difference which is largely responsible for the considerable decline in inequality. Weighting/not weighting does not appear to make much difference but this is not surprising since circumstance group sizes are fairly similar.

7.4 An Example in Portfolio Choice

When choosing between portfolio managers one can assess their effectiveness or performance by performing a risk–return analysis on their respective portfolios. However, as has been seen there are risks involved in summarizing their returns distributions in such a fashion. Here based upon the work of Anderson, Post and Whang (2018) and Anderson and Leo (2014) an approach to the problem using multilateral techniques is reported.

In the past, the Gini Coefficient has seen action in the realm of risk analysis and portfolio choice in quantifying the relative variability of average returns as a measure of risk (Fisher and Lorie 1970; Yitzhaki 1982; Shalit and Yitzhaki 1984; Shalit 2014). Here DISGINI is employed as a measure of risk in terms of the variability inherent in a collection of portfolio returns distributions. Choosing between alternative investment strategies represented by portfolio styles carries with it inherent risks dependent on the degree to which the returns distributions of the respective portfolios differ. If the returns distributions of all portfolio styles are identical to each other, it is of no consequence which investment style is chosen, their Distributional Gini would be 0. If, on the other hand, the respective portfolio returns distributions differ, arbitrary portfolio choice will carry with it inherent risks. At the other extreme, if the returns distributions are segmented any first order ranking would be unambiguous and the best portfolio would be unequivocally so since it would stochastically dominate all other portfolios and be Utopian (Anderson et al. 2018). This can be analyzed by assuming a particular probability distribution for portfolio selection and assessing the relative distributional variability inherent in such a choice. For example, if choice was arbitrary, a discrete uniform distribution would be applied in the DISGINI weighting process, if on the other hand choice was based on the ranking of the portfolio a distribution with probabilities ordered by rank could be used.

To explore the use of DISGINI in this environment, two benchmark sets of portfolios from Kenneth French's data library are used. Monthly percentage value weighted returns in excess of the monthly treasury bill rate from January 1927 to August 2016 are employed to construct Gaussian kernel estimates of the pdfs of six portfolio investment styles plus a passive market portfolio in each set. These portfolios are of interest because they have frequently been employed in empirical research (Banz 1981; Basu 1983; Jegadeesh 1990; Jegadeesh and Titman 1993). The six active portfolios of US common stocks in the first set are based on the market capitalization of equity ("size") and book-to-market equity ratio ("valuation") and labeled Small Growth (SG), Small Blend (SB), Small Value (SV), Large Growth (LG), Large Blend (LB) and Large Value (LV), reflecting their respective investment strategies. The second benchmark set consist of six portfolios based on market capitalization and recent past return labeled Small Loser (SL), Small Neutral (SN), Small Winner (SW), Large Loser (LL), Large Neutral (LN) and Large Winner (LW) (past return is measured using a one-month lagged trailing window of 11 months).

Precluding mixing portfolios and permitting selection of just one from the set of alternatives, two investment strategies are considered, one where selection is purely random with an equi-probable choice model, the other where choice is based upon the Second Order Utopian index value of the portfolio U_i (Anderson, Post, and Whang 2018) where P(Select $i = U_i / \sum_{i=1}^{7} U_i$) are reported in Tables 7.4 and 7.5. The latter generates a high probability of choosing better performing portfolios.

As may be seen, the Utopia index itself has a wider range for the History based portfolios than the Style based portfolios which is not surprising since French's History based portfolios can be construed as deliberately choosing historically bad and historically good performers for comparison purposes. The Transvariation and Distributional Gini coefficients are

Table 7.4 Style based portfolio Utopia scores and selection probability

	Passive market stocks	*Small growth stocks*	*Small blend stocks*	*Small value stocks*	*Large growth stocks*	*Large blend stocks*	*Large value stocks*
Second order index	0.5000	0.0612	0.6765	0.8502	0.2660	0.3304	0.5215
Selection Prob.	0.1560	0.0191	0.2110	0.2652	0.0830	0.1031	0.1627

Source: Authors own calculations

Table 7.5 History based portfolio Utopia scores and selection probability

	Passive market stocks	*Small loser stocks*	*Small neutral stocks*	*Small winner stocks*	*Large loser stocks*	*Large neutral stocks*	*Large neutral stocks*
Second order index	0.5000	0.0866	0.6418	0.9477	0.0702	0.4116	0.7004
Selection prob.	0.1489	0.0258	0.1911	0.2822	0.0209	0.1226	0.2086

Source: Authors own calculations

Table 7.6 Multilateral Transvariations and Distributional Ginis

	MTR	*Std error*	*DISGINI*	*Std error*
Style (equi-probable)	0.05704	0.01507	0.03775	0.00680
Style (index based probability)	0.24691	0.01407	0.03155	0.00650
History (equi-probable)	0.07022	0.01515	0.04485	0.00719
History (index based probability)	0.26218	0.01437	0.03897	0.00680

Source: Authors own calculations

reported in Table 7.6 and, consistent with expectations, record higher distributional variability for the History based as opposed to the Style based collections. Furthermore, when a higher probability is attached to choosing the better portfolios, DISGINI records reduced distributional variability for both Style and History strategies; however, MTR records increased variability due to the camouflaging of similarities.

7.5 Gender Equality in Sub Saharan Africa Irrigation Schemes

Irrigation scheme developments have been key in improving economic opportunity in Sub Saharan Africa agricultural households. That such opportunities should be equally shared among those groups is an equally important, though less frequently enunciated imperative. In facilitating efficiencies, diversification and off farm activity, the schemes improved food security and made a substantial contribution to poverty reduction in the area (Bjornlund et al. 2017). However, increasingly it was the case that males worked off farm leaving women as the principal farmer and de-facto household head complicating household decision-making processes. Bjornlund et. al. (2019) observed that female headed decision-making units tended to have lower incomes raising concerns regarding the extent to which the household decision-making structure constrained its ability to generate crop related incomes, especially with regard to female headed households. In a sense, this is an equality of opportunity issue and it was investigated as such in Anderson and Manero (2019).

Sen (2009) and Atkinson (2012) averred that the "Transcendentally Optimal" Equal Opportunity states are seldom attainable and argued for policies that progressively equalized such opportunities. This begs the question of how such progressivity can be quantified for policy evaluation purposes. Here instruments for measuring the extent to which such opportunities have been equalized are proposed and implemented in a study of Sub Saharan Africa irrigation scheme development. The data in this study was obtained from the research project "Increasing irrigation water productivity in Mozambique, Tanzania and Zimbabwe through on-farm monitoring, adaptive management and agricultural innovation platforms". Funded by the Australian Centre for International Agricultural Research, its focus was six smallholder irrigation schemes in Zimbabwe, Tanzania and Mozambique. (Given their limited number of female observations, the Mozambique schemes were excluded from this study.) The data is comprised of two rounds of household surveys conducted in 2014 and 2017, with questions on household structures and economic activities over the 12 months prior to the interviews (Manero 2017).

Equal Opportunity requires agent outcomes be independent of circumstances beyond the agents control. Agent outcome variable "X" should only depend upon individual effort. Given collection of K circumstance classes (k = 1,...,K), circumstance conditioned outcome distributions $f_{X,k}\left(x \mid k\right)$ should be identical. This has prompted two basic investigative approaches. Regression/treatment affects approaches (Mulligan 1997; Solon 1992, 2008) which seek statistical differences in conditional means. These approaches fall foul of the Carniero, Hansen, Heckman (2003) and Durlauf, Quah (2002) critique which is a "veil of ignorance" argument favoring comparison of distributional differences over their complete range. Alternatively, Lefranc, Pistolesi and Trannoy (2009) proposed distributional difference tests for Equality of Opportunity by exploring the prevalence of stochastic dominance relationships between the circumstance conditioned outcome distributions, (absence of dominance => Equality of Opportunity). The problem here is that dominance tests are just pairwise comparators; as has been seen in Chap. 4, these are cumbersome when applied to many circumstance classes, they give no sense of proximity to the "transcendentally optimal" state and are not really an equality in distribution test (non-dominance ≠> equality of distribution). An index of distributional difference is what is required.

Here Gini's (1916, 1959) Bilateral Transvariation measure GT is used to develop a Distributional Gini coefficient. For distributions $f_i(x)$ and $f_j(x)$, GT_{ij} is given by:

$$0 \le GT_{ij} = \frac{1}{2}\int_0^\infty \left| f_i(x) - f_j(x) \right| dx = \frac{1}{2}\int_0^\infty \begin{bmatrix} \max\left(f_i(x), f_j(x)\right) \\ -\min\left(f_i(x), f_j(x)\right) \end{bmatrix} dx \le 1$$

GT_{ij} attains 0 when $f_i(x)$ and $f_j(x)$ are identical and 1 when they are segmented. Noting that $GT_{i,j} = 1 - OV_{i,j}$ where $OV_{i,j}$ is the distributional overlap (Anderson, Linton, Whang 2012) implies it has a computable asymptotic standard error. Anderson, Linton, Pittau, Whang and Zelli (2019) provide an estimate (together with asymptotic standard errors) of a Distributional Gini coefficient DISGINI where, letting w_k be the relative size of the *k*th group:

$$\text{DISGINI} = \frac{1}{\left(1 - \sum_{k=1}^{K} w_k^2\right)} \sum_{i=1}^{K}\sum_{j=1}^{K} w_i w_j \left(1 - OV_{ij}\right) = \frac{1}{\left(1 - \sum_{k=1}^{K} w_k^2\right)} \sum_{i=1}^{K}\sum_{j=1}^{K} w_i w_j \left(GT_{ij}\right)$$

This measures similarities and differences multilaterally. Again, it is an index between 0 and 1 measuring the lack of commonality over all distributions. Unweighted comparisons (by setting w_j equal to $1/K$ for all i) are also considered.

The gender of the household head and the nature of the irrigation scheme can readily be construed as circumstances but can the same be said of land? Access to workable land is a major constraining factor in the households' ability to acquire wellbeing from agricultural activity. Inheritance is through agnatic kinship, and women are expected to marry someone with land—typically, they don't inherit it, so that female household heads rarely have choice over the land they cultivate. Aside from cultural norms, lower female education levels together with additional household responsibilities make off farm work less feasible for females so that wealth accumulation for the purpose of land purchase or rent is less of an option for them as compared to males. Anderson and Manero (2019) define an individuals' circumstance as their gender and the irrigation scheme they are located on, with gender used as a proxy for the land constraint.

To exemplify differences by gender in the land access and household net agricultural revenues, stochastic dominance tests are employed and reported in Table 7.7. As can be seen, male outcomes stochastically dominate female outcomes in all cases except net revenue per hectare

Table 7.7 Kolmogorov-Smirnov[a] 2 sample tests (male vs. female household head distributions)

Land distributions	*Unequivalized*	*Unequivalized*	*Equivalized*	*Equivalized*
	2014	*2017*	*2014*	*2017*
Differences	0.20448	0.38357	0.15800	0.35114
Stochastic dominance "+"	0.20448	0.38357	0.15800	0.35114
Stochastic dominance "–"	0.00317	0.00000	0.00000	0.00000
Household net revenue				
Differences	0.12205	0.16011	0.10749	0.18703
Stochastic dominance "+"	0.06220	0.04354	0.05146	0.05917
Stochastic dominance "–"	0.12205	0.16011	0.10749	0.18703
Household net revenue per hectare				
Differences	0.03141	0.06454	0.02508	0.07720
Stochastic dominance "+"	0.03141	0.06454	0.01712	0.07720
Stochastic dominance "–"	0.02414	0.00944	0.02508	0.01280

Critical Values for Alpha =	*0.10*	*0.05*	*0.025*	*0.01*	*0.005*	*0.001*
2014	0.12613	0.14389	0.15964	0.17833	0.19137	0.21841
2017	0.15672	0.17877	0.19834	0.22156	0.23778	0.27137

[a]The comparator. $D\left(\hat{F}_a(x),\hat{F}_b(x)\right)=\sup_x\left|\hat{F}_a(x)-\hat{F}_b(x)\right|$ is compared to a critical value $c(n_a n_b\alpha)=\sqrt{-0.5\ln(\alpha)}\left(\frac{n_a+n_b}{n_a n_b}\right)$, where n_a and n_b are the respective sample sizes and α is the chosen size of the test. The null hypothesis of commonality is rejected if $>c$. Stochastic dominance tests can be contrived using $D\left(\hat{F}_a(x),\hat{F}_b(x)\right)=\sup_x\left(\hat{F}_a(x)-\hat{F}_b(x)\right)$ and $D\left(\hat{F}_a(x),\hat{F}_b(x)\right)=\operatorname{Inf}_x\left(\hat{F}_a(x)-\hat{F}_b(x)\right)$. Rejection of one together with non-rejection of the other indicates a first order dominance relation

highlighting the substantial differences by gender across the various schemes. The exception of the net revenue per hectare example is interesting since it suggests that there is no difference in the productivity or efficiency of female as opposed to male head of household farms; it's just that female headed farms tend to be smaller in scale.

To explore the extent of equality of opportunity, eight circumstance groups are considered male headed and female headed households on the Magozi and Kiweri Schemes in Tanzania and the Silalatshani and Mkoba Schemes in Zimbabwe. To accommodate the fact that households varied in size adult equivalized and unequivalized access to land and crop revenues were considered. To get a sense of the distributional differences across the circumstance groups Figs. 7.1, 7.2, 7.3, and 7.4 illustrate the variation in adult equivalized access to land and adult equivalized crop revenue surplus per hectare for both 2014 and 2017.

Turning to the results for the eight circumstance groups reported in Table 7.8, it can be seen that there is evidence of inequality of opportunity in all cases (the Distributional Gini is significantly greater than 0) but the situation has improved over the 2014–2017 period with statistically significant reductions in the coefficient in all but the Net Crop Revenue measure where there was a reduction but it was not significant at usual levels of significance.

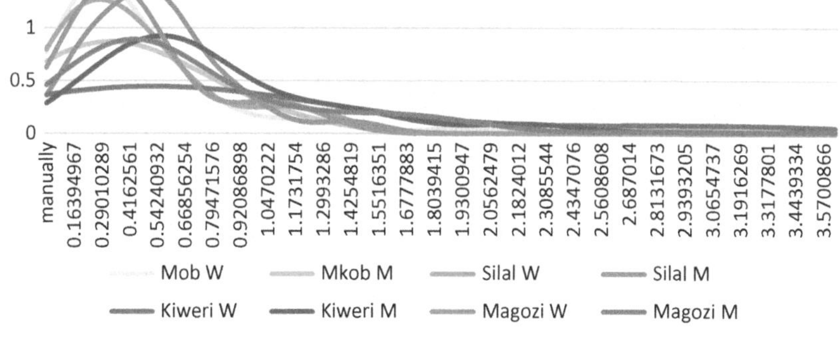

Fig. 7.1 Adult equivalized land access 2014. (Source: Anderson and Monero 2019)

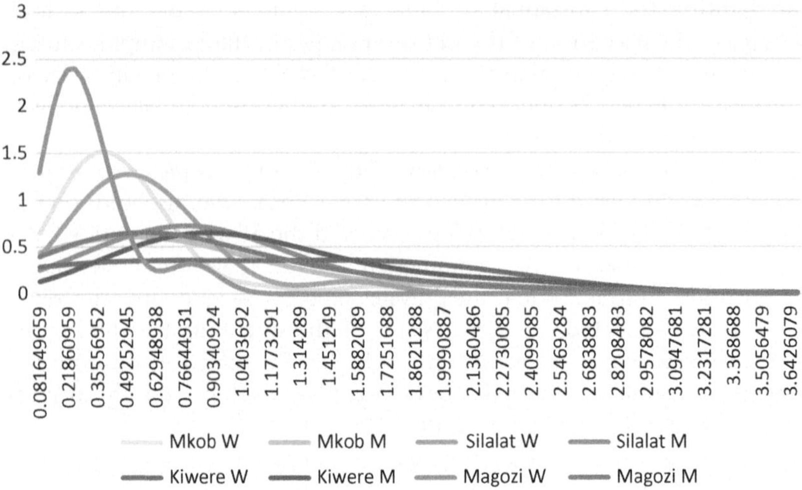

Fig. 7.2 Adult equivalized land access 2017. (Source: Anderson and Monero 2019)

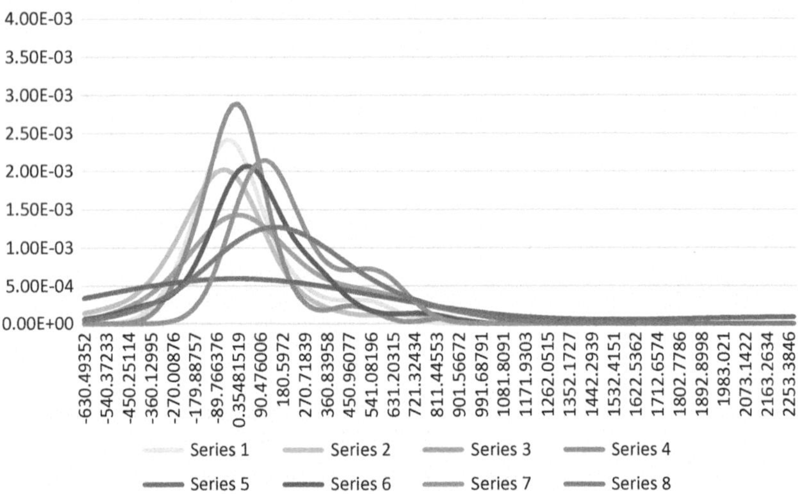

Fig. 7.3 Crop revenue surplus per hectare adult equivalized 2014. (Source: Anderson and Monero 2019)

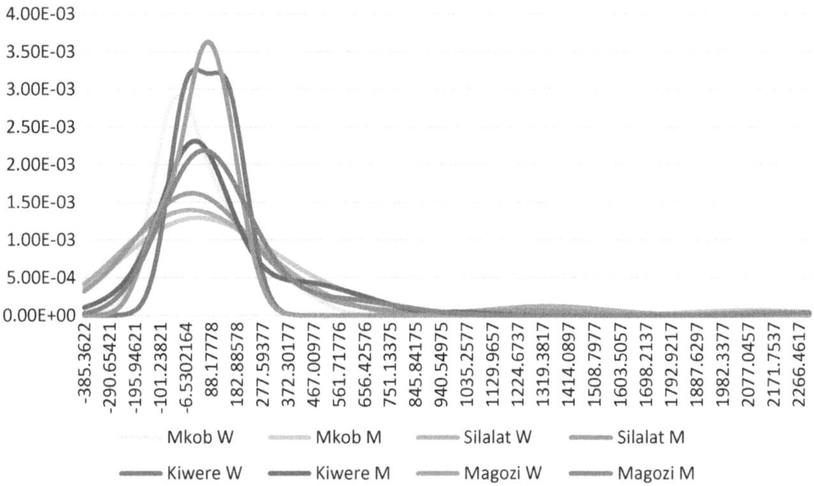

Fig. 7.4 Crop revenue surplus per hectare adult equivalized 2017. (Source: Anderson and Monero 2019)

7.6 A Multidimensional Human Development Example

The problem of categorizing groups when boundaries are ill defined is made much more complicated when the subject matter is multidimensional in nature and the number of groups is not determined. Here some results drawn from Anderson, Farcomeni, Pittau and Zelli (2019a) are reported which deal with the problem of determining the number and categorization of latent groups when the object of comparison is multivariate.

In the field of Economic Development, nations have frequently been categorized into groups for various ranking purposes. The World Bank has a fourfold classification of nation status (Low, Lower Middle, Upper Middle and High Income) based upon three Gross National Income (GNI) per capita (US$ equivalent) thresholds updated annually with an inflation adjustment. The thresholds were established in 1989 "based largely on operational thresholds that had previously been established". In terms of Human Development, there has been some concern regarding the adequacy of national income for nation comparison purposes (Stiglitz et al. 2010) leading the United Nations to develop its Human Development Index

Table 7.8 Distributional Ginis for eight circumstance groups (standard errors are reported in brackets)

	Land		*Net crop revenue per hectare*		*Net crop revenue*		*Net crop revenue ad equ.*	
	DISGINI	*WDISGINI*	*DISGINI*	*WDISGINI*	*DISGINI*	*WDISGINI*	*DISGINI*	*WDISGINI*
2014	0.2058	0.1692	0.3024	0.2409	0.4167	0.4371	0.3835	0.3993
	(0.0165)	(0.0174)	(0.0149)	(0.0176)	(0.0161)	(0.0133)	(0.0165)	(0.0137)
2017	0.3382	0.2698	0.2433	0.1750	0.3249	0.2662	0.3572	0.2983
	(0.0159)	(0.0145)	(0.0145)	(0.0166)	(0.0162)	(0.0149)	(0.0159)	(0.0145)

Source: Authors calculations

(UNPD 2016), a three component index covering health (life expectancy), education (aggregated levels of schooling) and per capita GNI.

Anderson, Farcomeni, Pittau, and Zelli (2019a) studied the progress of 164 nations over the period 1990–2014 in terms of these components of the Human Development Index in a semi-parametric multidimensioned mixture model. In contrast to the usual four group classification reported in World Bank (2017), three groups, Low Human Development (HD), Medium HD and High HD, each with a commonality of behaviors were established and in that context, measures of relative poverty, inequality, polarization and mobility were proposed and implemented. In implementing the modeling process, per capita GNI has been log-transformed[2] and all variables were standardized with respect to the initial year 1990. Thus, all analyses are performed relative to the base year weighted average. The multivariate subgroup distributions were assumed to be independently normally distributed though dependent over time. Tables 7.9 and 7.10 report the year-by-year means, standard deviations and relative group sizes of the subgroups.

While the mean group characteristics (mean log GNI, Life Expectancy and Education) improved systematically over the period for all groups, the transition analysis detected a slowly evolving, relatively immobile world, very different from the World Banks income based univariate analysis. Over the period, reflective of some downward mobility, the poor group increased in size, which may be interpreted as an increase in the multidimensional relative poverty rate. In concert with univariate analyses, there was substantial evidence of reduced inequalities both within and between groups over the period (though this was not universal the low HD group experience an inverted U shaped inequality profile over the period), the transition structure and the year-by-year analysis revealed substantive polarizing patterns. Increasing within and between-group equality did not inhibit the groups increased sense of segmentation or "differentness". In essence, groups were simultaneously becoming more equal and more polarized. For the most part countries stayed within their groupings though some deterioration was seen for some African nations (Table 7.11).

[2] Income is taken in logarithms "in order to reflect the diminishing returns to transforming income to human capabilities" (Anand and Sen 1994, p.10; see also Brandolini 2008).

Table 7.9 Estimated means (relative to the base year), standard deviations of the components in the year-by-year mixture model

	Means			*Std deviations*		
	Low	*Medium*	*High*	*Low*	*Medium*	*High*
GNI pc						
1990	−1.23	−0.02	1.15	0.287	0.253	0.308
1995	−1.18	0.02	1.31	0.431	0.187	0.172
2000	−1.11	0.09	1.36	0.417	0.172	0.186
2005	−1.00	0.24	1.41	0.402	0.157	0.174
2010	−0.91	0.39	1.44	0.328	0.149	0.137
2014	−0.81	0.46	1.46	0.332	0.138	0.133
Life Exp.						
1990	−1.41	0.23	0.91	0.219	0.194	0.236
1995	−1.25	0.41	1.09	0.299	0.130	0.119
2000	−1.16	0.52	1.18	0.295	0.121	0.132
2005	−0.92	0.65	1.28	0.317	0.124	0.137
2010	−0.60	0.75	1.41	0.268	0.121	0.112
2014	−0.38	0.84	1.50	0.261	0.108	0.105
Education						
1990	−1.40	0.25	0.87	0.167	0.147	0.180
1995	−1.04	0.39	1.22	0.536	0.232	0.214
2000	−0.78	0.59	1.47	0.549	0.226	0.245
2005	−0.43	0.82	1.61	0.459	0.179	0.198
2010	−0.12	0.97	1.74	0.383	0.173	0.160
2014	−0.03	1.03	1.81	0.385	0.160	0.154

Source: Anderson et al. (2019a)

Table 7.10 Relative group sizes of the components in the year-by-year mixture model

	Low HD	*Medium HD*	*High HD*
1990	0.26	0.45	0.29
1995	0.30	0.45	0.25
2000	0.31	0.41	0.27
2005	0.32	0.40	0.29
2010	0.31	0.41	0.28
2014	0.32	0.40	0.28

Source: Anderson et al. (2019a)

Table 7.11 Transvariations and within-group inequality measures of the year-by-year mixture model

Year	*Transv*	*Within-group inequality*		
		Low HD	*Medium HD*	*High HD*
1990	0.9884	0.1050	0.0072	0.0131
1995	0.8578	0.0691	0.0056	0.0044
2000	0.9018	0.0675	0.0047	0.0060
2005	0.8570	0.0585	0.0035	0.0047
2010	0.6705	0.0337	0.0031	0.0025
2014	0.6658	0.0334	0.0024	0.0022

Note: Computation of Transvariation is facilitated by noting that, given the present case of diagonal covariance matrices, these are differences of integrals of products of independent normal distributions which can be calculated by standard methods
Source: Anderson et al. (2019a)

References

Anand, S., & Sen, A. (1994, July). *Sustainable Human Development: Concepts and Priorities.* UNDP Human Development Report Office, Occasional Paper No. 12.

Anderson, G., & Leo, T. W. (2014). *Ranking Alternative Non-Combinable Prospects: A Stochastic Dominance Based Route to the Second Best Solution* (Working Paper 520, 2014-10-20). University of Toronto, Department of Economics

Anderson, G., & Manero, A. (2019). *Crop Based Incomes and Access to Land in Sub Saharan Africa Agricultural Irrigation Schemes: Assessing Equality of Opportunity Using Multilateral Distributional Comparison Techniques.* Mimeo University of Toronto.

Anderson, G., & Thomas, J. (2019). Measuring Multi-Group Polarization, Segmentation and Ambiguity: Increasingly Unequal Yet Similar Constituent Canadian Income Distributions. *Social Indicators Research.* https://doi.org/10.1007/s11205-019-02121-z.

Anderson, G. J., Linton, O., & Whang, Y.-J. (2012). Nonparametric Estimation and Inference About the Overlap of Two Distributions" Oliver Linton and Yoon-Jae Whang. *Journal of Econometrics, 171*(1), 1–23.

Anderson, G. J., Post, T., & Whang, Y.-J. (2018). Somewhere Between Utopia and Dystopia: Choosing From Multiple Incomparable Prospects. *Journal of Business and Economic Statistics.* https://doi.org/10.1080/07350015.2018.1515765.

Anderson, G., Farcomeni, A., Pittau, M.G., & Zelli, R. (2019a). Multidimensional Nation Wellbeing, More Equal Yet More Polarized: An Analysis of the Progress of Human Development Since 1990. Forthcoming *Journal of Economic Development*.

Anderson, G., Pittau, M. G., Zelli, R., & Fruehauf, T. (2019b). *Educational Reform and Equal Opportunity in Capability Acquisition in 21st Century Germany: New Tools for Quantifying Distributional Differences in the Absence of Cardinal Comparability*. Mimeo University of Toronto.

Anderson, G., Linton, O., Pittauz, M. G., Whangx, Y.-J., & Zelliz, R. (2019). *Segmentation or Convergence in European Household Income Distributions? New Tools for Analyzing Multilateral Differentness in Collections of Distributions*. University of Toronto, Economics Department. Mimeo.

Atkinson, A. B. (2012). Public Economics After the Idea of Justice. *Journal of Human Development and Capabilities, 13*(4), 521–536.

Banz, R. W. (1981). The Relationship Between Return and Market Value of Common Stocks. *Journal of Financial Economics, 9*, 3–18.

Basu, S. (1983). The Relationship Between Earnings' Yield, Market Value and Return for NYSE Common Stocks: Further Evidence. *Journal of Financial Economics, 12*, 129–156.

Battistin, E., Blundell, R., & Lewbel, A. (2009). Why Is Consumption More Log Normal Than Income? Gibrat's Law Revisited. *Journal of Political Economy, 117*(6), 1140–1154.

Bjornlund, H., van Rooyen, A., & Stirzaker, R. (2017). Profitability and Productivity Barriers and Opportunities in Small-Scale Irrigation Schemes. *International Journal of Water Resources Development, 33*(5), 685–689.

Bjornlund, H., Zuo, A., Wheeler, S. A., Parry, K., Pittock, J., Mdemu, M., & Moyo, M. (2019). The Dynamics of the Relationship Between Household Decision-Making and Farm Household Income in Small-Scale Irrigation Schemes in Southern Africa. *Agricultural Water Management, 213*(1), 135–145.

Blundell, R., & Preston, I. (1998). Consumption Inequality and Income Uncertainty. *The Quarterly Journal of Economics, 113*(2), 603–640.

Brandolini, A. (2008, April). *On Applying Synthetic Indices of Multidimensional Well-Being: Health and Income Inequalities in Selected EU Countries*. Banca d'Italia, Temi di discussione (Working Papers No. 668).

Browning, M., & Lusardi, A. (1996). Household Saving: Micro Theories and Micro Facts. *Journal of Economic literature, 34*(4), 1797–1855.

Carneiro, P., Hansen, K. T., & Heckman, J. J. (2003). 2001 Lawrence R. Klein Lecture Estimating Distributions of Treatment Effects with an Application to the Returns to Schooling and Measurement of the Effects of Uncertainty on College Choice. *International Economic Review, 44*, 361–422.

Durlauf, S. (1996). A Theory of Persistent Income Inequality. *Journal of Economic Growth, 1*(1), 75–93.

Durlauf, S. N., & Quah, D. (2002). Chapter 4: The New Empirics of Economic Growth. In J. B. Taylor & M. Woodford (Eds.), *Handbook of Macroeconomics*. Amsterdam: North Holland.

Fisher, L., & Lorie, J. (1970). Some Studies of the Variability of Returns on Investments in Common Stocks. *Journal of Business, 43*, 99–135.

Fortin, N., Green, D. A., Lemieux, T., Milligan, K., & Riddell, W. C. (2012). Canadian Inequality: Recent Developments and Policy Options. *Canadian Public Policy, 38*(2), 121–145.

Friedman, M. (1957). *A Theory of the Consumption Function*. Princeton: Princeton University Press.

Galor, O. (1996, July). Convergence? Inferences from Theoretical Models. *The Economic Journal, 106*(437), 1056–1069.

Gibrat, R. (1931). *Les Inégalités Économiques*. Paris: Librairie du Recueil Sirey.

Gini, C (1916). Il concetto di transvariazione e le sue prime applicazioni. In C. Gini (Eds.), (1959), *Giornale degli Economisti e Rivista di Statistica* (pp. 1–55).

Gini, C. (1959). *Transvariazione*. Rome: Libreria Goliardica.

Green, D. A., Riddell, W. C., & St-Hilaire, F. (2016). Income Inequality in Canada: Driving Forces, Outcomes and Policy. *Income Inequality: The Canadian Story* (pp. 1–73). Montreal: Institute for Research on Public Policy.

Hahn, F. H., & Matthews, R. C. O. (1964). The Theory of Economic Growth: A Survey. *Economic Journal, 74*, 779–901.

Hall, R. E. (1978). Stochastic Implications of the Life Cycle-Permanent Income Hypothesis: Theory and Evidence. *Journal of Political Economy, 86*(6), 971–987.

Jegadeesh, N. (1990). Evidence of Predictable Behavior of Security Returns. *Journal of Finance, 45*, 881–898.

Jegadeesh, N., & Titman, S. (1993). Returns to Buying Winners and Selling Losers: Implications for Stock Market Efficiency. *Journal of Finance, 48*(1), 65–91.

Lefranc, A., Pistolesi, N., & Trannoy, A. (2009). Equality of Opportunity and Luck: Definitions and Testable Conditions, with an Application to Income in France. *Journal of Public Economics, 93*, 1189–1207.

Manero, A. (2017). The Limitations of Negative Incomes in the Gini Coefficient Decomposition by Source. *Applied Economics Letters, 24*(14), 977–981.

Mulligan, C. B. (1997). *Parental Priorities and Economic Inequality*. Chicago: University of Chicago Press.

Quah, D. (1996a). Convergence Empirics Across Countries with (Some) Capital Mobility. *Journal of Economic Growth, 1*, 95–124.

Quah, D. T. (1996b). Twin Peaks: Growth and Convergence in Models of Distribution Dynamics. *The Economic Journal, 106*, 1045–1055.

Quah, D. T. (1997). Empirics for Growth and Distribution: Stratification, Polarisation and Convergence Clubs. *Journal of Economic Growth, 2*, 27–59.

Sen, A. K. (2009). *The Idea of Justice*. Cambridge, MA: Harvard University Press.

Shalit, H. (2014). Portfolio Risk Management Using the Lorenz Curve. *The Journal of Portfolio Management, 40*, 152–159.

Shalit, H., & Yitzhaki, S. (1984). Mean Gini, Portfolio Theory and the Pricing of Risky Assets. *Journal of Finance, 39*, 1449–1468.

Shorrocks, A. F. (1978). The Measurement of Mobility. *Econometrica, 46*, 1013–1024.

Solon, G. (1992). Intergenerational Income Mobility in the United States. *American Economic Review, 82*(3), 393–408.

Solon, G. (2008). Intergenerational Income Mobility. In S. Durlauf & L. Blume (Eds.), *The New Palgrave Dictionary of Economics* (2nd ed.). London: Palgrave Macmillan.

Solow, R. M. (1956). A Contribution to the Theory of Economic Growth. *Quarterly Journal of Economics, 70*, 65–94.

Stiglitz, J. E., Sen, A., & Fitoussi, J. P. (2010). Mis-measuring Our Lives: Why GDP Doesn't Add Up. In *The Report of the Commission on the Measurement of Economic Performance and Social Progress*. New York/London: The New Press.

UNPD. (2016). *Human Development Report 2016*. Washington DC: Communications Development Incorporated.

World Bank. (2017). https://datahelpdesk.worldbank.org/knowledgebase/articles/906519

Yitzhaki, S. (1982). Stochastic Dominance, Mean-Variance and Gini's Mean Difference. *American Economic Review, 72*, 178–185.

Index[1]

[1] Note: Page numbers followed by 'n' refer to notes.

G. Anderson, *Multilateral Wellbeing Comparison in a Many Dimensioned World*, Global Perspectives on Wealth and Distribution,
https://doi.org/10.1007/978-3-030-21130-1

The manufacturer's authorised representative in the EU is Springer Nature Customer Service Centre GmbH, Europaplatz 3, 69115 Heidelberg, Germany. If you have any concerns regarding our products, please contact ProductSafety@springernature.com

Printed and bound by CPI Group (UK) Ltd, Croydon, CR0 4YY
30/09/2026
02225439-0003